Presented to

Sir Dominic

By

The Packard Family

Date

May 30, 2005

Memorial Day
2005

Sir Dominic,

May the Lord on high bless you.

May you become All He has planned.

May you reach your dreams

May you touch the stars

As you become one unto yourself.

Love for you . . .

The Parkard Family

Villa Dio Vista

Cower Heights California

Wisdom and Inspiration from the Best Commencement Speakers Ever

GRADUATiON MOMENTS

Includes Powerful Insights from:

Barbara Bush

Bill & Vonette Bright

Billy Graham

Bob Hope

Chuck Colson

Condoleezza Rice

Gary Smalley

George Bush

Martin Luther King Jr

Mother Teresa

Oswald Chambers.

. . . and many more

HONOR **HB** BOOKS

Inspiration and Motivation for the Seasons of Life

An Imprint of Cook Communications Ministries • Colorado Springs, CO

08 07 06 05 04 10 9 8 7 6 5 4 3 2 1

Graduation Moments
Wisdom and Inspiration from
the Best Commencement Speakers Ever

ISBN 1-56292-987-9

Published by Honor Books,
An Imprint of Cook Communications Ministries
4050 Lee Vance View
Colorado Springs, CO 80918

Compiled and written by Jan Price, Tulsa, Oklahoma

Developed by Bordon Books

INTRODUCTION

You've worked hard all these years, and now you are ready to move out into the world and do the great things you have always dreamed about. Where do you want to go? What do you want to do? What do you need to know to accomplish your dreams? What do you need to know to nurture those dreams in the years ahead? Where does God fit into the picture of your life and your career accomplishments?

Graduation Moments is filled with the wisdom of people from all walks of life, who have stepped out, done great things, and also finished well. And now they share it with you. Inside you will find inspiring commencement speeches, powerful principles for achieving your life goals, and motivating quotations to help you in this next stage of your life's journey. We have also included stories of graduates just like you who pursued their dreams after graduation and, with diligence and persistence, found success.

After all, your graduation is a life-changing, life-affirming moment. And commencement speakers throughout the years have recognized this by distilling the most vital, motivating, and inspiring pieces of wisdom and advice to help graduates begin this new journey of their lives with the wisdom and the tools they need to succeed. In this book you will learn how to find your dream and your passion, how to maintain your integrity in the face of great pressure, and what you need to remember the value of your contribution to the world.

You know you want your life to count in the world today, so we invite you to turn these pages and be inspired by the wisdom of those who have done just what your are desiring. Grow, flourish, and influence your world—You Can Do It!

CONTENTS

STAND YOUR GROUND,
Let Your Light Shine!

"You are the light of the world. A city set on a hill cannot be hidden. Nor do men light a lamp, and put it under the peck-measure, but on the lampstand; and it gives light to all who are in the house. Let your light shine before men in such a way that they may see your good works, and glorify your Father who is in heaven.

MATTHEW 5:14-16 NASB

GOD IS WITH YOU

A native Kansan, Congressman Jerry Moran completed degrees in economics and law and presently teaches part-time at Fort Hays State University as well as represents the state of Kansas in the U.S. House of Representatives. Moran speaks of integrity, service, and family. As one who attained his goal to make it to Washington, he admits real satisfaction in life can only come from "satisfying the goals God establishes for our lives."

JERRY MORAN
Barclay College
May 3, 1998

Thank you President Moody. I am honored to be here for Barclay College's graduation ceremony and back in Haviland, a community I represented for four years in the State Senate and now in the United States Congress.

Being here today brings back memories of my own graduation, more years ago than I wish to remember. I recall my graduation as a day of mixed emotions. It was an odd experience filled with both anticipation and sadness, celebrating my graduation while simultaneously wondering what new things lay before me. The real journey of my life was about to begin. And now too, so will yours.

Like most of you, I hoped that our commencement speaker might provide some insightful commentary on the world and my role in it—And if at all possible, in fifty words or less. In other words, I hoped what many of you are hoping right now: may the speaker be meaningful—meaningful but brief.

And brief I promise to be.

It is rare that I ever agree to give a graduation address. And after struggling over the last several months about what to say, I resolved that this may be my last. My reluctance is rooted in feelings of inadequacy. What can I say that is equal in meaning to this day, this institution, and this graduating class?

The task was made more difficult after speaking with President Moody who indicated a preference for a speech about personal philosophy, rather than the garden variety, "Go forth and do great things," graduation speech. While everyone has a personal philosophy for their individual lives, it is very difficult to express one's personal view in a way useful to graduating seniors.

Having made all the appropriate disclaimers, I will do my best to share with you my thoughts on life, not as a member of the United States Congress, but as a person, a husband, and a father.

I can tell you from my own life's experiences that satisfaction does not derive from economic well-being, status on the social ladder, or power in nation's capital. Although I rarely admit it, for a very long time I had a goal for my life—the goal of being your congressman, of going to Washington to represent the people of Kansas. Well, with the help of a great number of people, I accomplished that goal in January of last year.

. . . in all your ways acknowledge him and he will make your paths straight.

But like so many of the goals we set for ourselves, even when they are accomplished, we are left feeling empty and unsatisfied. For the only satisfaction in life comes not in meeting the goals we establish for ourselves but instead living a life according to God's will and satisfying the goals God establishes for our lives.

I have often struggled to know what God has in store for me and my life. Are my goals compatible with God's goals for my life? In seeking an answer to this question I regularly look to Proverbs 3:5-6:

Trust in the LORD with all your heart;
Lean not on your own understanding;
In all your ways acknowledge him
And he will make your paths straight."

After the 1996 election and the excitement of being sworn in as a member of the United States Congress had worn off, I needed to ascertain the straightness of my paths.

Fortunately, I had friends in Kansas who knew I would need help in my new role. They let me know they were praying for me the prayer of the apostle Paul found in Colossians 1:9-12:

Since the day we heard about you, we have not stopped praying for you and asking God to fill you with the knowledge of his will. . . . And we pray this in order that you may live a life worthy of the Lord and may please him in every way; bearing fruit in every good work, growing in the knowledge of God, being strengthened with all power . . . so that you may have great endurance and patience, and joyfully giving thanks to the Father.

The fact that people were praying for me in my new job was, and is, of great comfort. I began to recognize that God had placed in my life a wonderful opportunity to be of service to my fellow man—that I was not elected to office to satisfy my own ego, but rather to live a life in service to the Lord, to the best of my human abilities.

We are often told that our country is in need of great leaders. I believe that we are in desperate need of servants—just as Jesus humbled himself to be a servant—not a leader who commanded an army, or who sat upon a royal throne; but a servant who washed his disciples' feet. So graduates, I would challenge you to imitate Christ's humility. Follow the instructions of Philippians 2:3-4: Do nothing out of selfish ambition or vain conceit, but in humility consider others better than yourself. Each of you should not look to your own interests, but also to the interests of others.

Today, we face new and greater challenges—challenges that affect each of us directly. Whether it's violence stemming from broken homes, drugs in our schools, gangs in our communities, or teenage pregnancies, the problems are evident in more and more places. And they are growing each and every day.

Morality is adrift, and for that we are paying a high price. For too long, right and wrong have been relative—not absolute. For the last thirty years, government has attempted to replace individuals, churches, and communities in addressing our social problems, only to fail miserably.

I believe the most successful health, education, and welfare programs ever created are moms and dads, families, churches, and communities. Government has no monopoly on compassion. Indeed, government is compassion's least able practitioner. It is up to us as Christians and citizens to renew our commitments, in not only caring for our own families, but also for our neighbors when our help is needed.

> **All of you here today can be the heroes of tomorrow — you can make a remarkable difference in this world.**

To be effective, our charity and assistance to others must be spiritual and personal. It must be done individual to individual, block to block, church to church, and community to community.

All of you here today can be the heroes of tomorrow—you can make a remarkable difference in this world. And I hope you will. Many Christians today are involved in a political movement—trying to change the human condition by governmental action. I believe this is important. But Christians should remember the human condition is one of sin and our primary mission is not at the ballot box, but at the altar of saving souls.

When I first engaged in public service, it was not as an elected official. And while I believe in the opportunities for service in elected office, I would not suggest that running for office is the only way or even the best way to positively serve our communities.

To the contrary, I believe it is those individuals who volunteer their time and efforts in our neighborhoods and communities and those who witness to their faith in Jesus Christ that will have the greatest effect on people's lives and on the direction of this country. Indeed, the effect of this involvement, this witness, is far greater than any government program or the result of any election. Do something to help someone else and you will continue to work towards your highest potential as servants of Christ and His Church. Recognize that His Word is unchanging and that right and wrong are absolute.

Your education at Barclay College has undoubtedly prepared you well for a job. But more importantly you are called upon to make a life. Not only to make a dollar, but to make a destiny. Not just to find happiness, but to pursue usefulness—to seek the good, the true, and the eternal. Success is not simply achieving wealth, power, or fame. Do not allow yourself to lose sight of what is truly important. Always remember that no job, regardless of money; no indulgence, however tempting—nothing can take the place of a life committed to something other than yourself. The real challenge is to seek a life that is something more than just being "comfortable."

This nation will not be better off because we have one more millionaire, but will be better if one more person lives his or her life with integrity serving his or her fellow man. One committed Sunday school teacher, one boy or girl scout leader, one big brother or sister, one loving mother or father, one dedicated teacher or faculty member of this college can make more difference in this world than all the members of Congress combined.

I don't mind saying that I have one of the most fulfilling and important jobs in the world. It requires responsibility, extensive knowledge, being on-call twenty-four hours a day, combining firm leadership with careful negotiations, and keeping one's word. The job I have just described, however, is not that of a member of Congress but that of husband and father to my wife and our two young daughters. Some of you may already be married and some of you may be parents. For others, marriage may be around the corner or down the road. Let me remind you, but for your obligation to God, no other responsibility is greater than your obligation to your family.

Throughout your lives, you will be faced with endless choices—some simple, some difficult. There will be plenty of both. Decisions will be made regarding how to spend your time, your energy, and what you hope to accomplish in your life. Please do not, except for your faith, place anything on a higher priority than that of your spouse and children. Nothing can ever compensate for the price of a ruined family.

What I am suggesting here this afternoon is that
- You should pursue God's goals for your life, not your own goals;
- You should live your life with humility;
- Service and charity to others is required of us;
- Right and wrong are absolute, integrity matters;
- A useful life is more important than a comfortable life; and
- Next to your commitment to God, commit yourself to your family.

The world is a large and wonderful place and it is your time to step into it boldly.

You are armed with your college education and the character bred into you by family, faculty, and friends. You are balanced on the threshold of the rest of your life. Have the courage to really live your life. The [possibilities] are large and the way uncertain, the challenges enormous, and our own abilities limited.

Our small voice tells God, " I don't know where we're going."

And God answers: "We're going forward, into the future I have shaped for you."

"But I don't know where that is."

And God answers, " I do, let's go."

"But I am afraid."

And God says, "Of course you are. Any sensible person would be. Let's go."

And we say, "But can I do all that is given to me to do?"

And God says, "I have made you, I am with you to the end. Take my hand. Let's go."

We need the chance to build a new world. And God has always given us that. Never have the challenges been greater. But go with the knowledge that God is with you.

INSIGHTS *for* LIVING

SO LET IT BE IN GOD'S OWN MIGHT
WE GIRD US FOR THE COMING FIGHT,
AND, STRONG IN HIM WHOSE CAUSE IS OURS,
IN CONFLICT WITH UNHOLY POWERS,
WE GRASP THE WEAPONS HE HAS GIVEN,
THE LIGHT AND TRUTH AND LOVE OF HEAVEN.
—JOHN GREENLEAF WHITTIER

Mercy comes down from heaven to earth
so that one, by practicing it, may resemble God.
—GIAMBATTISTA GIRALDI

ETERNAL BLISS IS ROOTED IN GOD ALONE AND NOTHING ELSE.
AND IF PEOPLE ARE TO BE SAVED, THIS ONE AND ONLY GOD
MUST BE IN THEIR SOUL. . . . FOR BLISS OR BLESSEDNESS DOES
NOT COME FROM THE WEALTH OF THINGS, BUT FROM GOD.
—THEOLOGICA GERMANICA

"MY ANXIETIES HAVE ANXIETIES,"

Harold T. Shapiro, former president of Princeton University since 1988 and a respected leader in American higher education for more than twenty years, questions the lack of moral and ethical convictions that our society seems to be embracing. Instead, he challenges the graduates to become anxious about "moral anxiety," to grasp the importance of serving others, and "push forward the boundaries of both knowledge and understanding."

HAROLD SHAPIRO
Princeton University
May 30, 2000

Commencement is always a joyous milestone, not only for the graduating students but for their families and friends, their teachers, and all who have nurtured them, mentored them, and cherished them.

Our justified pride in the achievements of today's graduates is buoyed up even further by our feelings of hope, of anticipation and of optimism as we welcome the next generation of leadership to the challenges and opportunities we all face. It is with great pleasure, therefore, that I join with all of you in celebrating the achievements of today's graduates.

I want to speak about anxiety and ethical controversy. Moreover, I will advance the notion that ethical controversy and at least a certain type of anxiety may be a very good thing.

The particular anxiety I have in mind is a moral anxiety, or a certain anxiousness or uneasiness regarding the nature of the moral responsibilities that accompany our rapidly expanding knowledge of the natural world, our developing moral sensibilities, and our ever larger accumulation of technology and resources.

The anxiety I wish to speak about, therefore, is not the everyday anxiety one may feel about, for example, taking exams or meeting deadlines for your senior thesis. These types of anxieties are real enough, but not the focus of my concerns this morning.

You may, however, remember the *Peanuts* cartoon where Charlie Brown is complaining to Linus that he is not only worried about his exams, but he is also worried about the fact that he is worried. As Charlie Brown explains, even his anxieties have anxieties!

The moral anxiety I will speak about concerns a deeper matter: namely, how we can build a better future by constructing social and cultural institutions and mechanisms that more fully reflect the interests of everyone.

The purpose of my brief remarks is to suggest that such moral anxiety and ethical controversy are essential to the dynamic evolution of our society, and each of us should consider them as welcome companions on our life's journey. I believe that a certain anxiety about society's current circumstance is a necessary ingredient of both a thoughtful life and our capacity to imagine a better future.

Each of us, as individuals, is invested with a great deal of moral autonomy but also moral responsibility. Indeed, the moral authority and responsibility that is now presumed to rest on the shoulders of each one of us is perhaps the most significant aspect of modern life. It is both the greatest source of our freedom and our freedom of conscience, and the most important foundation of our moral responsibility.

In order, therefore, for each of us to meet our moral responsibilities and protect our freedom, we must face and deal with the moral anxieties and ethical controversies of our time. . . .

Each of us, as individuals, is invested with a great deal of moral autonomy but also moral responsibility.

I grew up under the twin shadows of World War II and the Cold War. It seemed easier then to understand just who the major powers and ideologies were that were competing for our allegiance. Our contemporary situation has become much more complex.

Given all these new complexities and general uncertainty regarding our moral responsibilities, the *New York Times* did a national survey on the moral attitudes of individual Americans. The results were reported in the May 7 issue of the *New York Times Magazine*. Let me just quote from the headlines of that survey: "There is no strong god, no strong (moral) rules, and no strong superiors, moral or otherwise; and Americans are unwilling to follow anyone's party line regarding how they ought to behave."

The reporter concluded among other things that, unlike Socrates and Galileo, individual American "dissenters" had no need to escape from society, since society, in the sense of a common source of authoritative rules, had, to some extent, already evaporated. I would conclude that there is an urgent need to take our moral responsibilities more seriously than ever. . . .

You, who are about to become . . . alumni during this important rite of passage today will pass through our gates to raise families, to follow the paths of your careers, to lead your communities—perhaps even your countries— and to serve societies everywhere. I hope that your experience . . . not only helped you gain knowledge but prepared you to eagerly confront, consider, and debate the momentous moral and ethical questions that accompany the flood of new knowledge. It is my belief that these issues will ultimately determine the future of your generation and the many generations to follow.

It will be your task to chart an ethical course that encompasses the rich human diversity of our nation and the complex realities of our rapidly broadening global society. One of the important distinctions that makes us human is the capacity to put ourselves in the mind of another and to understand what they believe, what they need, and what they desire. This treasured human capacity is the source of both our ethical responsibilities and opportunities.

And in the midst of all the change, challenge, and anxiety, let me assure you that there is one thing that we are not anxious about—and that is how ready and able you are to undertake this task, to push forward the boundaries of both knowledge and understanding. . . .

I will close my remarks with the words of Princeton's great nineteenth-century scientist, Joseph Henry: "How short the space of an earthly career and yet what a universe of wonders is presented to us in our rapid flight through this space."

INSIGHTS *for* LIVING

SURELY THE SHORTEST COMMENCEMENT ADDRESS IN
HISTORY—AND FOR ME THE MOST MEMORABLE—WAS THAT OF
DR. HAROLD E. HYDE, PRESIDENT OF NEW HAMPSHIRE'S
PLYMOUTH STATE COLLEGE. HE REDUCED HIS MESSAGE TO THE
GRADUATING CLASS TO THESE THREE IDEALS:

KNOW YOURSELF —SOCRATES

CONTROL YOURSELF —CICERO

GIVE YOURSELF —JESUS CHRIST

—WALTER T. TATURA

As for me, I will see Your face in righteousness;
I shall be satisfied when I awake in Your likeness.

PSALM 17:15 NKJV

THERE'S NOT A SINGLE THING ON OFFER
IN THIS ALL TOO TEMPORARY WORLD FOR WHICH
YOU SHOULD EVER SELL YOUR SOUL.

ALAN KEYES

DREAM THE BOLD DREAM
OF A SERVANT-LEADER

Ann McGee-Cooper, Ed. D., educator, business consultant, and co-founder of Ann McGee-Cooper & Associates in Dallas, addresses graduates on the meaning of "servant-leadership." Just as Jesus washed His disciples' feet in servitude, so we, too, can defy the traditional understanding of leadership and become servant-leaders. "Through God's infinite wisdom, all my dreams and far more have been fulfilled," she says, as she shares what can happen when we "dare to become servant-leaders."

DR. ANN MCGEE-COOPER
Sterling College
May 19, 2001

This is a very special occasion as we come together—family, faculty, college community—to honor and celebrate you, our graduates, poised to now move out into the world in Christian service. Nothing can be more blessed than to choose a life of stewardship through the love of Christ. And you have chosen to prepare yourself in a four-year community of believers where you have studied and lived your faith. So what lies ahead?

In the book of John we are told, "When Jesus had washed the disciples' feet, He sat down and said, 'Do you realize what I have done? You call me 'teacher' and 'Lord' and you are right. If I, your teacher and Lord, have washed your feet, you must be ready to wash one another's feet. I have given you this example so that you may do as I have done.'"

Robert K. Greenleaf, a Quaker by faith, accepted a challenge from one of his professors to go find work in a large corporation and bring change from within. He took that as his calling and from his career of many decades within AT&T created the writings and tradition of Servant-Leadership. He rose through the ranks to become Director of their Management Center and from that position he carefully studied the leadership styles that had the greatest impact, not just on the bottom-line, but on the quality of life for those led by building teamwork, life/work balance, and health of the business for both employees, customers served, and the extended community.

He knew that a new term was needed to describe this profoundly different way of being a leader. In his words, "It begins with the natural feeling that one wants to serve, to serve first. Then conscious choice brings one to aspire to lead. This is sharply different from the person who is leader first, perhaps because of the need to assuage an unusual power drive or to acquire material possessions." He gave this very different form of leadership the name, Servant-Leadership. This very name stops many people in their tracks. They are repelled by the word servant and find this to be the last thing they would want to call themselves. I believe this would please Bob Greenleaf. He knew that we must unlearn all the selfishness and self-serving motives of traditional leadership if we are to truly become Servant-Leaders.

So often we find ourselves conflicted as we dream of the future. We may want to put service first yet still long for all the benefits of becoming a top leader in our field. I have found that if I put my trust in the Holy Spirit, the best will happen. I may not understand early on, but even what I first considered to be tragedy in my life, later I recognized to be significant preparation for what would come next. The pain, loss, and injustices I have experienced gave me the compassion and will to make a positive difference in the lives of others. Dr. Jean Houston calls this "sacred wounding." I now realize that God's infinite love and wisdom

> **I now realize that God's infinite love and wisdom have and are preparing me for my calling.**

have and are preparing me for my calling. "All things work for good for those who love the Lord" (see Romans 8:28) may be another way of acknowledging that truly, all things are possible through faith and God's love.

I have been lucky many, many times throughout my life. I count it a great blessing that I am here with you now and that our team has joined with Sterling College in a partnership pledged to share the spirit of Servant-Leadership through our work and role models, individually and collectively.

I was mentored by Bob Greenleaf the last decade of his life. I remember most of all the spirit of deep listening and challenging questions he would pose. "What are your dreams for your life, Ann? Nothing much happens without a dream. For something great to happen, it takes a great dream." I challenge each of you now to dream a great dream for your life. Do so without editing. Trust your heart to show you and tell you your sacred calling. Don't try to understand. Let it be a leap of faith. Simply listen and be with whatever comes to you.

Early in my career I worked with NASA in Clear Lake just outside of Houston. It was there I first learned of the field of accessing our higher intelligence through imaging. This was used with scientists, engineers, and the astronauts to create and prepare for journeys never taken before. May I invite you to tune into your higher self through this experience? And be assured that if you are more comfortable with prayer, it brings the same deepening experience. Trust your own sense of what is right for you.

Begin with several slow deep breaths to relax yourself and open your mind. Gently close your eyes to shut out other distractions. Relax and get comfortable where you are. Feel your heart beating. Now, gently go into the future and pose the question. If you were to make your life count, if you were to dare to live into your sacred gifts, if you were to become the best of who you are, a blessed child of God, a true messenger of divine love, where would you go, what might you do? What are the issues and challenges that call to you? Is it protecting the environment? Teaching? Serving in a non-profit organization? Founding your own business or finding a career within a large corporation? Medicine, law, the arts, music . . . simply notice what fills your imagination? How will you choose to serve?

Go also to your personal life. Finding a loving mate, perhaps having a family together, creating a lovely and loving home. Simply allow the dreams to find you. I have learned that this is a way to become still and hear or sense the will of God for my life.

One mistake I made early on was to believe that if I claimed one part of my dream, I would have to give up another. This was my lack of faith. The amazing thing is that through God's infinite wisdom, all my dreams and far more have been fulfilled. What I used to regard as frivolous and wishful day-dreams, I now recognize as God whispering in my ear.

May I share with you one story to illustrate the abundant miracles that await us if we only dare to become Servant-Leaders.

In 1970, I was guiding a Master's level, graduate practicum in art therapy for one of my students in a children's psychiatric unit in Children's Medical Center, Dallas. My student had been assigned to work with a ten-year-old boy, I'll call David, who had been abandoned repeatedly in his early life, first by his mother, then grandmother, then passed around to any number of foster homes. David looked like a normal ten-year-old from the waist up. But from the waist down his growth had been stunted at about age five and his legs were like those of a midget. No one seemed to know why his legs stopped growing but now, with each year, he became more and more disproportioned. And as a result, other children shunned him, and David was very withdrawn.

In the early briefing, David's psychiatrist explained that this child had such a fear of being hurt by getting attached to anyone that he could be expected to do something very hurtful to Nancy, my student, if he felt him-self beginning to care about her. The doctor explained that her test would be to not turn away when this happened but to find the courage to continue to care about David beyond his repelling behavior, whatever that might be.

Nancy and I would go to the psychiatric unit once a week for art therapy with David. There was a small room where she would set up art supplies. David would come in and be invited to either paint, work in clay, or build with other materials. Nancy would bring some motivation such as a story about animals, a circus, or other theme to stimulate ideas for making art. I would observe behind one-way glass so that I could coach Nancy before and after each session. At the close of each session, Nancy would ask David if there was a story that went with his work. Almost always there was, and Nancy would write the story as David told it. Then together they would clean up, Nancy would display his work and his story, we'd say goodbye, and then debrief with the medical team.

After almost a semester of art therapy sessions, which David seemed to really enjoy, one day David was painting. He had finished his painting, and as Nancy wrote down the story David was telling her, without warning David doubled up his fist and, without looking up, hit Nancy as hard as he could in the face. She staggered a bit. I was not sure whether to rush in or wait. Nancy recomposed herself and finished writing. David, again without making eye contact, said, "I'll never see you again will I?"

Nancy said calmly, "I'll be back next week. But I hope you won't hit me. That really hurt."

David said quietly, "I won't hit you."

At the follow-up staffing session, we were told that Nancy had successfully passed David's test. He was subconsciously trying to drive her away, testing her commitment to their relationship. When she returned the next week, he began to believe he could trust her to not abandon him as had happened so many times before in his young life.

In the next few weeks, David began to change remarkably. He talked more, laughed often, and became more animated. For the first time, he would even hug Nancy as he greeted her and said goodbye. What astounded even the medical team was the fact that within three months, David's legs began to grow. As his spirit dared to stir, his body seemed to also awaken and become whole.

In a field now called psychoneuroimmunology, we have learned that our emotions, nervous system, and immune system are all connected. And as David began to trust and even allow himself to love and be loved, his body began to grow in a normal way.

My dream as I left college was to make a difference, somewhere, somehow. I wanted to find those being forgotten by others and find ways to give them hope. I wanted to live a life of full-time Christian service. I wanted to dare to believe in and live from the genius that God gives to each of us, that specialness that makes us each unlike any other. Many times each day I pray, "I will, to will, Thy will." And as I let go of my will and trust the Holy Spirit, again and again miracles happen through God's presence and love.

I urge you to dream bold dreams.

And dare to make your part of the world better by choosing to be a servant-leader.

Robert Greenleaf said, "Too many settle for being critics and experts. There is too much intellectual wheel spinning, . . . too little preparation for and willingness to undertake the hard and high-risk tasks of building better institutions in an imperfect world, too little disposition to see 'the problem' as residing in here and not out there. In short, the enemy is not the evil people but the strong natural servants who have the potential to lead but do not lead, or who choose to follow a non-servant."

And so, my friends and special graduates, I urge you to dream bold dreams. And dare to make your part of the world better by choosing to be a servant-leader.

INSIGHTS *for* LIVING

*I am not ashamed, for I know whom I have believed
and am persuaded that He is able to keep what I have
committed to Him until that Day.*

2 TIMOTHY 1:12 NKJV

THE CHRISTIAN IDEAL HAS NOT BEEN TRIED AND FOUND
WANTING. IT HAS BEEN FOUND DIFFICULT AND LEFT UNTRIED.

—G. K. CHESTERTON

*A person who lives right and is right has more power in his
silence than another has by words. Character is like bells
which ring out sweet notes and which, when touched—
accidentally even—resound with sweet music.*

—PHILLIPS BROOKS

IN THE WORLD BUT NOT OF IT

Dr. Gerald Kieschnick, president of the Lutheran-Church Missouri Synod, tells the graduates that in spite of life's many challenges ahead, the relationship with their Savior and God is what will see them through. They must bear their faith before the world with confidence and leave the future to God.

Dr. Gerald Kieschnick
Concordia University at Austin
May 11, 2002

Your parents know as well as anyone what sort of world awaits you out there. It's a far more complicated world than the one they knew when they were your age. There's war and terror. There's economic instability and job insecurity. There are children gunning down other children in schools and people putting poison and pipe bombs in the mail. There's a sea of broken human relationships. There's an upside-down view of what's right and wrong, moral and immoral, acceptable and unacceptable.

That's the way it is in the year 2002, but it is not something you need to fear. You have your faith, you have your church, you have your families—all of them reminding you that, in Christ, you have perfect righteousness before God. As Martin Luther said, "This righteousness is your ground and anchor-hold in life." This relationship with your Savior and God is what will see you through, no matter what you may encounter in the days and years ahead.

And you will encounter very real and certain challenges. For one, as you go out into the marketplace of America, you will discover—if you haven't discovered it already—that Christianity is not held in the highest regard by everyone. Many people in our society do not necessarily appreciate our Christian faith and values.

But this is nothing new. As Billy Graham said, "It is not unnatural for Christianity to be unpopular."

One reason Christianity is unpopular with some is that we Christians believe that our faith is the one and only true pathway to God and salvation. We base this belief on the words of Jesus Christ Himself, who said, "I am the Way and the Truth and the Life. No one comes to the Father except through me" (John 14:6 NKJV).

This truth seems clear to us, who believe it with all of our hearts, but it flies in the face of our increasingly diverse and permissive culture. This culture insists that all faiths are equally valid, all different routes to the same goal. In the eyes of this culture, it is the height of arrogance and narrow-mindedness for anyone to suggest that his or her faith is the only true one.

One of the most influential people in our country, Oprah Winfrey, recently said: "One of the biggest mistakes humans make is to believe there is only one way. Actually, there are many diverse paths leading to what you call God." We Christians respectfully but strongly disagree.

Again, however, this is hardly new thinking. In fact, 300 years ago, Frederick the Great, King of Prussia, wrote: "All religions must be tolerated. Every man must get to heaven in his own way."

What I believe you'll find, as you go out into the world, is that every religion is being tolerated—with the exception of Christianity. Not along ago, a U.S. congressman from Texas gave a speech to a private group of evangelical Christians. The congressman, a devout Christian himself, said the following:

Christianity offers the only viable, reasonable, definitive answer to the questions of "Where did I come from? Why am I here? Where am I going? Does life have any meaningful purpose?" Only Christianity offers a comprehensive worldview that covers all areas of life and thought, every aspect of creation. Only Christianity offers a way to live in response to the realities we find in this world. Only Christianity. . . .

When his critics heard about this speech, you would have thought the congressman had just committed the most villainous, treasonous crime imaginable, when in fact all he had done was share his personal testimony in a private setting of fellow Christians. His critics thundered that the congressman had shown a shocking, callous disregard for the religious pluralism of the United States.

To which the congressman replied, "No, that's not the case at all. In sharing my own experience and personal beliefs, I was emphasizing the need for Christian people to get involved in this country. I was emphasizing the need for them not to segregate their religious worldview from their outward, daily lives."

Actually, in a nutshell, this is probably the main point of my talk to you today. Don't segregate your religious worldview—your precious Christian faith—from your outward, daily lives in this world. Bear your faith proudly, always on the lookout for ways to share it, and always on the lookout for those who would seek to marginalize you, or even harm you, because of it.

A week or two ago, NBC-TV aired a special celebrating the network's seventy-five years in the radio and television business. I didn't see much of the program, but one clip I did see featured a scene from a popular police show of several years ago called *Hill Street Blues*. In this scene, which recurred every week, the sergeant tells the officers, who have just received their day's assignments, to "be careful out there." I would encourage you, too, to be careful out there. At the same time, I would also encourage you not to be overly gun-shy or apologetic about who you are, what you believe, and what you, as a Christian, stand for.

There is a place at the table for you as Christians, even in this wide-open, anything-goes, nothing-is-shocking-anymore society of ours in the year 2002. Some voices at the table will disagree with you. Others will ridicule you. Others will try to shout you down. But you can handle all that.

You will do your best if you can respect, at least outwardly, the spiritual views of others, while holding firm to your own. Think of the Apostle Paul, in Athens, in the Areopagus, as your model. Paul knew that the beliefs of the Athenians were false, and that the people there would not be saved eternally if they did not come to saving faith in Jesus Christ. But he didn't start off by hitting them over the head with this news. Rather, he sought to connect with them in various ways. He even flattered them by saying, judging from all the altars to their pantheon of gods, they must be "a very religious people." Only when the time was right did Paul make his move. Happily, owing to his patience, diplomacy, and resolve, he met with some success.

The Areopagus of ancient Greece was not unlike the marketplace of modern America. It teemed with any number of competing philosophies and religious ideas. But of course—then as now—there was, and is, only one right idea: the free gift, given to all the world, of God's grace and mercy through faith in Jesus Christ.

If you will seek to comport yourself like Paul, I think you will find that the marketplace—or at least part of it—is prepared to listen to your reasoned defense of the hope that lives within you. Some will scoff, of course; they always have and they always will. But others, as with Paul, will be intrigued and say, "We want to hear you again on this subject. Will you come back and talk to us another day?"

My dear graduates, it is imperative that each of you, it is imperative that all of us, our entire church, pastors, and laypeople alike, continue to carry the cross of Christ into the marketplace. Remember the command of the hymn "Lift High the Cross." The cross of Jesus is not personal property of ours that we are to protect and keep to ourselves. It is not something that we are to reflect on only with like-minded people on Sunday mornings.

Let me share with you some words from the twentieth-century Scottish clergyman George MacLeod:

> I argue that the cross be raised again at the center of the marketplace as well as on the steeple of the church. Jesus was not crucified in a cathedral between two candles, but on a cross between two thieves, on the town garbage heap; at a crossroads so cosmopolitan they had to write His title in Hebrew and in Latin and in Greek; at the kind of place where cynics talk smut, and thieves curse, and soldiers gamble. Because that is where Jesus died, and because that is what He died about, that is where churchmen [and churchwomen] of today should be.

So, to you graduates of Concordia University at Austin, in the year of our Lord 2002, I appeal to you, in the words of Christ, to be in the world, but not of it. (see John 17:14.) I entreat you, in the words of Peter, to "save yourselves from this corrupt generation," (see Acts 2:40) while at the same time helping to save that corrupt generation from itself.

Do your best with this. Be winsome and effective witnesses to your Lord and to your faith. At the same time, don't feel that the weight of the world—the weight of saving the world—is entirely on your shoulders. Don't feel too much pressure. You have just come through four years of pressure, and you are about to enter a new phase of life that will bring pressures of its own.

So, enjoy your life. Enjoy your friends and loved ones. Enjoy your new pursuits, your new jobs, your new independence. And when opportunities do arise for you to share your faith, to stand up for your Christian principles, to shoulder the cross of Christ and carry it into the marketplace, remember that you do all these things with God's help and blessing.

God loves you right down to your soul. He loves you with a passion. He loves you with the adoring, cherishing love of a parent for a child. He will never heap more expectations on you, He will never give you more burdens or pressure, than you can handle.

> **You have reached a key milestone, a key crossroad, in your walk through time. I am confident that, as you continue that walk, you will leave worthy evidence of your passage.**

As someone once said, no man or woman ever sank under the burden of the day. It is when tomorrow's burden is added to today's that the weight becomes more than you can bear. Never load yourself that way. And if you do find yourself so loaded, remember that it is your doing, or the world's doing, not God's doing.

Jesus Christ Himself tells you to leave the future to Him. You just worry about the present, and even then He will be there to help you. Seek first His kingdom and His righteousness, and all the things you find yourself worrying about will be given to you as well. (See Matthew 6:33.)

These wonderful proceedings today are a celebration of what you have accomplished and a festival of the future you are about to begin. Concordia University now sends you off, with Godspeed, into that future.

Of course, no one knows what that future holds, or how much time it contains before the Lord returns. But, again, we are not to worry about that. Rather, we are to be about our business as Christ's agents and ambassadors on this earth. "As long as it is day," Jesus says, "We must do the work of him who sent me. Night is coming, when no one can work"(John 9:4 NASB).

So, graduates, while it is day, be about your business, guided by the Light of the world, Jesus Christ, the Savior of the world and the Lord of the universe. You have reached a key milestone, a key crossroad, in your walk through time. I am confident that, as you continue that walk, you will leave worthy evidence of your passage.

THANK YOU, AND GOD BLESS YOU ALL.

INSIGHTS *for* LIVING

THE SUPREME END OF EDUCATION IS EXPERT DISCERNMENT IN ALL THINGS—THE POWER TO TELL THE GOOD FROM THE BAD, THE GENUINE FROM THE COUNTERFEIT, AND TO PREFER THE GOOD AND THE GENUINE TO THE BAD AND THE COUNTERFEIT.

—SAMUEL JOHNSON

Youth is not a time of life but a state of mind,
a temper of will, a quality of the imagination,
a predominance of courage over timidity, of the appetite
for adventure over the love of ease.

—ROBERT KENNEDY

WHEN YOU WERE BORN,

YOU CRIED AND THE WORLD REJOICED.

LIVE YOUR LIFE IN SUCH A WAY THAT WHEN YOU DIE

THE WORLD CRIES AND YOU REJOICE.

—INDIAN PROVERB

Commune with your own selves, for the kingdom of God is
within you. See with whom you associate, with whom you
readily stay; and examine the reasons and the tendency to all
evil habits. For if a person gives way to a fault for a year or
two, that fault takes such deep root in their heart, that they
can scarcely overcome it with all their might.

—JOHANN TAULER

TO SERVE AND NOT BE SERVED

Diana Chapman Walsh, alumna and twelfth president of Wellesley College, tells graduates that yes, they are ready, they are equipped to walk "the next step of their journey." Walsh encourages graduates to exercise patience, confidence, and balance as they move forward. She closes her message with words of advice from those alumnae who graduated fifty years ago.

DIANA CHAPMAN WALSH
Wellesley College
May 29, 1998

W ell, my charged up [graduates in the] . . . class of 1998, we are fast approaching the point of culmination. The moment has come now for me to bid you good bye and good luck.

This is a bittersweet moment for those of us you are leaving behind. We will miss this class of '98, your spark and your spirit. And I know from our conversations that many of you are leaving with your own mixed feelings: great excitement intermingled with just a touch of apprehension about what the future may hold, and a sense of loss as you take your leave from your friends, your professors, and this beautiful campus that has been "home" for the past four years.

This section of the program is the traditional president's "charge to the seniors"—the president's last official opportunity to address you as . . . students. (You don't have your diplomas yet; I still have your attention). Soon you will . . . fan out all over the country, all over the world—indeed, as we now know, into the solar system—and you'll begin to work the magic you have worked here.

My heart is full of things I want to say to you in this moment laden with meaning and with expectation, in this momentary pause in your life's journey from challenge to challenge, from lesson to lesson, from strength to strength. I want to tell you how grateful we are for each of you, for who you have been and who you are becoming, for the many talents you have brought to this place, for your energy and your commitment, for your creativity and the countless ways you showed us that you cared.

I want to tell you how hopeful we are for the difference we know you will make in this world that so badly needs the gifts you now carry forth. During your four years here—as throughout history—people all over this country and this world have fought, killed, abused, neglected, and harmed

My heart is full of things I want to say to you in this moment laden with meaning and with expectation, in this momentary pause in your life's journey from challenge to challenge, from lesson to lesson, from strength to strength.

one other, brutally and inconceivably, day after day, brutalities so commonplace that we become inured to them.

And, at the same time, other people—often unheralded—have patiently persevered in setting the world right, in protecting the weak and powerless, in preserving those things that are beautiful, irreplaceable, good, and true. I know you will align your lives with stewardship for the future. . . . Knowing that you will carry on gives us hope.

I want to tell you how ready you are, how well equipped for this next stage of your journey. You take a cargo that will serve you well—the ability to read critically, write persuasively, speak cogently, reason analytically, a knowledge base from which to think historically, spatially, cross-culturally, comparatively, and (not least) with empathy. You take habits of mind that will always remain fundamental to your sense of self—a habit of questioning assumptions, avoiding bias, prejudice, and rigidities of thought, a habit of learning—forever learning, never give that up—of listening well and always imagining the ways you may be wrong. And you take the incomparable treasure of the extraordinary women—your Wellesley sisters from all over the country and the world—in whose company you have spent the past four years.

I want to tell you to stay in touch with each other and with us. As you prepare now to commence the next stage of your lives—to continue your education, to begin careers, to put down your roots and build families and communities. . . . These connections will remain an extraordinary resource for you. Keep them alive, cultivate and nurture the bonds—and values—you share.

I want to tell you to be patient with all that is unresolved in your hearts. There will be hard times ahead, just as there have been here, times when you will feel as though you have lost your way, lost your grasp of the meaning of it all, lost your belief in yourself. Often those painful times are the sources of greatest learning. You will feel like a fraud sometimes, someone who doesn't belong, someone in over her head—feelings I know you have experienced on occasion here.

But also you have experienced here your largest, fullest self—a person of intellectual passions, promise, and discipline, a person who honors diversity, embraces ambiguity, practices honesty, experiences humility, and exercises great care for the things you value most. You have memory anchors rooted in this place for that person of integrity. When you feel lost you can call them forth. Those anchors in memory will remain here for you throughout your lives.

Finally, I want to urge you to relax, take your time, keep your balance and perspective. I know how hard it is for you to hear that message now, in this hypercharged world that awaits you impatiently, so it seems. With everything moving so fast it is excruciatingly difficult to hold to the belief that life is long and there is time.

To anchor that message in a more concrete reality, I bring you, in closing, greetings from fifty years out, from the class of '48. In anticipation of their fiftieth reunion next week, they filled out a survey developed by Judith Krantz, the best-selling author, whom (you may not know) is a member of that Wellesley class.

One of the questions she asked her classmates to address was for you— their "best single piece of advice" on the occasion of your graduation. I wish I could read you all of what they said, across this span of half a century of . . . experience. I can tell you that many counseled you to give yourselves some margin for error, be comfortable with yourselves, to savor life's small pleasures, keep your sense of humor, reach for your dreams and yet be ready to change, "play the hand you're dealt with patience, strength, courage and good cheer," one wrote. Learn to prioritize. "You *can* have it all," several said with the wisdom of hindsight, "just not all at once."

"Take your time finding out what you want to do with your life," another wrote. "Try out many things; don't panic and make a commitment too early. It took me twenty years and a number of false starts to find the right kind of teaching and the perfect setting for me. But I found it." "Second choices are sometimes excellent choices," another wrote as she described a series of life choices she had made; "Flexibility is essential to a happy and productive life." "Know yourself, like yourself, and always be yourself."

"Enjoy every precious moment of your life and loves, keeping all that you hold dear very tenderly in your heart," another said, and two wanted you to remember that it's more important to love than to be loved. "Know that it is better to love well than to guard a fearful heart," another added. "I'm not a religious person," said another, "but I often think of those great gold letters in Wellesley's chapel which proclaim that 'God is Love'. I have found that to be extraordinarily true."

These older [graduates] urge you to find balance in your lives, to work and be proud of your accomplishments, to achieve the utmost without expecting too much of yourselves or others, and to have friends and loved ones whom you trust. They hope you will discover, as they have, "the simple truth that everyone—each one of us—is born both gifted and handicapped. It is up to us to celebrate the gifts and help each other with the handicaps."

They especially hope (as I do) that you will never forget "our Wellesley motto," to serve and not be served.

And finally, they want you to know how impressed they are with you. One spoke for many when she wrote on her survey form, "the recent . . . graduates I meet fill me with awe. With their calm collectedness, sense of timing and direction and their accomplishments, it's they who should be giving the advice to us, not we to them."

Fifty years from now it *will* be you giving the advice, reading your class-mates' accounts of twists and turns in their lives, of their triumphs and pas-sions, sorrows and disappointments, all they have learned, and the work that absorbs them still. May the years ahead be filled with much joy and happi-ness, many successes and satisfactions, many . . . connections and many visits back to campus.

We'll miss you Class of '98. You go with our admiration, our aspirations for the future, and the pride of this institution—you go with our best wishes and with our love.

GODSPEED TO YOU ALL.

PUTTING THE BIG ROCKS FIRST

*Currently the President of International Operations at MIC Industries
and formerly Chairman of the Joint Chiefs of Staff, General Henry
Shelton focuses on the elements of a strong moral character, the "big rocks
of life," as he calls them. "Be excited at the journey you are beginning
today," General Shelton says, "but I hope you will also embrace the
responsibilities that these diplomas endow."*

GENERAL HENRY H. SHELTON,
*Auburn University at Montgomery
March 14, 2000*

I'm not going to talk about the battle against terrorism, military budgets,
or the latest world crisis. Instead, I want to focus on the future—*your*
future—and specifically, about the need for perseverance, courage, and
character.

I am sure that when you look back on the hours of study and hard work
it took to graduate, that all of the graduates here are very happy, and possibly a bit relieved. You can remember well, I'm sure when many obstacles
stood between you and a diploma. There were many books to read, numerous
papers to write, and dreaded exams to pass. And for some of you this effort
was done while you were working to support yourselves and your families.

But you *persevered* and *survived.*

It reminds me of the story about the man who arrived late to his son's
little league game. He sat down behind the bench and asked one of the boys
what the score was. The boy answered with a smile; "We're behind fourteen
to nothing.""

The man said, "Really? You don't look very discouraged."

The boy replied, "Why would I be discouraged? We haven't been up to
bat yet."

Now that's perseverance, and in a similar way, you have demonstrated
this same spirit.

You have also proven that you possess the drive and the determination
required of our most successful leaders.

Success in the future will require the same kind of perseverance as well
as a healthy dose of courage.

I'm not talking about the type of courage you see on the battlefield,
although at some point you may be called on to show that type of courage.

Instead, I'm talking about the type of courage that allows you to take chances and make mistakes. I'm talking about having the courage to believe in yourself and about having the courage to adjust and adapt to this ever-changing world.

I'm talking about the "two o'clock in the morning" kind of courage that turns defeats into victories, frustration into satisfaction, and visions into reality.

The courage to believe in yourself, and do the right thing.

Since the course of progress is rarely a straight line you will often need a compass to guide and focus your courage.

That's where character comes in.

Character is your moral compass. It sees you safely through the storms of life by providing you with *direction*.

I'm convinced that you cannot be a great scientist, nurse, parent, teacher, or soldier for that matter, unless you possess a strong ethical character. Or as Benjamin Franklin said, "It is a grand mistake to think of being great without goodness."

The values that form your character are not grown overnight, but are assimilated over a lifetime. I once heard a story that illustrates how you should live your life to build the right kind of character.

An expert in time management was speaking to a group and put a one-gallon, wide-mouth Mason jar on the podium. He pulled out a dozen rocks, about the size of your fist, and began putting them into the jar. When the jar was filled to the top and no more rocks would fit inside, he asked, "Is the jar full?"

Everyone answered: "Yes."

The time management expert reached under the podium and pulled out a bucket of gravel. He dumped some gravel in and shook the jar so that the gravel worked its way down into the spaces between the rocks. He asked the group again, "Is the jar full?"

By this time, they were on to him. "Probably not," someone yelled.

"Good," he replied and he brought out a bucket of sand. He started dumping the sand into the jar and it went into all of the spaces left between the rocks and the gravel. Once more he asked, "Is the jar full?"

"No," they shouted.

Then the expert grabbed a pitcher of water and began to pour it in until the jar was filled to the brim. Then he looked at the group and asked, "What is the point of this illustration?"

One person said, "It shows that no matter how full your schedule is, if you try really hard you can always fit some more things in it."

"No," the speaker replied, "that's not the point. What this illustration teaches us is that if you don't put the big rocks in first, you'll never get them in at all."

The BIG ROCKS in your life are those things that form your character—time with your loved ones, practicing your faith, improving your education, or working on a worthy cause. Remember to put these BIG ROCKS in first or you'll never get them in at all.

So later tonight or tomorrow morning when you think about this story, ask yourself this question: What are the BIG ROCKS in my life? Then put those in your jar first.

Well, I can see from the look on the faces of the graduates that they are hoping the big moment will arrive *sooner* rather than *later*. So, let me close by saying that you should be excited at the journey you are beginning today, but I hope you will also embrace the responsibilities that these diplomas endow.

The BIG ROCKS in your life are those things that form your character—time with your loved ones, practicing your faith, improving your education, or working on a worthy cause.

All of the changes we have seen in the past decade—the end of the Cold War; the technological advances in electronics, medicine, computers, and the Internet; and the possibility of a more peaceful and prosperous world—have came from the labors of generations that passed before.

You graduates are the beneficiaries of their wars, their struggles, their inventions, the knowledge they created the universities they founded.

It is up to you to continue to build on the foundation they have provided.

In a large part, what the future will be like, the future of your family, your community, and your country will depend on you.

And it is clear to me, as I look out at this diverse group of the Class of 2000, that the future will be in good hands.

I hope that you will look back to this day and remember that your commencement speaker was the Chairman of the Joint Chiefs of Staff, who spoke not of war, the defense budget, or the threats to our national security—Rather, that he spoke about perseverance, courage, and character—and about putting the BIG ROCKS in your life first.

Good luck to you, and may God Bless you and your families—and may God bless the United States of America.

ONE INDIVIDUAL—A WORLD OF DIFFERENCE

Having served three United States Presidents in various political positions and a Republican candidate for President herself, Senator Elizabeth Dole asks graduates a question: what choices will you make? Will they be ones of ambivalence or will they be choices of courage and honesty? "[For] wherever you go, you will be leaders. And the decisions that you make will have tremendous impact."

ELIZABETH DOLE
Notre Dame
May 16, 1999

G raduates—this is your day! My heartfelt congratulations! . . .

You know, it is not often in life we have a chance to sit down and think about our future. This is a turning point for you, and it comes at a time that is a turning point for our nation and our world. . . .

As a young woman, looking forward to my life's work, I found my highest ideals in public service. I believed, and still believe, that the greatest life is a life of service, and that public service, in a democracy such as ours, is one of the most satisfying ways to give back. . . .

What choices will you make?

Somewhere in the Class of '99 is a man or woman who will schedule a prime-time television show that beams into millions of homes. Another will be behind a corporate desk, wrestling over where to locate a new factory, and whether to close an old one. A school administrator will put in a purchase order for textbooks that an entire city's students will turn to for the truth. A military officer will say good-bye to spouse and child to meet a crisis overseas. Journalist, physician, musician, scientist, each with his or her own special challenges, I can't even begin to imagine all the possibilities. Some of you may even become politicians.

Indeed, if current trends are any indication, many of you will begin one career, then change, then change again. But wherever you go, you will be leaders. And the decisions that you make will have tremendous impact.

Since earliest childhood, I'm sure you've been told how important it will be to live good lives, lives of honesty, integrity, and civility—within your families, as neighbors, as students. But how important it will be—to carry your character and values into the world.

Many good people look around at our society and decide: "The most I can do is take care of myself and my family. Let somebody else deal with the mess in city hall or Washington or Kosovo" or wherever the problems lie.

If you fall prey to this mistaken idea, we're in trouble. Our country is built on what we, as individuals, bring to the public arena. "A nation, as a society, forms a moral person," Thomas Jefferson once wrote, "and every member of it is personally responsible for his society." And let me assure you, one individual can make a world of difference . . . even, I might say, a different world. . . .

> **Let us live in the harness, striving mightily. Let us run the risk of wearing out, rather than rusting out."**

Graduates, may you live by the words of Teddy Roosevelt. These are favorite words of mine. This quotation hangs on the wall of my office: "We are face to face with our destiny, and we must meet it with a high and resolute courage. For ours is the life of action, of strenuous performance of duty. Let us live in the harness, striving mightily. Let us run the risk of wearing out, rather than rusting out."

Thank you so very much. God bless each and every one of you. Thank you very, very much.

FOLLOW TO LEAD

Robert Ballard, the leader of the expedition to recover the sunken R.M.S. *Titanic and a participant in almost one hundred other deep-sea expeditions, speaks of dreams and heroes. But instead of focusing on success and leadership, Ballard emphasizes the importance of knowing how to follow and "how to get back up after being knocked down." "How strong is your heart?" he asks.*

ROBERT D. BALLARD
Worcester Polytechnic Institute
May 23, 1992

To me, life is a great adventure. A series of journeys within journeys, circles within circles. And like all great journeys, they begin with a dream. When I was growing up, dreams were, and still are, a major part of my life. Everyone should dream and then try to make those dreams come true. For me, my dreams dealt with adventure. My heroes were people like Marco Polo, Captain James Cook, and mythical characters out of Jules Verne's novels. . . . My biggest dream was to build a submarine myself and sail around the world underwater—to be Captain Nemo and look out of his magical window to see things no one had ever seen before. . . .

In an epic journey, after you have a dream, you begin to prepare yourself to pursue that dream. That is what many of you have been doing for the last four years. . . .

To me, life is a great adventure. A series of journeys within journeys, circles within circles. And like all great journeys, they begin with a dream.

Your childhood is spent dreaming, your young adulthood preparing. The moment finally comes when it is time to venture forth. If your dream is a big one, you will need help, you will need to be part of a team. Initially, you will follow, but then you will lead. You will never make a good leader unless you have learned to follow. On those initial journeys when you are asked to pull your oar while another leads, learn what it takes to be a team player. Learn how to get along with others. Learn what loyalty and honesty are all about. Anyone can get to the top by taking shortcuts by climbing over the bodies of others. But if you take that route, your time at the top will be short-lived.

Finally, after working for years to help someone else live their dream, your turn will come. And when you lead your team on its first adventure in life, be prepared to fail initially. For no quest is worth pursuing that does not require you to pass many tests, take numerous risks. . . . Every major adventure I have been on over the years has tested me severely with violent storms and lost equipment. My first voyage to find the Titanic ended in failure. My first expedition to find the Bismarck failed as well. The test you must pass is not whether you fall down or not but whether you can get back up after being knocked down. The journeys you will now begin in life will test you to find how well you prepared your mind, but the hardest tests of all will look to see how determined you are to live your dream, how strong is your heart. . . .

The journeys you will now begin in life will test you to find how well you prepared your mind, but the hardest tests of all will look to see how determined you are to live your dream, how strong is your heart. . . .

Your journey is not over once your goal is reached, your dream fulfilled, the truth attained. The journey is never over until you share what you have learned with others. Then and only then can you begin preparing yourself for your next adventure. Sharing is the final step, when you give up what you have learned. Giving is not something that may interest you right now, but always remember life is never fulfilled, your journey never over until you take time to give back a portion of what has been given to you.

I congratulate all of you for dreaming dreams and preparing yourself to live those dreams. This is at hand to move on to the next phase. When life knocks you down, which it will, lay there for a second and reflect upon what has happened. Learn from your mistake, but then get back up. Do not let anyone stop you from fulfilling your dreams.

INSIGHTS *for* LIVING

THE LOGIC OF WORLDLY SUCCESS RESTS ON A FALLACY: THE STRANGE ERROR THAT OUR PERFECTION DEPENDS ON THE THOUGHTS AND OPINIONS AND APPLAUSE OF OTHER MEN! A WEIRD LIFE IT IS, INDEED, TO BE LIVING ALWAYS IN SOMEBODY ELSE'S IMAGINATION, AS IF THAT WERE THE ONLY PLACE IN WHICH ONE COULD AT LAST BECOME REAL!

—THOMAS MERTON

Remember the truth that once was spoken: To love another person is to see the face of God!

—VICTOR HUGO, *LES MISERABLES*

HE IS RICH OR POOR ACCORDING TO WHAT HE IS, NOT ACCORDING TO WHAT HE HAS.

—HENRY WARD BEECHER

I am not bound to win, but I am bound to be true. I am not bound to succeed, but I am bound to live by the light that I have. I must stand with anybody that stands right, stand with him while he is right, and part with him when he goes wrong.

—ABRAHAM LINCOLN

CHRIST, THE GROUND OF OUR TOLERANCE

Dr. John Piper, preaching pastor of Bethlehem Baptist Church in Minneapolis, Minnesota, writer of more than twenty books, and well-known speaker, addresses an important issue in our world today: "what is the relationship between Jesus Christ and religious pluralism and tolerance?" Religious tolerance will ultimately end, he says, when Jesus Christ returns but for now, we must "become unshakeable trees of conviction and courage and love" to those around us.

JOHN PIPER
Wheaton College
May 12, 2002

The events of September 11th last year unleashed in the Christian community a tidal wave of compassion and cowardice. The compassion at ground zero and beyond has been beautiful and is owing to the life that remains in the tree of conviction concerning Jesus Christ. The cowardice is owing to the fact that for many, the root of the tree of conviction has been severed. A long time before September 11th, the ax of unbelief had been laid to the root of conviction, and the withering of courage was predictable.

The cowardice I have in mind, of course, is not the daring of Todd Beamer on United Flight 93 over Pennsylvania (class of '91). The cowardice I have in mind is the fear in the hearts of Christian clergy to make the supremacy of Jesus Christ central in the public, religious events that followed the calamity, especially when Muslims were present. When Jesus Christ himself, the crucified God-man and the Lord of glory, is made subordinate to the cultivation of amicable, patriotic, religious feeling, He is crucified afresh on the altar of clerical cowardice. It was a sad spectacle.

And it has set many of us to pondering with more urgency than we ever have the issues of tolerance and religious pluralism in national and global perspective. There are not many issues that the class of 2002 needs to have more clear than this: what is the relationship between Jesus Christ and religious pluralism and tolerance?

The issue of religious pluralism and tolerance in the world is tremendously complex for

. . . what is the relationship between Jesus Christ and religious pluralism and tolerance?

several reasons. One is that religion is woven into life and produces behaviors that may meet intolerant legal regulation: letting your child die rather than using medical treatment, smoking Peyote as part of a religious rite, practicing polygamy, refusing to pledge allegiance to the American flag. And the issue is complex because with the rise of Islamic states and the civil implementation of Sharia, the assumptions that we have of separating church and state are increasingly challenged. And we find ourselves today, for example, pouring billions of dollars into the creation of a state in the Middle East that is committed to religious intolerance.

But complexity or no complexity, the members of the class of 2002 will have to take a position on this issue because neutrality is a position on this issue, and a very radical one. What is the relationship between Jesus Christ and religious pluralism and tolerance? In the few minutes I have, I want to plant a seed in the soil of your mind and heart in the hope that they will grow up and become a tree of unshakable Biblical conviction and courage and love.

> **Christianity will spread not by killing *for* Christ, but by dying *with* Christ— that others might live.**

Here's the seed: Jesus Christ, the source and ground of all truth, will himself one day bring an end to all tolerance, and He alone will be exalted as the one and only Lord and Savior and Judge of the universe. Therefore, since Jesus Christ alone, the Creator and Lord of history, has the right to wield the tolerance-ending sword, we dare not.

To put it another way: All religious tolerance will end because Christ will come. And therefore it dare not end until He comes.

To put it a third way: Because Christ alone is absolute and infinite in his wisdom and power and justice and grace, He alone is the final end of tolerance, and therefore the present ground of tolerance.

Or to put it more personally, you not only may, but must, make room for religious pluralism in the world, not in spite of, but because of, the absolute Lordship of Jesus Christ over all false religions.

Or, to put it most radically and most violently—and most Biblically— since the wrath of Jesus will consign to everlasting punishment all who do not obey the gospel, therefore we must give place to wrath, and love our enemies. Since Christ alone, crucified-for-sinners, has the final right to kill his religious enemies, therefore Christianity will spread not by killing *for* Christ, but by dying *with* Christ—that others might live. The final triumph of the crucified Christ is a call to patient suffering, not political success.

Listen to the apostle Paul in 2 Thessalonians 1:7-10:

The Lord Jesus [will be] revealed from heaven with his mighty angels in flaming fire, inflicting vengeance on those who do not know God and on those who do not obey the gospel of our Lord Jesus. They will suffer the punishment of eternal destruction, away from the presence of the Lord and from the glory of his might, when he comes on that day to be glorified in his saints, and to be marveled at among all who have believed.

Wheaton College embraces this terrible and glorious truth with these words:

"WE BELIEVE in the blessed hope that Jesus Christ will soon return to this earth, personally, visibly, and unexpectedly, in power and great glory, to gather His elect, to raise the dead, to judge the nations, and to bring His Kingdom to fulfillment.

"WE BELIEVE in the bodily resurrection of the just and unjust, the everlasting punishment of the lost, and the everlasting blessedness of the saved."

In other words, Wheaton College does not believe in eternal tolerance. Wheaton College and every honest professor who signs this statement believe that religious tolerance will one day end. And, unless I judge wrongly, Wheaton College also believes that religious pluralism and tolerance in the world will remain, and must remain, until Christ himself, in person, puts it to an end.

In the last hours of his life in answer to Pontius Pilate, Jesus said, "My kingdom is not of this world. If my kingdom were of this world, my servants would have been fighting, that I might not be delivered over to the Jews. But my kingdom is not from the world" (John 18:36).

This does not mean that the kingdom of Christ has no impact on this world. The salt and light and truth and beauty that the kingdom of Christ brings to this world are inestimable. What it means is that this kingdom does not advance by the sword. To spread the gospel and establish the church of Christ and transform the world, Christ puts one sword into the hands of his people: the Word of God.

And in that Word he says, "Repay no one evil for evil . . . Beloved, never avenge yourselves, but leave it to the wrath of God, for it is written, 'Vengeance is mine, I will repay, says the Lord'" (Romans 12:17, 19). The vengeance of Christ, and the final end of tolerance, is the ground of love, not violence.

Therefore, Christian graduates of Wheaton College will not play the Joshua of the conquest of Canaan, which was a redemptive-historical season of savagery and judgment, appointed by God for a limited time and place. But now with the coming of Jesus into the world and the kingdom of God being taken away from Israel (Matthew 21:43) and given to a people bearing the fruits of it from every tribe and tongue and nation—Palestinian, Jew, Saudi, Afghani, Latino, Chinese—a new time and a new way is here: The way of suffering and patience and love and courage, persuading and pleading

Don't kill to spread your faith. Die to spread your faith. Christ is the end and the ground of your tolerance and your suffering. Give place to wrath. Love your enemies.

with the world to be reconciled to God.

"Lord, do you want us to tell fire to come down from heaven and consume them?"

"No, you don't know what spirit you are of. Come, walk with me toward Jerusalem, we have other villages to reach." (See Luke 9:54-55.)

"Lord, an enemy has sown weeds with the wheat in the world. Do you want us to go pull them up?"

"No. Let them grow. At harvest time, I will tell the reapers to gather the weeds first and bind them in bundles to be burned, but gather the wheat into my barn." (See Matthew 13:30).

"God, should we fight to spare our Christ the shame of rejection and the cross?"

"No. Put your sword away. Join my Son on the Calvary road."

Show by your willingness to rejoice in unjust treatment for Christ's sake that your treasure is in heaven, and that you know the day is coming when all tolerance will cease, and Christ alone will be exalted.

Let that be your joy and your hope, class of 2002. Follow the crucified Christ in patient suffering. Don't kill to spread your faith. Die to spread your faith. Christ is the end and the ground of your tolerance and your suffering. Give place to wrath. Love your enemies.

May the seed of this message find good soil in the class of 2002 so that you become unshakeable trees of conviction and courage and love.

INSIGHTS *for* LIVING

Education does not develop your character, until it merges with integrity and wisdom. . . . The future of our nation will be affected by our education, our wealth, and our technology, but our survival as a free society will be determined by our wisdom, our integrity, and our character.

—SAM NUNN

THE TEST FOR THIS CENTURY IS WHETHER WE MISTAKE A GROWTH OF WEALTH AND POWER FOR A GROWTH IN STRENGTH AND CHARACTER.

—VINCE LOMBARDI

In matters of principle, stand like a rock; in matters of taste, swim with the current.

—THOMAS JEFFERSON

INTEGRITY IS THE FIRST STEP TO TRUE GREATNESS.

—CHARLES SIMMONS

SEIZE THE OPPORTUNITY IN TODAY'S CHALLENGES

J. Kerby Anderson, President of Probe Ministries, lecturer, visiting professor, and radio commentator, speaks of the hostility of the world toward godly virtues, likening today's culture to that of the Israelites thousands of years ago. Yet, Mr. Anderson encourages the graduates that they can "seize the day because this is a great opportunity that God has placed in [their] hearts."

J. KERBY ANDERSON
Washburn High School
May 6, 2001

Congratulations to you graduates. It has often times been said that there's nothing like a high school graduation, and I think that's true. This will be perhaps the last time you have a chance to graduate with all sorts of people that you know. If you go on to college, sometimes you graduate at different times or with people you don't know. If you don't go on to college, this will be the last time you have a chance to be with people who are your peers. This is a very significant passage. . . .

A rabbi awhile back put it this way. He said,

You know life is tough. It takes up all of your time. All of your weekends. What do you get at the end of it? I think the life cycle is all backwards. You should die first, get it out of the way, then live twenty years in an old age home, then you get kicked out when you're too young, you get a gold watch, you go to work, work forty years until you're young enough to enjoy your retirement. You go to college, you party until you're ready for high school, you go to grade school, you become a little kid. You play, you have no responsibilities, you become a little baby, you go back into the womb, and you spend the last nine months floating as you finish up as a gleam in somebody's eye.

> **It's often times been said that life is a lot easier lived backwards but we have to live it forwards.**

It's often times been said that life is a lot easier lived backwards, but we have to live it forwards. You are in the midst of an incredible and very important transition. Congratulations on passing all of those tests, of enduring all of those late nights, of passing many exams, writing essays, and doing all the things necessary for you to appear right here. I want to spend a good portion of our time tonight talking about the world that you are going to enter. I'm going to suggest that this is a very different kind of world. My theme is the idea of being Christian in a secular world.

... We really are living in a secular world. We're living in a world that is oftentimes more hostile to Christian values. We're living in a world where there are a lot of problems. I see these as great opportunities as well as great challenges for you graduates. I see this as an opportunity for us to begin to think clearly about the world that we live in and to recognize that just as each generation has had to face challenges, whether it was the challenge of the Civil War or World War I or the Great Depression ... or World War II or Desert Storm, this generation is going to have to face challenges as well. ...

Seize the day for the glory of God. Seize the day because this is a great opportunity that God has placed in your heart. . . .

Hear the verses from Isaiah 5:18-21:
Woe to those who drag iniquity with the cords of falsehood, and sin as if with cart ropes....Woe to those who call evil good, and good evil; who substitute darkness for light and light for darkness; who substitute bitter for sweet and sweet for bitter! Woe to those who are wise in their own eyes, and clever in their own sight!

... The problem was not the external threats; the problem was internal. Almost every great nation has fallen from within. What was happening in the nation of Israel is happening in our nation today.

There were five different challenges that the nation of Israel had to face that you, too, will have to face. ...

1. [The Israelites] were a nation of skeptics ... I haven't seen God so I don't believe He exists. ...
2. They were a nation of deviants, ...individuals who were willing to call evil good. ...
3. They were prideful, wise in their own eyes ... pride bordering on arrogance, pride that says "I did it all by myself, I didn't need help from my parents or God.". ..
4. They were drunkards or to be politically correct, they were users of "controlled substances.". ..
5. They were purveyors of injustice. ... Does that sound like the United States? ...We have a society that has decided it's no longer going to follow moral principles. ... It's turned its back on biblical morality. ...

What is our challenge as we head into the twenty-first century? Our challenge is to begin to model godly behavior, to be people who are motivated by moral principles, by following moral guidelines and applying the very important principles we find in the Scriptures to our lives. . . .We need to come back and devote ourselves to the important principles of virtue, integrity, and stability. . . .

You live in a wonderful time, a time that is brimming with opportunities. This is an exciting time. I hope that you will grab for this exciting time with all that you can. . . . Seize the day for the glory of God. Seize the day because this is a great opportunity that God has placed in your heart. . . . Use these challenges to bring glory to God.

It's said that the Chinese word picture for "crisis" is really two words: the word picture for "danger" and the word picture for "opportunity." I think that's where we are right now. We're in the midst of crisis. There are dangers and challenges, but there are also opportunities. . . . I challenge you to take those opportunities and use them for the glory of God.

MAINTAIN YOUR INTEGRITY

Most well known for his Hollywood roles as Superman in both the movie and television show, Christopher Reeve continues to act and speak throughout the country. In his speech to the Ohio State University graduates, he refers to the challenges and newly found priorities discovered after his 1995 accident when he became paralyzed after falling from a horse. Mr. Reeve has offered awareness and funding to numerous spinal cord research projects as he works to find a cure for paralysis. "Never forget human compassion," he tells the graduates, "and the desire to make a difference."

CHRISTOPHER REEVE
June 13, 2003
Ohio State University

Before I begin, you should know that I have enjoyed watching Ohio State football on television for many years, but I never knew what a buckeye was. I always assumed it was a common name for a species of a little known but dangerous wild animal. I recently learned that it's just a tree. At first glance, it appears to be useless: the wood doesn't burn well, the bark smells, and the meat of the nut is bitter and mildly toxic. Yet it grows where others cannot, it's difficult to kill, and adapts to its circumstances. So much for first impressions.

I am extremely honored to address more than five thousand of you who are graduating from the bachelors, masters, and doctoral programs of OSU. I wanted to be here today to pay tribute to the longstanding ideals of the University: compassion for our fellow human beings, the aspiration to be champions in all arenas of life, and the desire to make a difference. . . .

[I] congratulate you for your outstanding achievements. But I also want to sound a note of caution as you leave this sanctuary of learning, self-discovery, and ethical conduct to make your way in the outside world.

You have been taught to work hard, not to cheat, and to balance your own advancement with service to others. But when you look beyond this campus, you witness seemingly endless examples of questionable conduct in government, religion, business, the media, and even sports. Our intelligence agencies are being challenged to explain their recommendation for the invasion of Iraq. The Catholic Church is embroiled in a crisis of misconduct and cover-ups. CEOs of major corporations are facing fines and imprisonment for their greed at the expense of the employees who helped create their success.

The reputation of one of the most respected newspapers in the country has been severely damaged by a reporter who could not resist plagiarizing in his zeal to succeed. Even the achievements of one of our favorite baseball players will probably be eclipsed by controversy over his use of an illegal bat.

The challenge before you will be to maintain your integrity in a culture that has devalued it. You will have to bring your own personal and professional ethics with you on the journey when you leave here today, because you may not find anyone to guide you. Living a moral life in an indifferent world is likely to be more difficult than you can imagine. How will you succeed?

> **The challenge before you will be to maintain your integrity in a culture that has devalued it.**

The answer may be found in a few simple words written by Abe Lincoln: "When I do good I feel good. When I do bad I feel bad. And that's my religion." All of us have a voice inside that will speak to us if we let it. Sometimes it's easy to hear; sometimes we have to turn down the volume of the distracting noise around us so we can listen. That voice tells us if we are on the right track. It lets us know if we give as much as we take, if we welcome the opinions of others, and at least accept diversity even if we are not able to embrace it.

As you go forward, hopefully that inner voice will remind you of some of the points of pride that bring such distinction to OSU. You'll discover that you can go far by being conscientious, but you will go farther and find true satisfaction by being conscious. If you have already achieved self-awareness and set specific goals for yourself, that's fine. If you don't know who you are or what to do next, don't worry about it. Your life shouldn't run on a schedule, and you may go down some dead end streets until you find the right road. . . .

Perhaps the greatest reward for living a conscious life is that it prepares you to cope with adversity. If you are open to change and new experiences, if you are accustomed to self-discipline, if you respect others and nurture your relationships, then you will have built a solid platform that will support you and help you deal with anything that comes your way. I'm not saying all of that is easy. But sitting here today I can honestly tell you that you don't need to break your neck to learn the value of living consciously. I was lucky to grow up unthreatened by change and eager for new experiences. Thirty years as an actor before my injury taught me self-discipline and helped me cope with rejection and failure. My marriage and my relationships with friends and family were alive and well before the accident; since then, they have grown even stronger and given me the ability to recover and go forward.

That catastrophic event also changed my perspective about other things in life. Outside of my circle of family and friends, I didn't appreciate others nearly as much as I do now. Once I trained with actual paraplegics to portray one in a film. Every evening as I drove away from the rehab center, I quickly pushed those suffering patients out of my mind, relieved that I was not one of them. Less than a year later, I became paralyzed myself. Did I need to learn something about compassion and humility? No doubt about it.

. . . you have already learned some of the most important principles you will ever need to know . . .

It was not until I was immersed in my own rehabilitation that I realized an apparent tragedy had created a unique opportunity. Spinal cord patients like the ones I once dismissed were now in the next room, traveling down the same hallways, and struggling right beside me in physical therapy. I came to know people of all ages and from all walks of life that I would otherwise never even have met. For all our differences, what we had in common was our disability and the desire to find a reason to hope. I was inspired by so many and gradually discovered that I had been given a job that would create urgency and a new direction in my life: I could do something to help.

Thanks to the education you have received here at Ohio State and the ideals that guide this distinguished university, you have already learned some of the most important principles you will ever need to know: compassion for our fellow human beings, the aspiration to be champions in all arenas of life, and the desire to make a difference. To all of you leaving today I can only say, on behalf of all those who will look to you for guidance and leadership, take those principles with you and hold them close.

Congratulations on all your achievements. I wish you the best of luck.

PLAYING FOR KEEPS

Sidney Rittenberg, author of The Man Who Stayed Behind *and recipient of the first "Bridge Builder for Peace" award from Pacific Lutheran University and its Wang Center for International Programs, served the United States Army in China as a Chinese language expert in 1945. Working with such Chinese leaders as Mao Zedong and Deng Xiaoping, Rittenberg was twice arrested in China on charges of being a CIA agent at the demand of Stalin, and held in solitary confinement for a total of 16 years. He challenges graduates to ask themselves what success looks like, urging them to use the untapped strength and talent that lies within them.*

SIDNEY RITTENBERG
Pacific Lutheran University
May 25, 2003

"Commencement of What?" This is the beginning—the end of school is just where you arrive at the start line—whether or not you go on to graduate school.

We're both very fortunate to be at a school that believes in education for service, not a huge factory for stamping out career patterns. I am privileged and honored to be teaching at this school and to be able, in all humility, to share some thoughts with you today.

First of all, commencement of what? Of playing for keeps, of life in earnest. Now it's up to you, to make your life meaningful or meaningless, happy or miserable, winning or losing.

So that's what's really happening today. But as you commence, seeking success and happiness, I wonder how much you've thought about this, about what success would look like? What the picture of a happy life would be for you? Everyone has thoughts about what they want to do, and you may even spend time figuring out what kind of car you want to buy—but have you considered carefully not just what you want to do, but who you want to be? I mean, a car is great—but this is your one life! Is it worth giving some thought to?

I am someone very ordinary—not particularly tough, and not particularly ingenious. Less than eight years after my own commencement, I began the first of sixteen years locked up in a tiny little prison cell, in solitary confinement in Chinese prisons, on suspicion of being an American spy—

which I was not. But, you say, why are you telling me this? Sitting in solitary isn't part of my plans for the future—what does that have to do with the commencement of my adult life?

I argue that it might have something to do with it, because the questions that I had to grapple with in solitary are the same ones that confront you on the streets and in your homes and workplaces every single day—questions about what it all means, about where happiness lies, about how you can possibly win in a world that is often unfair.

The difference is that in solitary you have no diversions, so that you have no choice but to face these basic issues and try to work them out, if you want to survive. You have to decide mighty fast, what are the really important things in life. What is it that I can't live without, as opposed to the things that I *thought* I couldn't live without, but that don't really matter much at the end of the day?

That first year, when I wasn't being grilled, I was totally alone, with a tiny space and no idea of time, except that it was endless, and in total darkness. But strangely enough, out of that darkness came light. It lit up my human ability to analyze and to reason, and my faith in the true, the good, and the beautiful, as I understood them.

Some people get so battered and confused by the underside of everyday life that they think there is no truth—"You have your truth, and I have mine," they say. They suffer from a sort of mental combat fatigue, they give up the battle for truth, and they say, "There is no objective truth." I say, "Don't you believe it!" Truth is what is (unless you believe, like Bill Clinton, that "it depends on what *is* is"), truth is what counts, truth is what wins. Truth is not easily come by, but it is the one thing in life worth pursuing to the death. And every single day I savored thankfully the dictum, "You shall know the truth, and the truth shall set you free." (See John 8:32) And in looking for ways of dealing with the devious, hectoring ways of the interrogators, I found the answer in those great lines from Hamlet, which I recommend to you: "This above all, to thine own self be true, and it must follow as the night the day, thou cans't not then be false to any man." Shakespeare told what is really important—it is integrity. Integrity, the simple business of practicing what you preach.

In those long and lonely years, I actually learned to enjoy the challenge of being by myself, drawing on my education, on my inner resources, and on the inspiration of wonderful people I had known. I realized that all I had to do was to hold on, to keep going, to fight, and, to paraphrase Winston

> **I was totally alone, with a tiny space and no idea of time, except that it was endless, and in total darkness. But strangely enough, out of that darkness came light.**

> **I found that reason and faith could manage moods and control emotions, that . . . through all the misery ran a defiant little thread of happiness and confidence in victory.**

Churchill, never never never never never never never never NEVER!!! to give up—and finally to win. I found that reason and faith could manage moods and control emotions, that even though every day in the solitary confines of a bare prison cell was misery, yet through all the misery ran a defiant little thread of happiness and confidence in victory. As long as I lived, in whatever circumstances, I would keep learning and keep trying to make some contribution to the human race—even if it was only keeping my Chinese prison cell squeaky clean. In other words, no matter how many years I spent locked up by myself, I would find ways to make it an addition to my life, not a subtraction.

I learned that it really is better to give than to receive—that this was not just a pious statement, but what actually works in real life. Only by giving do we open ourselves up to receive.

I learned that every situation, no matter how bad, also has another side that offers good possibilities and that you can turn disadvantages into advantages, stumbling blocks into stepping stones, bad things into good things—I could take the peephole in the door that deprived me of privacy and turn it around to break through my isolation, to show who I was to a captive audience, the guard watching on the other side of the peephole, who had to report on my behavior every day. I could take the curiosity of some of the guards about this supposed foreign enemy who was so-o-o respectful, so positive, and so well-behaved and turn it into an opportunity to catch their ear, to tell them enlightening stories about America. I could turn the crushing loneliness into an opportunity to train myself so that I learned to overcome depression and do away with the panic syndrome that attacked me repeatedly for a time.

I assure you friends, that you are much stronger than you think. You have resources within you that can produce great strength and talent. You need never despair. You do not need to take refuge in drink or drugs. Don't believe you are helpless victims of hormones—Sorry, not true. Do not listen to any voices who tell you differently. The strength I found is available to one and all, if only you believe in yourself and are guided by the Truth.

We have a switch in our minds that we can control. One night, after the interrogators kept saying that I would never again go free, even if I confessed, I went back home to my little cell and lay there thinking to myself, "If I'm never going to get out of this place, what's the point in this kind of life?" I felt really down. But then, a little voice said to me, "You're supposed to be dedicated to serving the freedom and happiness of other people. How come, now that 'Me' is in trouble, you forget about the millions of people in the world who have suffered much worse than you, about your beloved wife and your four little children who are being persecuted out there, and all you can do is worry about 'Me'?" Then, guess what—The minute that change of focus took place, the minute I turned my attention to the fate of other people, my mind moved away from my own troubles, my heart lifted up like a bird released from a cage, my mind's eye grew clear—and I knew immediately that the interrogators were lying—that the evil dictatorship of the Cultural Revolution could not last for long, and that they would not be able to keep me imprisoned forever.

I assure you friends, that you are much stronger than you think. You have resources within you that can produce great strength and talent.

And so I learned that the central point is to not be concerned for yourself alone, but to expand your little self into a big self by trying to love your neighbor as yourself—this is the central point, love your neighbor as yourself—that determines the quality of your entire life, this is what decides whether your life will have meaning and whether you will be a consistently happy person. People may differ widely in their skills, knowledge, and talents, but that doesn't matter. If you have this basic orientation of caring for others as you would for yourself—then the light of understanding can shine on you, and you will be a success as a human being. The road to happiness runs through other people's hearts.

The first thing that sprang into my head when the door slammed shut behind me on the first day of darkness was four lines from the poet Edwin Markham, that my sister used to read me when I was a sickly little boy in Charleston:

They drew a circle that shut us out,
Heretic, rebel, a thing to flout.
But Love and I had the wit to win,
We drew a circle that took them in.

Love is the key—Love, the process of deriving happiness from bringing happiness to the object of your love. What about hatred, twin brother of love? Yes, we hate the narrow, petty, selfishness and human meanness that are the enemies of love. But we hate the error, not the erring persons, and we work to release them from their narrowness and meanness.

Today, the dogs of war are howling again, and there are those who seek to prevail by visiting terror on innocent people, as well as those who would follow imperial ambitions in the guise of combating terror. You will face the complicated task of eliminating the matrix that breeds terrorism, the poverty and oppression of billions in the present-day world. You will take the side of history, reflected in the United Nations Charter, which declares that war is not an acceptable solution. You will work with China, the oldest country now becoming the newest—and with Japan and with Europe—to build a strategic partnership for peace.

I learned in solitary that when you as an individual run into problems, fears, conflicts—just sit quietly, try to calm down the noise in your mind, and look down into yourself, see what exactly is going on, what is wrong down there, what is it that you fear, what is it that you want, what is it that is blocking your way, how can you remove the blocks? No one else can tell you, only your own quiet thinking and your faith.

Every time you help dig a well for some Third World village where the children are without clean water; every time you comfort someone in distress and help them find their way forward; every time you contribute to enlightening the confused; every time you take a stand against injustice, prejudice, violence, wrong; every time you help the sick get well and the sorrowful lift up their hearts;—every time you put a drop into the long river of human progress, that drop is a part of your immortality. It will live and grow, wave upon wave, forever and ever, and your life will have made a difference and will live and grow with it.

So, back to the previous question—what is it that commences today? It is your life as a real person. Today is your rite of passage, you are now a full member of the tribe, with all the rights and responsibilities thereof. You will be tested and tried by the same challenging issues. How will you move towards your goals? What are the truths, the knowledge of which can make you free?

Finding the answers will make you happy, productive, blessed men and women.

Now, go out there and win!

GOOD LUCK!

REACH FOR THE SKY
Never Stop Learning or Growing

Listen carefully to wisdom; set your mind on understanding. Cry out for wisdom, and beg for understanding. Search for it like silver, and hunt for it like hidden treasure.

PROVERBS 2:2-4 NCV

INSIGHTS *for* LIVING

A wise man *will hear and increase learning, and a man of understanding will attain wise counsel.*

PROVERBS 1:5 NKJV

I URGE OUR GRADUATES HERE TO REGARD THE ACHIEVEMENTS WE ARE MARKING . . . NOT AS THE END, BUT RATHER AS THE BEGINNING, OF A CONTINUOUS PROCESS OF LEARNING.

—NELSON MANDELA

I hope that you will abandon the urge to simplify everything, to look for formulas and easy answers and begin to think multi-dimensionally, to glory in the mystery and paradoxes of life, not to be dismayed by the multitude of causes and consequences that are inherent in each experience—to appreciate the fact that life is complex.

—M. SCOTT PECK

THE MAN WHO GRADUATES TODAY AND STOPS LEARNING
TOMORROW IS UNEDUCATED THE DAY AFTER.

—NEWTON D. BAKER

*God has designed the human machine to run on Himself. He
himself is the fuel our spirits were designed to burn or the
food our spirits were designed to feed on. There is no other.
That is why it is just no good asking God to make us happy
in our own way.*

—C.S. LEWIS

THIS GRAND SHOW IS ETERNAL.
IT IS ALWAYS SUNRISE SOMEWHERE, THE DEW IS NEVER ALL
DRIED AT ONCE, A SHOWER IS FOREVER FALLING, VAPOR IS EVER
RISING. ETERNAL SUNRISE, ETERNAL SUNSET, ETERNAL DAWN
AND GLOAMING, ON SEA AND CONTINENTS AND ISLANDS,
EACH IN ITS TURN, AS THE ROUND EARTH ROLLS.

—JOHN MUIR

CELEBRATING HOW LITTLE WE KNOW

Dr. David Hoekema, Academic Dean and Professor of Philosophy at Calvin College, celebrates with graduates not how much they have learned and accomplished but how "little [they] have learned." Indeed, when we place our achievements against the backdrop of a living and holy God, all works pale, fading "into insignificance in comparison to the glorious transformation that God works in our lives. . . ." How encouraging it is to know that our wisdom is ultimately in the hands of our Creator.

> DR. DAVID A. HOEKEMA
> *Honors Convocation Address*
> *Calvin College*
> *April 25, 1996*

The purpose of this Honors Convocation is to recognize the remarkable achievements of students at Calvin College and to offer thanks for the gifts and talents with which you have been entrusted. I have a slightly different purpose in mind in this address, however. First, I want to celebrate how little you have learned. And then, before I conclude, I will point out with gratitude how little you have achieved.

In fact I am speaking as much to my colleagues on the faculty as to those of you who are students. To be sure, we have spent even more of our lives and our fortunes in the pursuit of knowledge than you have thus far. Books and articles on our shelves attest to our professional accomplishments, and diplomas on our walls confer the right to attach little bouquets of letters behind our names—Ph.D., M.F.A., M.B.A., Th.M.—that impress the folks back home and may even help get a bank loan. Yet it is the ignorance of the faculty no less than that of students that I celebrate this evening.

Exactly two weeks ago at this very hour of the evening, Madeleine L'Engle sat right here, in the wheelchair to which recent surgery has confined her, and offered us at Calvin a glimpse of the joys and challenges of her vocation as a writer of fiction that explores the spiritual dimensions of life. All her life, she said, she has been obsessed with hard questions about who we are, what happens when we die, and why God permits so much suffering. Yet she has recoiled from those who pretend to have wholly satisfactory answers to such questions, from theologians and preachers who claim more wisdom than anyone can truly offer.

This week on "All Things Considered" I heard a strikingly parallel warning against the dangers of facile answers to difficult questions—this time in the voice of the popular writer Erma Bombeck, whose passing was marked by clips from previous interviews. A friend, she recounted, sought to comfort her daughter when a favorite pet died by assuring her, with more compassion than theological warrant, "We shouldn't be sad—after all, Frisky is in heaven with God."

"But Mom," her five-year-old philosopher answered in a matter-of-fact tone, "what does God want with a dead dog?"

But do you have any answers yet to the really important questions?

In your programs of study at Calvin you have asked a great many difficult questions, and for some of them you have found answers. Let us suppose that you are a senior and have had the good judgment and courage to complete a major in philosophy, for example. No doubt you can tell me, if I ask you, about Heraclitus' conception of the natural world as the interplay of opposing forces in perpetual flux, and you can describe Parmenides' insistence that an eternal and unchanging unity can be discovered by the soul. You can recount Socrates' search for a ground on which to build our moral lives. You can explain, too, how Plato united Heraclitean plurality and Parmenidean unity in his system, which held that the true, the good, and the beautiful lie concealed beneath the surface of the world of experience. You can explain further how Aristotle took the world apart once more and put it back together, shaped neither by a personal God nor by an eternal realm of the Forms where the soul dwells but rather by an all-pervasive orderliness in nature. . . .

You can trace the ways in which the thinkers of our own century continue to probe the nature of the person, the relationship between us and our world, the place of language, and the meaning of history. Think back to the first weeks of your first philosophy course—remember how puzzled and frustrated you were by your first Philosophy 153 test?—and you can measure how far you have come.

But do you have any answers yet to the really important questions? Can you tell me who we are as persons, and whether there is a self that is distinct from the body? Can you explain what makes the testimony of our senses a reliable basis for knowledge? Can you even give a satisfactory answer to the question that Socrates put to his fellow Athenians so many centuries ago: What sort of life ought a human being to strive for? . . .

Alas, you cannot, and neither can I, nor any of your professors. In one sense, the history of philosophy is a history of continual progress, as each generation discovers the errors of its predecessors and formulates theories that build a more satisfactory foundation for further reflection. Yet the questions persist. Those for which we still have no fully satisfactory answers are at least as numerous, and perhaps more important, than those we can answer.

But not all of you are philosophy majors, more's the pity. And the rest of you may be thinking to yourselves: Yes, yes, that's why I didn't major in philosophy. At least in history, or biology, or engineering, we can get some answers!

But let's look a little deeper. First, what about you history majors? No doubt you could provide a brilliant and lucid account of the economic and social forces that drove European explorers out onto the oceans in the sixteenth century, of the ways in which the African-American family has been shaped by the experience of slavery and Reconstruction, and of why Japan closed its ports to European vessels for so many centuries and finally let Commodore Perry break the wall of isolation in the 1850's. But these are easy questions, warm-up pitches for the real game. Try your hand with some real questions. . . . Can you tell me why the Western societies that have attained the highest levels of individual freedom and prosperity still struggle with deeply rooted divisions of race and class, or why the growing wealth of some seems only to plunge their neighbors a few miles away deeper into poverty? Why is it that human societies seem never to live up to the promises that emerge from the brightest moments of their history?

But these are easy questions, warm-up pitches for the real game. Try your hand with some real questions.

Perhaps we need to leave the domain of the humanities for the sciences, where both questions and answers lie nearer to hand. . . . What is it that causes some cells to ignore the normal internal signal to stop multiplying, causing the fatal excesses that we know and dread as cancer? Why do some individuals destroy their own pancreatic cells for the production of insulin, causing diabetes? In response to such questions we can offer enormous quantities of data but no real answers. What is the impact of environmental pollutants on human and animal reproduction? We are scarcely any farther along the path to an answer to this urgent question than the ancient Greeks were in trying to explain communicable diseases.

By now the senior engineering majors may be sitting smugly in their seats. . . . In engineering, you may be thinking, we tackle concrete problems and find real solutions. We don't spend our time worrying over the nature of knowledge, the meaning of history, or the functioning of biological structures too small to be seen. We make stuff, and we make it work. Sure, there are lots of questions we cannot answer. But give us an appropriate question and we'll give you the answer. Can you build a bridge at this spot to carry four lanes of traffic, within the limits of this year's county road budget? Can the structural supports in that bicycle rack be made of composite plastic instead of steel? Will the pollutants we have detected in the topsoil leach into the aquifer from which the wells nearby draw their water? Give us the facts—the capabilities of the materials and the relevant specifications—and we will find the answer. But do these answers really provide the whole story? Will the bridge simply help move people to their destinations more efficiently, for example, or will it open up a delicate ecosystem to heavy use that may destroy its character? What is an acceptable level of pollution in a drinking water source? Does technology itself sometimes threaten the quality of human life? Are some projects technically feasible but morally objectionable? . . .

Let me return to my title and invite you to celebrate with me how very little we know. We can give thanks for such a wonderful profusion of ignorance, such a rich offering of questions that demand our attention even while they yield no satisfactory answers. What a blessing it is, after all, to have come so far in our learning that we can understand and puzzle over these questions and their importance! Before you began your college study, how many of these questions would you even have understood? How many do you understand now? (I will not answer that question myself.)

We might think of education as adding valuable items to two baskets, a basket of answers and a basket of questions.

If the former becomes filled while the latter is frequently empty, you are not truly receiving an education in the liberal arts, an education that lays the foundation for a life of learning and for spiritual and intellectual growth. As you carry on your studies and follow your vocation in later life, you should strive to keep adding to the contents of both baskets.

Once in a while you may hear a professor or even a resident advisor—trying to persuade you to spend less time in the coffee shop, perhaps—tell you that most of what you need to learn in college is between the covers of your textbooks. Don't believe it for a moment. Textbooks are not divinely revealed sources of authority: they are highly selective attempts to persuade you that what the author thinks you should study is what you should really study. What you find between the covers of the text is deeply shaped by the author's questions—and its value lies as much in the questions that the text leads you to ask as in any information it contains. . . .

Your education may indeed begin with careful study of texts. Learning to read critically and intently is an essential discipline in every field of study. But texts come to life and have meaning when you interpret and apply the information and the ideas that you find there. This process begins in the classroom, no less when students are speaking than when the instructor holds the floor. By no means does it stop when the class disperses. The real work of learning—formulating questions, seeking answers, testing ideas against those of others—goes on also in the residence hall, library lounge, the dorm Bible study, the van heading for the track meet, and the planning meeting for a service-learning project. Most of our learning comes not simply from reading texts but from conversation with each other, students and staff and faculty alike, and above all by putting our growing understanding to use in class presentations and writing. Bit by bit, lab by lab, assignment by assignment, coffee-shop session by coffee-shop session, term paper by term paper, we become more deeply aware of who God is, who we are, and what sort of world we have been placed in. And the more we learn, the more clearly we discern how vast is our remaining ignorance.

> **. . . we become more deeply aware of who God is, who we are, and what sort of world we have been placed in. And the more we learn, the more clearly we discern how vast is our remaining ignorance.**

Recall the excitement when, months after the Hubble space telescope was launched, and its repaired mirror at last yielded images of breathtaking clarity from the farthest reaches of the universe. And what did these images show? Did they finally penetrate to the limits of space and show us everything that there is? Far from it: instead we saw millions more stars and galaxies than we can see from earth's surface, a profusion of richness in the created order that boggles the imagination. It is the same with all learning. The finer our tools of analysis become, and the greater the reach of our means of inquiry, the greater the number of unknown regions and unanswered questions that will come into view for the first time.

If you have caught the spirit of love for learning that underlies everything we do at Calvin College, you will never stop challenging yourself to consider questions that you cannot answer—to ensure that your basket of answers does not become full while the other basket empties out. . . .

[Whatever you may have accomplished,] I insist that in a larger sense you have really achieved nothing of lasting significance. The reason is that, for all our ignorance, there is one thing that we know at Calvin College, and it is this: we know that every human endeavor, no matter how grand or how trivial, how successful or how disastrous, fades into insignificance in comparison to the glorious transformation that God works in our lives through the teaching, the sacrifice, and the living presence of Jesus Christ. Of course we should strive to do our work well, and help each other when we fall short. Certainly we do well to acknowledge and celebrate the outstanding achievements of some among us. But even as we do this we need to remember that in the largest sense not a scrap of all that we do is of ultimate importance. Of our own initiative and by our own powers, we can accomplish nothing of lasting significance. Yet in all that we do God works through us, reconciling us to God in Jesus Christ and advancing the kingdom of righteousness and peace. . . .

Please join me, therefore, in a joyful celebration of how little we know and how little we can achieve. For from that knowledge flows the joy of a life dedicated to hard tasks and hard questions, confident in the knowledge that neither our wisdom nor our achievements are finally in our hands but in the hands of the One who made us and sustains us daily in love.

INSIGHTS *for* LIVING

A THOUSAND VOICES CLAMOR FOR OUR ATTENTION AND A
THOUSAND CAUSES VIE FOR OUR SUPPORT. BUT UNTIL WE HAVE
LEARNED TO BE SATISFIED WITH FELLOWSHIP WITH GOD, UNTIL
HE IS OUR ROCK AND OUR FORTRESS, WE WILL BE RESTLESS
WITH OUR PLACE IN THE WORLD.

—ERWIN W. LUTZER

*The things taught in schools and colleges
are not an education, but the means of education.*

—RALPH WALDO EMERSON

I HAVE NEVER LET MY SCHOOLING INTERFERE
WITH MY EDUCATION.

—MARK TWAIN

*A college education is not a quantitative body of memorized
knowledge salted away in a card file. It is a taste for
knowledge, a taste for philosophy, if you will; a capacity to
explore, to question, to perceive relationships between fields
of knowledge and experience.*

—A. WHITNEY GRISWOLD

LIVE, LOVE, LEAD

When Dr. Bill Bright retired, he knew the international organization Campus Crusade for Christ would be in good hands. For thirty years, Mr. Stephen Douglass has been involved in Campus Crusade, now serving as its president. He has also authored several books including How to Achieve Your Potential and Enjoy Life. *Mr. Douglass reminds graduates that it will be the light of Jesus Christ in them that will shine into the darkness of the world. Through love and courage, he says, live out your lives for Christ.*

STEVE DOUGLASS
Biola University
May 2001

Soon-to-be-honored graduates, it's a privilege to be here with you. I have some flavor for what you've just gone through from my own educational experience. And do I sense on your faces a measure of relief? Even joy?

What can I add to the many years of education represented here? My conclusion is: not much. Another source of great relief to you, no doubt. Rather than trying to add to all those concepts you've managed to cram into your brain even in recent weeks, let me instead help you apply what you have learned—what it is when you leave here that you should do with what you've learned. My outline is quite simple . . . just three syllables: *live, love, lead.*

First, *live.* I don't need to tell you that the ambient holiness in America is not very good. Let me read to you a couple of statistics from several years ago. In America there was a murder every 23 minutes, a rape every 5 minutes, a violent crime every 17 seconds, and a property crime every 3 seconds. In one year (1996), 538 children were killed by their parents. In that same year, 308 parents were killed by their children.

America is not shining brightly with the light of Jesus Christ. But, there is some good news in that. As you graduate from here you can benefit from the fact that the darker that darkness is, the brighter your light will be . . . if you just *live* your life for Jesus Christ. The more stark the sin, the greater the contrast with the righteousness of Jesus Christ.

In Matthew 5:14, we find these words, "You are the light of the world." As far as righteousness is concerned, you *are* the light. Then in verse 16 we find, "So let your light shine that men will see your good deeds" and give you a pat on the back. Is that the rest of that verse? No. Wouldn't that have been fairly normal? You do something "good," and someone gives you a compliment. No, that's not what that verse says. It says, "and praise your Father in heaven."

The righteousness that people will see, they will *know* you couldn't do. They will be looking for who did it and they will conclude, "There must be a God. Could you tell me about your God?"

There was a Christian woman living in a condo in England. There was just a wall between her condo and the one next door, where a woman lived who was not a Christian. This second woman was quite ill both mentally and physically. The woman who was a Christian made it her practice every morning to go over to that wall and very quietly just pray for the woman in the other condo, that she would be healed and that she would come to know Christ in a personal way.

> **The righteousness that people will see, they will know you couldn't do. . . . . they will conclude, "There must be a God. Could you tell me about your God?"**

Months later, there was a knock on the door of the Christian woman, and who should be there but the woman next door. The Christian woman said, "Why are you here?" And the other woman said, "I'm here to say thank you." She asked, "For what? What have I done for you?" The reply was, "*Every* morning you prayed for me, didn't you?" The Christian said, "Yes, I did. How did you know that?" She replied, "I could *feel* your prayers coming through the wall between our condos and your prayers, to be more accurate, your God healed me. And I'm here to say thank you and ask you how I could know your God."

It was the summer of 1967. I had just finished four years at MIT, thinking that success was the secret to satisfaction and discovering that it was not. I was dating a young woman named Cathy. If I wanted to be with Cathy on Tuesday nights, I had to go to this Bible study sponsored by Campus Crusade for Christ.

Let me just tell you, that wasn't my idea of how to have fun on Tuesday night! But I was surprised. I saw not only people who were studying the Bible but were also so filled up with the joy of Jesus Christ it showed. It was just shining out like a beacon light, all over me. After about four weeks of that, I found myself sitting up in bed one night and I said, "*God, that's what I want. Could I have that kind of a relationship with you through Jesus Christ?*" . . .

That leads to my second point. *Love.* Jesus was asked by one of the experts of the law in Matthew 22:36, "Teacher, which is the greatest commandment in the Law?" Jesus said in verse 37, "Love the Lord your God with *all* your heart, and with *all* your soul, and with *all* your mind. This is the first and greatest commandment. And the second is like it: Love your neighbor as yourself."

Why love? If Jesus chose to name it as the one that summarizes all the law and the prophets, why did he pick love? Well, for one reason, because it gives motive for obeying God. Love gives similar motivation in human relationships. You see, if I *love* you, I'm not going to *lie* to you, I'm not going to *cheat* you, I'm not going to *hurt* you.

In addition, love communicates. A number of years ago a couple from Wycliffe Bible Translators was placed in a remote region of Guatemala. Before long they found themselves in the midst of a conflict between the government and those who wished to overthrow it. Many men from the village where they were working were killed.

Since the Wycliffe couple had one of the only vehicles in the area, often they were called upon to go out and retrieve the bodies of husbands and brothers of families in the village. Shortly after such an act of kindness toward one wife and mother, one of the woman's other sons joined the rebel ranks.

But he never forgot the kindness of the Wycliffe couple. On several occasions, the couple was at the top of the rebel list of people to assassinate, only to have the young man from their village push them down to the bottom of the list.

True love communicates! And that kind of love can only be explained by the presence of Jesus Christ in your life.

The third point is *lead*. In Joshua 1 we find, "Be strong and courageous because you will lead these people to inherit the land I swore to their forefathers to give them."

I must confess when I first read that verse, my mind is called to many great leaders in history. For example, Winston Churchill inherited the leadership of England in a very dire and dark time during World War II. I'm quoting from a speech in June of 1940 when things looked particularly bad. He said, . . . "We shall defend our island whatever the cost may be. We shall fight on the beaches, we shall fight on the landing grounds, we shall fight in the fields and in the streets. We shall fight in the hills. We shall never surrender." Of course, history records that Winston Churchill helped lead England to victory.

> **True love communicates! And that kind of love can only be explained by the presence of Jesus Christ in your life.**

Certainly, that is leadership! But what I'm talking to you about happens much more often in less dramatic ways. It can happen in the context of the local church. A number of years ago I had the occasion to be in a church that split and some months later lost their pastor besides. Although I wasn't on the leadership board of the church at that time, they called me in to advise them, since they had no full-time pastoral staff left. My advice was simple:

Forgive the people who split off from the church a few months before. "Oh, you don't know what all they have said and done!" was the response to my suggestion. "Well," I said, "that's true, but I do know that the Bible teaches us to forgive as the Father has forgiven us."

Finally, they did send a letter to the group that split off—offering and asking forgiveness. God must have been very pleased because within a week after the letter was received, God sent the church an excellent interim pastor, whom they had been praying for over several months. In whatever circumstance you find yourself, you can point to God's Word. It may take courage because people don't want to hear it. But God has called and equipped you to lead.

But God has called and equipped you to lead.

Live, love, lead. Not a long outline . . . actually pretty simple and easy to remember. Yet it does highlight the importance of doing the right things with all that you have learned—all that the faculty and administration here have sought to pour into your hearts and minds. And if you do these three well, you will likely hear these words from the Lord at life end, "Well done, good and faithful servant. Enter into the joy of your Master."

YOU CAN SOAR!

From sleeping in bombed houses of refugee camps to calculating one hundred math problems in his head three hours straight for his father, Philip Emeagwali from Nigeria understands the importance of learning. "Life is a journey and we should spend the early years preparing for it. To become a scientist required many years of education. I never accepted defeat. I kept trying."

PHILIP EMEAGWALI
Willingboro High School
Willingboro, New Jersey
February 25, 1999

Everyone of you has the potential to achieve anything you want in life. You were born with many talents that you don't even know you have. Someone in this audience may become a famous writer, may travel to the planet Mars or discover the cure for AIDS.

However, to become successful requires that you set personal goals for yourself and then study and work hard to achieve them. Setting personal goals is very important because those who do not have goals in life do not know where they are going. Those who do not know where there are going could end anywhere. They could end [up] in prison. They could end [up] on illegal drugs.

You must never, never, never experiment with any illegal drugs. It will ruin your life and the lives of those that love you. Those drug dealers standing in your street corners are trying to sell you a one-way ticket to nowhere.

My advice to every one of you is to write down your goals on a piece paper. Then discuss your goals with your friends, parents, and teachers. You should read your goals to yourself at least once a week. Reading your goals aloud helps you to stay focused. It creates a positive attitude that is necessary to overcome the obstacles that you will encounter along the way.

A question that students often ask me is: "How can I overcome the major obstacles in life?"

When I was twelve years old, I lived in a new African country called Biafra, which was at war with Nigeria. Because of the thirty-month Nigerian-Biafran war, my family became homeless. We slept in abandoned school classrooms. We were refugees, our schools were closed, and I was forced to drop out of school for six years, when I was still in the eighth grade. We ate only once a day. Some days we had nothing to eat. We were among the poorest families in the world. Growing up poor and overcoming several obstacles made me a stronger person. I became more determined to succeed in life.

Similarly, the obstacles that you will encounter in your life should make you a stronger person. Overcoming obstacles is your preparation for the challenges that you will encounter in the future.

I . . . recommend that you write your plan of action for overcoming any obstacle that comes in your way. After dropping out of school in the eighth grade, I developed a plan of action. I planned to pursue my education by self-study. I studied from six in the morning to midnight, until I earned my high school equivalency.

Earning my high school diploma opened a lot of doors for me. It enabled me to enroll in college and eventually earn graduate degrees in five different fields and become a scientist.

> **. . . the obstacles that you will encounter in your life should make you a stronger person.**

Another question that students often ask me is: "What did it take you to reach your goals in life?" The answer is that I stayed in school and completed my education. I always put in the necessary study time. I limited my associations with undesirable friends. I never smoked or used drugs, and I avoided alcohol. I learned from my mistakes and from the mistakes of others. I tried to be persistent and accepted disappointments and failures as a learning experience.

You must always do your homework. My personal experience with doing my homework is that practice makes perfect. This is especially true for difficult subjects such as mathematics and science.

When I was ten years old, my father insisted that I solve one hundred mathematics problems each day. Due to my daily practice, I became very good in mathematics. You will become very good in mathematics when you solve one hundred problems each day. Today, I solve more than one hundred mathematics problems a day. I use supercomputers to solve billions and billions and billions of mathematics problems each day. . . .

To get back to my original point, I was a student doing my homework when I broke the world's computational speed record. Not only did homework help me improve my grades, it also taught me discipline, responsibility, a love for learning, and how to work independently.

Each evening and no matter how tired you are, you must set aside three hours for homework. During this period, you cannot receive telephone calls, watch television, or play video games. During the weekend, you can complete sixteen hours of homework. Japanese students study every evening, weekends, and holidays. You too should study every evening, weekends, and holidays.

In Japan, students from third to nineth grade enroll in private lessons called juku. These lessons start after school and continue until dinner time. Japanese students attend juku full time during the holidays and summer vacations. Since Japanese students spend more time studying than American students, they are better in mathematics and science subjects. Similarly, you can improve your grades by studying as hard as the Japanese students. You can become the most brilliant student in Willingboro. But you must study in the evenings; study on weekends; and study on holidays.

I want to close with one important message: Education is our investment in your future. For that reason, we expect you to study hard. You should study hard not because it is easy, but because you will be the beneficiary tomorrow of the homework that you completed today. Education will bring the best out of you and enable you to fulfill your potential, achieve your goals, and live your dreams.

THANK YOU AND GOD BLESS YOU ALL.

INSIGHTS *for* LIVING

THE MOST IMPORTANT ASPECT OF FREEDOM OF SPEECH IS
FREEDOM TO LEARN. ALL EDUCATION IS A CONTINUOUS
DIALOGUE—QUESTIONS AND ANSWERS THAT PURSUE EVERY
PROBLEM ON THE HORIZON. THAT IS THE ESSENCE OF
ACADEMIC FREEDOM.

—WILLIAM O. DOUGLAS

*Give thanks for sorrow that teaches you pity; for pain that
teaches you courage—and give exceeding thanks for the
mystery which remains a mystery still—the veil that hides
you from the infinite, which makes it possible for you to
believe in what you cannot see.*

—ROBERT NATHAN

OUR KNOWLEDGE COMPARED WITH GOD'S IS IGNORANCE.

—AUGUSTINE OF HIPPO

LEARNING IS THE ANTIDOTE

Elie Wiesel, a Holocaust survivor and 1986 Nobel Peace prize recipient,
speaks openly to the graduates of hardship, poverty, and racism. You are at
a Christian university, he tells them, and this sends the message of
openness, an openness to learning and to respecting others. "Learning is
what brings people together," he says. "Continue to learn."

ELIE WIESEL
DePaul University
June 15, 1997

Reverend President, Rabbi Furman, clergy, distinguished members of the faculties, deans, parents, friends, and students; to be honored by this very great university is special to me, a Jew who comes from far away. When I was young, I was afraid of whatever had to do with Christianity. It inspired only fear in me.

I have learned since, that every religion, and those who believe in it, are to be respected and not feared. Therefore, today, I find it symbolic that we are here—you students and I, still a student although I have been a teacher—trying to see in each other, not strangers, but fellow sojourners who try to transcend all that separates human beings from one another. We are all still learning eternal truth from the same books. You have worked hard for four years. You have spent many sleepless nights, either worrying about grades or worrying how to get up in the morning, having had too much fun. From now on, no more exams, no more apprehension. Still, I hope you will not stop being students. The fact that you will not have exams does not mean that you should not go on learning. You must continue to listen to Plato or to Jeremiah or both; you must continue to come closer to other fellow human beings, just as you have been closer here among yourselves or with your fine, inspiring teachers.

What do you take with you from here? A story, a formula, maybe a handshake, a special encounter, a friendship. What will remain except a diploma? Much must remain because when two persons meet, a mystery is born. Take that

What will remain except a diploma? Much must remain because when two persons meet, a mystery is born.

> Learning is an
> antidote because
> when we learn, no
> matter who we are
> and where we come
> from, we still are
> marveling at the
> beauty of a sentence
> or cadence by
> Shakespeare, or an
> idea by Plato. .

mystery and respect it; and if possible, invest it with more meaning, with more miraculous significance. The world outside is a cold world, a cynical world. I imagine that you will stumble upon the same difficulties that my students stumble upon, as I do, when we have to express our faith in books and their authors; when we have to believe that those whom we have elected are not cynical, not hypocrites, that they in truth are our representatives, in spite of what we read in the papers. That to be a civil servant, or a political representative anywhere, is still a noble vocation. We must believe that in spite of our limitations, you and I must realize that there isn't much we can do to act on history in its shaping up for the next century.

However, there are certain things we can do and, therefore, to paraphrase Kant, we must do. There are so many prisoners in the world. We cannot free all of them, maybe not even one. But one thing the prisoner always suffers from is feeling abandoned, feeling given up, that he or she doesn't count anymore—to anyone! That is our work. We must see to it that that prisoner should know that there is always one person, or one group, dealing with human rights—who thinks of him or her in prison. Those who are sick, who are prisoners of their disease, be they victims of Alzheimers—the worst of all diseases because it attacks identity—or patients with AIDS or cancer; or victims of poverty, despair, racism; they should know that they are not alone. If I cannot, and you cannot, cure and help all of them, or not even one of them, at least we can be present to them in their special situation, their condition of suffering.

You studied here in a Christian school. I know not all of you are Christians, but nevertheless the school is a Christian institution, and I applaud the school for having you. Because it shows its openness. It shows the emphasis on learning. Learning is the best antidote to and against ignorance and fanaticism and hatred. How is it that all racists are so stupid? To believe that because one has a different color of skin, or comes from a different ethnic origin, or belongs to a different religious group, one is superior or inferior is stupid. Learning is an antidote because when we learn, no matter who we are and where we come from, we still are marveling at the beauty of a sentence or cadence by Shakespeare, or an idea by Plato. Learning, therefore, is what brings people together. Continue to learn.

Furthermore, children. You have been young, younger, and soon you are going to have children, too. You must be responsible for the world into which these children are being brought. When adults make war, children die. Adults fight and children suffer. While you are here celebrating, rightly so, your great achievement, somewhere in the world, in Africa and Asia, every minute a child dies of hunger or disease. I repeat, every minute a child dies of hunger or disease. Don't you think that is scandalous? It is—because that can be helped. If only our governments all over the world could be aware of the weight of suffering of children. Dostoyevsky said, "If one child dies, it calls into question the existence of God." And I would say if one child dies, it calls into question the humanity of the human being. You have learned the value of humanity, that is the goal of learning—learning means to be sensitive—sensitive to other people's pain and suffering and joy and happiness. And when children die, and we do not do enough to save one child here and one child there, something is wrong with our humanity.

. . . there is one sin we must never commit and it is to humiliate another person or to allow another person to be humiliated in our presence without us screaming and shouting and protesting.

Furthermore, humiliation. Always remember, my good friends, that there is one sin we must never commit and it is to humiliate another person or to allow another person to be humiliated in our presence without us screaming and shouting and protesting. Learn that. Poverty is humiliation. There is absolutely no reason in the world why some people should be poor when we are not. Exclusion, discrimination, is humiliation. There is absolutely no reason in the world why I should be happier than anyone else, in my place, in my home, and in my work. . . .

I wish you years of joy, years of serenity, years of friendship. Thank you.

INSIGHTS *for* LIVING

Every now and again take a good look at something not made with hands—a mountain, a star, the turn of a stream. There will come to you wisdom and patience and solace and, above all, the assurance that you are not alone in the world.

—SIDNEY LOVETT

The fear of the Lord is the beginning of knowledge. Fools despise wisdom and instruction.

PROVERBS 1:7 NASB

JOB—HOW TO SUFFER
PSALMS—HOW TO PRAY
PROVERBS—HOW TO ACT
ECCLESIASTES—HOW TO ENJOY
SONG OF SOLOMON—HOW TO LOVE

—OSWALD CHAMBERS

Wisdom is the right use of knowledge. To know is not to be wise. Many men know a great deal, and are all the greater fools for it. To know how to use knowledge is to have wisdom.

—CHARLES HADDON SPURGEON

THE DAY YOU STOP LEARNING IS THE DAY YOU BEGIN DECAYING, AND THEN YOU ARE NO LONGER A HUMAN BEING.

—ISAAC ASIMOV

AN ALTERNATE DESTINY

"Stick with those things that have eternal value, not the love of yourself, or the love of the world, but the love of God and what is right," cautions Alan Keyes, a U.S. Representative to the United Nations during the Reagan administration, before an audience of graduating seniors. God has singled out each of you, he says, to walk the road of conviction and faith in the midst of challenge. "God has remained faithful in the past, so He will not desert you in the future."

ALAN KEYES
Grove City College
August, 2000

As graduates in the year 2000, you are faced with a world in which, to put it mildly, there is a lack of respect for truth. Many speakers at commencement exercises this year will tell the graduates to commit themselves wholeheartedly to whatever it is that they define as success. "If they believe in themselves, they can go anywhere and do anything.

While many regard the process of education as preparing people to succeed, I guess today I have to be a little ornery. Knowing what I do of Grove City College, I am very certain that you have been fully prepared to succeed. But what I respect more about the principles of this institution is that you have also been prepared to fail in seeking success as the world defines it. According to the world, advancement comes in terms of honors, and material wealth, and all the other baubles that our culture considers true success. In this regard, Grove City College has also prepared you to fail. It has prepared you to fail to win the applause of those who have respect for nothing but the lie. It has prepared you to fail to win the applause of those who will not honor people who have the integrity to believe in and stand for truth. It has prepared you to fail to win the regard of those who no longer respect anyone who will stand forthrightly for the name and for the will of Almighty God.

I am happy today to stand on the platform of an institution that believes, as I do, that the real definition of success is not what the majority of commencement addresses will say it is. They will encourage the graduates to believe in themselves if they want to achieve success. Rather, I am pleased to be addressing graduates who have been taught by this institution that stands for a different belief. Here you were taught that true success is achieved only when and if you are prepared to act consistently and without equivocation on your faith and belief in the goodness, the authority, and the will of God. I am pleased to speak to graduates who believe in that Power which lies beyond your power, who believe in that truth which is defined by a Will that goes beyond your will. As you leave this place, attach yourself to an ideal that will, in that spark of divinity that is in you, survive through all eternity, unlike your body, which will perish and turn to dust.

> . . . true success is achieved only when and if you are prepared to act consistently and without equivocation on your faith and belief in the goodness, the authority, and the will of God.

I shall never forget what I was told when I first arrived at the United Nations. I was working then for a woman for whom I have much respect, Jean Kirkpatrick. We were serving Ronald Reagan, a president who will always remain for me "the President." When I started my job as Ambassador to the U.N. Economic and Social Council, I was young for the job, one of the youngest who had ever been promoted into such a position. As I was beginning, I sat down to talk with Jean, and she gave me some advice that I will never forget. She said that it was not only how well I handled the job, but how well I handled myself in performing the job, that would be important.

That advice bears consideration in terms of life itself, as you apply the knowledge and technical skills you have acquired in your education. Whatever vocation you choose, whatever path you walk, it is far more important for you to focus on what kind of person you are becoming as you live this life. For, all of us are building the work, not only of our own hands, but also of the hope and grace of Almighty God. He has in mind for you a magnificent destiny. At every stage, with each step, it is far more important to consider how much of that destiny you are achieving, than to contemplate whether or not the world approves, as you walk the walk He requires of you.

I think that this consideration is going to be particularly important these days, because there are so many ways in which the prevailing winds of our time blow in a direction that is contrary to truth, and to faith, and to justice, and to dignity. The gnawing temptation will be to fall away from a path of conviction.

Now, that may be hard for some of you to hear. Generally speaking, it is the prerogative of youth to believe that things will go well, that all one has to do is the right thing and everything will turn out fine.

As God measures things, that is true. We know how the story turns out—because Christ lives, the story ends well for His followers. But as the world measures things, it is not true. As you walk the walk, you have to remember that many times in the course of this human saga, those who were willing to stand with integrity for the things that God required of them were thrown on the ash heap of human history. They were passed up by those who were building the great edifices of empire and material success. They had to risk everything—honor, and life, and reputation, and dignity—and hold on only to this: what they valued in the end was not the world's opinion of their work, but rather, God's opinion.

So, I can't stand here and promise that if you take that path, everything is going to be wonderful. Instead, it might be very difficult, because I think we've come to a time different than some other eras in human history. People don't even pretend to care about what is right. Whatever one feels like doing today is set up as the current "god" to worship. If you look around, you can see that, little by little, it's a path leading to our destruction. That's particularly true if we care about the heritage and legacy of freedom into which all of us were born.

I am afraid, however, that this legacy is facing an uncertain future. We are surely in the generation that will decide the fate of this American republic, and of the ideas of self-government and liberty upon which it was founded. I think this nation now stands, as it were, on the precarious edge of its destruction. We are turning our backs on fundamental truths and principles.

This nation was not founded on the belief that if one just cares about himself enough, makes money, and builds knowledge in a scientific sense, everything will be fine. It was founded on an idea of justice which acknowledged that the source of human dignity and human rights and human hope was not the decision and will of human beings, but the power and will of Almighty God, the Creator. That's what was said in the beginning. And everything we hope for, everything we're supposed to represent in terms of the world's hope for a decent life and freedom, all depends on that premise. We are all created equal, all endowed, not by human will and self-esteem, but by God's will. In spite of all our human frailties and temptations, there remains the prospect that some semblance of justice can be achieved for us in the light of God's grace and will. I don't know in this generation if we shall, as a people, have the wisdom, and the courage, and the integrity to reclaim our allegiance to that great principle. I don't know if we will have the courage to restore it to its rightful place as the foundation of our policies, our laws, our habits and our character.

But there is a special word I want to bring to

> . . . those who were willing to stand with integrity for the things that God required of them were thrown on the ash heap of human history.

you graduates here today. I hope it's not a word that will burden you too much. I have felt compelled to challenge you with the difficulties of this path. You have come through an institution that is still dedicated to the importance of these fundamental principles of which I speak. This college seeks to shape in the hearts and minds of those who pass through its portals, an allegiance and respect for those principles. To go out now and remain true to that education places a special burden and responsibility on you. Not every graduating class this year will bear this responsibility. There are some who are in the darkness of confusion, who have been denied the light of that exposure to an authoritative moral tradition that has made our nation, in the truest sense, possible.

> **. . . you have marked out a different road. It is a road that calls on you to lead this nation in a direction that it does not want to follow, to be unto the world a light that it does not wish to see.**

As the scriptures tell us, of those to whom much has been given, much will be required. Those stumbling around in ignorance of this principle don't have to feel a special responsibility to be its champion. But I think you do.

In God's sovereignty, He has singled you out in your path. You could have walked into another institution that was filled with confusion, and you would have left four years later perfectly at ease with everything that goes on in our culture. But through the love and grace of God, and of your parents, and of your own decent inclinations and character, you have marked out a different road. It is a road that calls on you to lead this nation in a direction that it does not want to follow, to be unto the world a light that it does not wish to see. You must have the courage to stand for those convictions that will earn you contempt today from all the powers that be. Still they are the truths which alone shall win the smile we long for from the face of God.

With this special challenge and call upon your lives, you will scatter your talents and abilities into all those walks and areas of life where people can have an influence. And I don't mean just from the big platforms and podiums of our society. Some of you will certainly be called to walk in those arenas, but what I really mean is to be an influence, as well, in all those ways that we don't think of often enough but which are really the ways in which the world is shaped. You will need courage to stand with conviction and integrity for the faithful love you ought to bear for your spouses and the unyielding commitment that your marriage ought to demonstrate in spite of the sickness of our time.

You will need courage to stand with integrity as you parent your children, while the world tempts them at every crossroad. In spite of how it may tear at your heart and how it may momentarily affect your friendship with them, you must stand with integrity for those things that you know God requires in your children's lives. That's a special kind of courage, one that will be written of in no history books, that will not go down in any great annals. You will not be sung about, nor will you be remembered by any except those whose lives you shaped for the better, and whose hopes you kept alive for their salvation. You will not be praised by the world, and, in its eyes, you may very well die in a kind of obscurity.

But this special virtue and this special faith, I believe, offers the greatest hope that we have. Somewhere in this nation's life, it will be the leaven that will allow our hopes for liberty to rise again. You are that yeast. You are the seeds of that better future. And whatever it takes, I pray for you today that, by the grace of God, you will have the courage, conviction and integrity to walk the walk that Providence has set out for you. Stick with those things that have eternal value, not the love of yourself, or the love of the world, but the love of God and what is right. There is much reason in our world today to believe that we have wonderful prospects and potential, with all the scientific knowledge we are accumulating. But what worries me is that the more knowledge we gain, the more power we gain over nature, and over biology, and over genetics, the more God-like we become in our own eyes. As this occurs, the future that awaits us becomes more dangerous and precarious.

We are, as it were, at a great moment of choosing. Many nourish strong hopes for this new century, but because of our overwhelming pride and our abandonment of faith in God, we also face prospects of horror and human degradation. It may, in the end, make the twentieth century, for all its tragedies, look like a dress rehearsal.

And why is that possible? Because great knowledge and great power in the hands of people with no conscience and no respect for truth can only lead to humankind's destruction. We are in a world in which so many are simply giving in to that temptation to believe in themselves to the exclusion of that Power beyond

If you draw upon that instrument of faith and lift your hearts in humble prayer, I believe, as God has remained faithful in the past, so He will not desert you in the future.

themselves. You still have that true faith, but you move in a time when that faith must be tested. If it stands the test, then you will represent a light of hope to discipline this human knowledge and power that, by the grace of God, our reason opens up to us. Through the eyes of faith, you will not only understand how to better use this knowledge, but you will also recognize its limits in the light of His will. This is, in many ways, a task that goes beyond any that has been faced thus far by previous human generations.

I want to leave with you this thought about your special vocation. Every generation has a calling. Every generation faces special challenges and difficulties. This will be true, I think, especially for your generation. The challenge will be to remain faithful to truth in those small things that make life wonderful and in the large things that make it whole. It's a wonderful challenge. It will also be a difficult burden. But you must remember, as all generations have had to remember, that in meeting this challenge of your humanity, you are not alone. If you draw upon that instrument of faith and lift your hearts in humble prayer, I believe, as God has remained faithful in the past, so He will not desert you in the future. And I believe that parents and others sitting here today, as they look upon your shining faces, can nourish the hope that what shines there is the promise and fruit of that faith which alone will be the salvation of our world.

GOD BLESS YOU.

INSIGHTS *for* LIVING

When I was a boy of fourteen, my father was so ignorant, I could hardly stand to have the old man around, but when I got to be twenty-one, I was astonished at how much the old man had learned in seven years!

—MARK TWAIN

NEITHER A LOFTY DEGREE OF INTELLIGENCE NOR IMAGINATION NOR BOTH TOGETHER GO TO THE MAKING OF GENIUS. LOVE, LOVE, LOVE, THAT IS THE SOUL OF GENIUS.

—AMADEUS MOZART

Imagine yourself as a living house. God comes in to rebuild that house. At first, perhaps, you can understand what He is doing. He is getting the drains right and stopping the leaks in the roof and so on: you knew that those jobs needed doing and so you are not surprised. But presently, he starts knocking the house about in a way that hurts abominably and does not seem to make sense. What on earth is He up to? The explanation is that He is building quite a different house from the one you thought of—throwing out a new wing here, putting on an extra floor there, running up towers, making courtyards. You thought you were going to be made into a decent little cottage: but He is building a palace.

—C.S. LEWIS

FIGHT THE GOOD FIGHT

Greg Laurie, senior pastor of Harvest Christian Fellowship in Riverside, California, serves as a featured speaker on an international daily radio program, A New Beginning *and as a board member of the Billy Graham Evangelistic Association. In his speech, Pastor Laurie warns graduates of our "world of nuclear giants and ethical infants"; but with the foundation of Jesus Christ, we must dare to be Daniels and make the right choices before God.*

> GREG LAURIE
> *Biola University*
> *1999*

You are the last graduating class of the 90s but more than that, you are the last graduating class of the 20ᵗʰ century! What kind of world are you going into to "make your mark?"

I am reminded of the opening statement of Charles Dickens' classic *A Tale of Two Cities* in which he says, "It was the best of times, it was the worst of times." In many ways, that is an apt description of our time right now. On one hand, the world we live in is a frightening place. We have adversaries on other shores with increasing nuclear capabilities. We have unprecedented violence on our own shores as kids shoot kids on high school campuses. We are reaping the consequences of a culture that for all practical purposes has forgotten God. Then when a crisis like we just saw in Littleton, Colorado, happens we ask, "Why?" When the real question should be "why not?" What did you expect? After all, here is a generation that has been raised to believe that "we are all products of the evolutionary process." They are told that there is no God, plan, or purpose for our lives. They tell us that "we make our own luck, fate, etc." We are told "there are no absolutes. We all have our own truth. It's moral relativism, complete freedom from all restraint."

Where has this kind of thinking gotten us? Right where we are today.

General Omar Bradley said in an Armistice Day speech in 1948, "We have grasped the mystery of the atom and rejected the Sermon on the Mount. The world has achieved brilliance without conscience. Ours is a world of nuclear giants and ethical infants."

We have made breath-taking advances in science and technology but in the process, we have forgotten God. As news anchorman Tom Brokaw said to a graduating class recently, "It is not enough to wire the world if you short-circuit the soul."

A Barna report showed that the generation leading the way toward moral relativism is Generation X. This generation rejected absolute truth by a staggering 78 percent! You might say, "Well, that's just the way it is. It's not going to change!"

Some might throw in the towel but I have hope for our future today. Because of you.

Because of this graduating class and the ones to follow. Because you have been trained in a "national university." One of 229 out of the 3,300 institutions of higher learning in the United States that are called the "major leagues" of higher education. . . .

You are charting a course and running a race that you will hopefully continue to your last day on this earth, whenever that will be.

You have been preparing for this day. You have spent literally thousands of hours studying. You've been tested time and time again. You've prayed for the return of Christ preferably before exams! You've made countless runs to Taco Bell and In-N-Out Burger. Now the time has come to graduate. To go and make your mark on the world. You are charting a course and running a race that you will hopefully continue in to your last day on this earth, whenever that will be.

The Apostle Paul said in 2 Timothy 4:7-8, "I have fought the good fight, I have finished the race, I have kept the faith. Finally, there is laid up for me the crown of righteousness, which the Lord, the righteous Judge, will give to me on that Day, and not to me only but also to all who have loved His appearing."

Paul made this statement at the end of his life. Looking back over what he had lived, he sums up his priorities. He says, "I fought the good fight." It's a good reminder that the Christian life is not a playground but a battleground. There are going to come times in your life where your faith will be tested. Times when people will challenge what you believe. Temptations that will be very strong to do the wrong thing. You might ask, "Will I be able to stand strong spiritually when this happens?"

That's entirely up to you. The stand you make today will determine what kind of stand you will make tomorrow. When one is building a house, the most important time is not when we put up wallpaper or choose what color the outside will be. It is when the foundation is laid. Because if that is not done properly, all the rest is of no consequence.

Why? In the early years the dye is cast. The course charted. The path followed. You will decide what the evening of your life will be by the morning of it. Or the end by the beginning. It's not some "mystical thing" you have nothing to say about. You decide what principles you will live by, what road you will take.

Deuteronomy 30:19 says, "This day I call heaven and earth as witnesses against you that I have set before you life and death, blessings and curses. Now, choose life, so that you and your children may live."

We all know the story of those three courageous teenagers Shadrach, Meshach, and Abednego. We remember their courageous stand before Nebuchadnezzar when all the kingdom was commanded to bow before the golden image he had erected. He gave them one more change but still they would not bow.

> **The stand you make today will determine what kind of stand you will make tomorrow.**

Where did they get the courage to stand up for their faith like that? It was a bit earlier in their life, when they were taken into the king's court as some of the most promising sons of Israel. Nebuchadnezzar's objective was to get them to abandon their faith and embrace the pagan Babylonian culture and religion. It was the intention of Nebuchadnezzar to erase every vestige of identification between these boys and their people and God. He even changed their names, but he could not change their hearts.

Or the heart of their friend, Daniel. [They] "purposed in their hearts to not eat of the king's table."

This is what we need a lot more of today—Purpose. Dare to be a Daniel. Dare to stand alone. Dare to have a purpose firm. Dare to make it known. Paul wrote to Timothy, "You have fully known my purpose.". . . Could you say that to someone? What would you say your purpose is? Paul said, "My determined purpose in life is to know Him.". . .

What is yours? My purpose in life is to . . . Be successful? Make money? Become famous? Have fun? Experience pleasure? Solomon who in his quest for fulfillment and meaning in life had it all, including unparalleled wealth, yet he wrote, "Whatever my eyes desired I did not keep from them. . . . I did not withhold from my heart any pleasure, then I looked on all the works my hands had done and all was emptiness."

Yes, "life and death," "blessings or curses" are before you. The foundation has been laid. Now make the right choices. Be young men and women of purpose. Your life and future have been given to you by God. It is to be used for His glory! We often say, "What I plan for MY future, and MY career, and MY family, etc." Yet Scripture reminds us, "You are not your own, you have been bought with a price. Therefore, glorify God with your body!"

Your life is a gift from God, go bring Him glory in whatever field He leads you! This world of ours desperately needs your influence! In the education system, in politics, in law, in the arts, in business, in the medical field, and in the ministry. Men and women, who like Shadrach, Meshach, and Abednego who will stand their ground.

I think of the story of a young lady, age 17, who reminds me of these three. She went to Columbine High School. Her name was Cassie Bernal. She was in the library studying, and apparently one of the gunmen knew she would be there. He walked in with his black trenchcoat, pointed his semi-automatic weapon at her and asked the question, "Do you believe in Jesus Christ?"

Your life is a gift from God, go bring Him glory in whatever field He leads you!

What would you have said knowing the possible consequences? He shot back, "There is no God," and killed Cassie. You may not face the same challenge as Cassie Bernal. Then again, maybe you will. But you will be challenged wherever you go and you will be asked the question, "Do you believe in God?" Follow Cassie's example wherever you go. Impact this world of ours. We need you now more than ever! Because one day you, like Paul, will say, "I fought the good fight. I finished the course." But you do not know when that day is. So make each day count! May you cross the finishing line with flying colors!

INSIGHTS *for* LIVING

Never despise the acquisition of knowledge.
However much the map of learning changes,
you will find yourself at sixty living off some, at least,
of the intellectual capital that you acquired when you were
twenty. The kinds of things you thought important now,
the conflicts, arguments, beliefs which you held or against
which you reached, will mark you for life.

—NOEL ANNAN

BE OPTIMISTIC

Captain Andrew Gerfin from the United States Coast Guard offers graduates advice for personal growth: confidence, accountability, and optimism serve as key elements in their new journey.

CAPTAIN ANDREW GERFIN
Academy West Graduation
Coast Guard
May 19, 1999

Greetings. You are all distinguished guests this evening and I am pleased and honored to be here with you. . . . I reviewed your curriculum when I found out I would be here this evening. I would like to review some of the advice which was included in the . . . "Learning Insight" of the Increasing Human Effectiveness course and add a couple of my own bullets gathered over the years.

- Be someone's friend as you want them to be for you.
- Seldom do we exceed our self-imposed limitations or expectations.
- Accept 100 percent accountability and demand it of others.
- Have a positive expectancy of reaching your goals.
- Bounce back quickly from temporary setbacks.
- Enter situations with confidence and optimism.
- Be confident of your decisions.
- Communications is everything.
- Read and aspire . . . and finally,
- Be optimistic about life, keep your [colleagues] optimistic, and look forward to and enjoy the challenges.

In closing, an unknown author once penned "A Philosophy for Life." It reads:

Keep your thoughts positive . . . because your thoughts become your words

Keep your words positive . . . because your words become your actions

Keep your actions positive . . . because your actions become your habits

Keep your habits positive . . . because your habits become your values and

Keep your values positive . . . because your values become your destiny.

THE ULTIMATE EXAM

An internationally known Christian educator, Dr. Howard G. Hendricks is the founder and former chairman of the Christian Education department of Dallas Theological Seminary. He now serves as Distinguished Professor and Chairman of the Center for Christian Leadership at Dallas Seminary. He urges graduates to consider three important questions at this turning point in their lives: Is the Lord well pleased? Is the work well done? Is the Word well used?

Dr. Howard Hendricks
Multnomah Bible College and Biblical Seminary
May 2000

I'm profoundly impressed by graciousness because one of my heroes is Sir Winston Churchill, an incredibly gifted human being—gracious, he was not. Particularly with Lady Astor, first woman elected to Parliament. They were constantly at each other's throats; in fact, on one occasion, she said to him, "Sir Winston, if I were your wife, I would put arsenic in your tea." To which he responded, "Lady Astor, if YOU were my wife, I would drink it." On another occasion, they met on a lift; he was slightly to the wind and she said to him in disgust, "Sir Winston, YOU are drunk." He was equal to the occasion because he responded by saying, "Lady Astor, YOU are ugly. But tomorrow, I will be sober."

What a delight and an honor it is to bring the commencement address at Multnomah Bible College and Biblical Seminary.... I would like to say to you, the graduating class, we are proud of you. We have and will continue to make intercessory investments on your behalf. We pray that God will give you a life and ministry far beyond anything you have ever dreamed.

Ours is a generation in which everything nailed down is coming loose. In which the things that people said could not happen are happening. And thoughtful . . . individuals are asking where is the glue with which to reassemble the disintegrating and disarrayed parts? Eugene O'Neill makes one of his characters say it so graphically: "You cannot build a marble temple out of a mixture of mud and manure."

But we continue to try. Man is almost insanely committed to the proposition that he has the answers to his problems. He's forever building his little sand castles only to discover the inundating tides of reality washing them out to sea, and then he seeks someone to blame. I saw an intriguing piece of graffiti in Philadelphia a number of years ago. Scratched across the wall were these words: "Humpty Dumpty was pushed."

This forces a question: What kind of a man, what kind of a woman graduating from Multnomah in 2000 does it take to make a permanent impact on our kind of society?

I think I've discovered the answer in an ancient text. It's more relevant than this morning's newspaper. It's relevant because it's revealed. It's found in 2 Timothy. 2:15: "Do your best to present yourself to God as one approved. A workman who does not need to be ashamed and who correctly handles the word of truth."

Has the Spirit of God etched on the ledger of your life those words that fell from the lips of our Savior, "Without Me, you can do nothing"? "When I try, I fail. When I trust, HE succeeds."

"Do your best," put everything you have into it. Concentrate. Make it your aim. It was Aristotle who said, "Like archers, we shall stand a far greater chance of hitting the target if we can see it." And so, the Apostle Paul delineates the lines of the target for his young protégé Timothy.

When I was a student, I was always convinced that teachers were perverse because they gave exams. Now that I AM a teacher—I'm convinced. So I want to take my professorial prerogatives tonight; and I want to give you, the graduating class, an exam. What I believe is the ultimate exam. There are only three questions. Please keep your eye on your own paper. No cribbing please.

Question number one: is the Lord well pleased?

Did you pick it up as I read the text? "Do your best to be approved by God." Have you discovered yet that it is possible to be eminently successful in the evangelical community and be a total failure with God? Three times in the gospels the heavens are opened, and we hear those remarkable words: "This is my beloved Son in whom I find ALL of my delight." Why was that true?

We really don't have the answer until we come to the book of Hebrews where we are informed that before Jesus invaded our planet, He paused on the threshold of heaven and said, "Lo, in the volume of the book it is written of Me. I delight to do thy will, O God."

Did you catch the connection? God found all of His pleasure in the Son because the Son found all of His pleasure doing the Father's will. Has the Spirit of God etched on the ledger of your life those words that fell from the lips of our Savior, "Without Me, you can do nothing"? Oh, the awful finality of that word. SOMEthing! [But the word is] "nothing." Shortly after I became a Christian, someone wrote in the flyleaf of my Bible these words: "When I try, I fail. When I trust, HE succeeds."

Men and women, there is a WORLD of theology wrapped up in that couplet. You see, the flesh only knows one thing and that's failure and by the way, God has no self-improvement program for your flesh. If you should know the Savior for thirty, forty, fifty, sixty years, you will still be capable of all of the heinous sins described in the Scripture.

> . . . the Christian life is not difficult, it's IMPOSSIBLE. It's a supernatural life and it is not until the Holy Spirit takes up His residence in you and lives the life of Christ through you. It's everything coming from God and nothing coming from you."

But in contrast, the Spirit only knows one thing and that's success. And to the extent that you and I take each and every step by means of the Holy Spirit, THEN and only then will your life and ministry please the High God.

I had the privilege of leading one of the Cowboys to Christ a number of years ago before I became involved as their chaplain. He called me up one day and said, "Hey, Doc, I'm going out to Thousand Oaks, California—give me an assignment."

I said, "Okay. Why don't you study and read the book of Ephesians."

"The what?"

"Ephesians."

I found out later this guy read the book of Ephesians SIX times every single day in training camp. When he came back to Dallas, he called me up and said, "Hey, you know that assignment you gave me? . . . Boy, what a wipe out!"

. . . I said, "What do you mean" He said, "You got some time"?

I said, "Yeah, there's nobody here. Come on over."

He came over to my office, opened his Bible and read this verse: "Husbands love your wives even as Christ also loved the church."

"Whoo! That's impossible," he said.

"Fantastic, man, you're on the verge of the greatest breakthrough of your new Christian life," [I said].

He said, "Really? What did I learn?"

I said, "You learned what 80-85 percent of the body of Christ have never learned. And that is that the Christian life is not difficult, it's IMPOSSIBLE. It's a supernatural life, and it is not until the Holy Spirit takes up His residence in you and lives the life of Christ through you. It's everything coming from God and nothing coming from you."

My greatest fear for you, graduates, is not that you will fail. My greatest fear for you is my greatest fear for myself— and that is that you will succeed . . . in doing the wrong things—with the wrong means.

You see, I spend a lot of time with people just like you. And what has disturbed me over the years is to find students from schools like this and my own who go out and depend on their giftedness, on their personality, on their education and training, on their experience. In fact, on EVERYTHING except God. To be sure, God will use your training: you've never had one that's better. God will use your giftedness; some of you are gifted beyond description. God will use your experience . . . because He's the one who gave it to you. He will use your personality—some of you to reach people who the rest of us could not reach with a twenty-foot pole. But for God's sake, don't depend on it. USE it, but come with that humility that recognizes in every scene and circumstance of your life, Lord, without You, I can do nothing. George McDonald said it: "God is easy to please, but hard to satisfy."

There's a second question in the exam: is the work well done?

Notice how [Paul] puts it. "A workman who does not need to be ashamed." In Ephesians 2:8-10 we read, "For by grace are you saved through faith and that not of yourselves. It is a gift of God, not of works lest any man should boast. For we are His workmanship, created in Christ Jesus to do good works which God prepared in advance for us to do." . . . Perhaps the greatest question you need to come to grips with is why did God put me on the planet? What's the one thing that He has gifted me to do without which I will never have the fulfillment designed in Christian life and ministry?

I'm discovering an increasing number of people, business people, professional people, athletes, people in a variety of settings who are ending their lives at the top of the pile in their field and at the bottom of life in terms of fulfillment. They're successful . . . but they're not significant. They are famous . . . but they are not fulfilled. They're rich . . . but they're poor when it comes to meaning. They've been climbing the ladder of success only to discover that ultimately it's leaning against the wrong wall.

Every time I come back to this verse, I'm compelled to ask the question—I'm sure many of you have already—why will I be ashamed? I suggest two reasons to provoke your thinking.

First of all . . . you will be ashamed because you are ministering without standards. You're aiming to love. You all know Michelangelo, but do you know Bertaldo? For there's a constant argument and discussion in arts circles as to who was the greater? Michelangelo, the pupil, or Bertaldo, the teacher who produced him? And like the great teacher he was, he discovered that men and women who are gifted often ride on their giftedness rather than develop. And he warned him repeatedly.

One day [Bertaldo] came into the studio, and he watched Michelangelo as he piddled with a piece of statuary that he'd been working on for months. He went over and picked up a sledgehammer and batted that thing into a thousand pieces and as they ricocheted all over the studio, he was heard to shout, "Michelangelo, talent is cheap. Dedication is costly."

I have never found a successful significant servant of Jesus Christ . . . who did not pay a very high price. [Service to Him] is not available on a bargain basement sale. Not only will we be ashamed because we're operating without standards, but also because too often we're ministering without sacrifice. We're aiming too low, and it's costing too little.

> **. . . the service that counts is the service that costs. It'll cost you to serve the Lord with significance. [But] it will cost you more not to.**

During David's reign, people were dying like flies. He came to the high priest and said, "What shall I do?" And he said, "David, you'd better offer up sacrifices to the Lord our God."

David shows up outside the property of a man by the name of Araunah. I'm sure his heart leaped a couple of beats when he looked out from the flaps of his tent and there's the king with all of his entourage. He rushes out and says, "David, what can I do for you?"

And David says, "I want to buy a piece of property."

You can almost hear, "you've got to be kidding." "[But] you're the king. I'll give you the property, I'll give you the sacrifice, I'll give you everything you need."

But David said, "No, you won't."

You see, David would not make a good American because he was not a free loader. I think some of the most significant words that ever fell from his lips were uttered in 2 Samuel 24:24: "Neither will I offer unto the Lord my God of that which costs me nothing." [David] knew that the service that counts is the service that costs. It'll cost you to serve the Lord with significance. [But] it will cost you more not to.

. . .There's a third and final question for your ultimate final: is the Word well used?

Truth is always a return to reality. If you cannot take it any other way, take it by faith. It will stand you in good stead in the ministry to which God is calling you . . . When you and I come to the Word of God; and there are things [we] can't understand, the greatest mark of maturity is to say, "I don't know. I'm going to have to study that, or maybe we don't have enough evidence at this point time to give you all of the data related to it." But the one conviction you have is the conviction that your source of authority is the Word of God. And by the way, if God is no longer your source of authority, then YOU will be the authority to the people to whom you minister . . . and that's lethal.

Well, you say, "How, Prof? How can I become a spiritual craftsman?" As the text says . . . there are three things. [First], you have to KNOW the Word of God. You cannot communicate out of a vacuum . . . I hope you don't think you know it all now. See, if you stop learning today, you stop teaching and ministering tomorrow. . . . Paul says, "All scripture is given by inspiration by God and is profitable." That includes Habakkuk. Been in there lately? Second Chronicles. I said that in a men's group some time ago and a guy said, "I didn't know there was a first one." . . . By the way, if your knowledge, if your ability to defeat the Enemy depended on your knowledge of Deuteronomy, how would you make out? No, that's too convicting . . .

[Second], you must live the Word of God. Too many Christians today are like poor photographs. They're overexposed and they're underdeveloped. My friend, the Bible was not written to satisfy your curiosity; it was written to transform your life. It was not written to make you a smarter sinner but to make you like Jesus Christ. You are living in a generation, I guarantee you I'm immersed in it, that is WEARY of words, that's starving for reality. They've heard every rhetoric show that comes down the pike but what they're looking for is a woman like you, a man like you—not perfect but progressing. Somebody who fleshes out the life of Jesus Christ. . . .

Now, you show me a person who knows the truth and who lives the truth and I will show you a person who is eminently equipped to share the truth, to communicate it as God is calling you. Whether you're in business or the professions or in education or in marriage and family, wherever, you know what God has said: you are in the process of incorporating that truth in your lifestyle, and you have something to say to your generation.

That's the ultimate final. I have these three questions printed by a printer friend of mine which I have in my car, the most prominent places in my home, on my desk at the seminary. I never let a day go by but that I take the exam.

Is the Lord well pleased? A lot of people will not like you. I hope you're not hooked by an obsession to be liked, but I do hope you're hooked with an obsession that Jesus Christ finds His delight in you.

Is the work well done? [We live] in a generation where we suffer from a mania of mediocrity—anything is good enough for God—but not for one committed to Him and loved by Him.

And finally, is the Word well used? The answers to those three questions will determine if you hear the words, "Well done, good and faithful servant, enter into the joy of your Lord."

One of my favorite poems is entitled "The Night They Burned Shanghai." There are just a

You are living in a generation, I guarantee you I'm immersed in it, that is WEARY of words, that's starving for reality.

few lines that stick in my mind like a piece of glass:

> Some men die in ashes
> Some men die in flames
> Some men die inch by inch
> Playing silly little games

Men and women, die you will! We have a 100 percent probability apart from our blessed Lord's return. But the question is HOW? Your life is like a coin. You can spend it any way you want, but you can only spend it once. Our prayer is that you will make an eternal investment with dividends that will pay throughout the ages of eternity. I love you, and God bless you.

BE AFRAID—THEN DON'T BE AFRAID

Elisabeth Elliot, a well-known Christian speaker and writer, was born in Brussels, Belgium, where her parents served as missionaries. She and her husband, Jim Elliot, worked together on translating the New Testament into the language of the Quichua Indians of Ecuador. Ten months later while attempting to take the Gospel to the Auca Indians, Jim was killed by the primitive tribe. In her speech, Ms. Elliot refers to the obstacles of her life and how she has learned to not be afraid and at the same time, to be afraid.

ELISABETH ELLIOT
Moody Bible Institute
1994

I want to address two questions this afternoon: what do you fear and what are you sure about? One day when a shoving, elbowing mob of many thousands had gathered around Jesus, he began to speak not to them but to the smaller group of his disciples. And He said, "Don't be afraid"—and— "be afraid." Don't be afraid. Be afraid. . . .

It was forty-six years ago that I graduated from a small college about twenty-five miles west of here. I was as relieved as you are . . . but I was also afraid. I believe that I honestly wanted more than anything else the will of God, God's holy will for my life. But what if I missed it? Suppose I went to the wrong mission field or the right field but the wrong tribe?

I was quite sure that I was meant to be a jungle missionary, one of those who lived under a thatched roof, far from civilization but might I misinterpret God's leading? And then there was one particularly scary thought: would I always be single? I was afraid . . . but of the wrong things.

Hear the words of Jesus: "I tell you, my friends, do not be afraid of those who kill the body and after that, can do no more. But I will show you whom you should fear. Fear Him who after the killing of the body has power to throw you into Hell; yes, I tell you, fear Him. Are not five sparrows sold for two pennies, yet not one of them is forgotten by God? Indeed, the very hairs of your head are all numbered. Don't be afraid. You are worth more than many sparrows."

Fear God and fear nothing else. Fear Him who's got the whole world in His hands, and you'll never find anything else *in* the world worth fearing. The more deeply we recognize Jesus Christ as Lord of the universe, Lover of souls, the more He becomes to us the one essential, the less concerned we'll be about everything else. When everything in our world is shaken, our feet will still be firmly placed on an unshakable foundation, the Rock of eternal indestructibility.

If a sparrow worth less than half a cent is under a heavenly Father's watchful eye every second of his life, and if each separate hair of your head has a number on it, shall we suppose that we who are made in His image will be overlooked or forgotten? Are we perhaps at the mercy of chance? That question strikes fear enough to turn our knees to water. What if the universe is nothing but a chaotic jumble?

Having grown up in a very strong Christian home, I took it for granted that I was well prepared for life. Whenever one of us children complained about weather, chores, unfair treatment or whatever, someone in the family was bound to remind him of a family byword—"GMT"—good missionary training. We had a lot of that, and I'm thankful for it. But then there are God's mysterious ways—unpredictable, unexplained. He plants His footsteps in the sea. Ever seen any footsteps in the sea? He brings us face to face with His inscrutability and our fallibility.

You remember Burns' poem about the farmer who turns up a mouse's nest with his plow and begins to ponder the panic that he has caused this "wee, sleeked, cowering, timorous beasty." The poor little creature had worked hard on that "wee bit housy," and all his plans went to smash as do often the best laid schemes of mice and men.

> **Fear God and fear nothing else. Fear Him who's got the whole world in His hands, and you'll never find anything else IN the world worth fearing.**

It took me four years to get to Ecuador. When I got there, I didn't know which of the nine Indian tribes I should work in. That answer came when God's answers always come—in His time, not mine. I went to the west jungle and began work on the unwritten language of the Colorado Indians. Before I had been there one full year, three things brought me to the brink of the abyss of the unexplained, where faith is most rigorously tested. They were three stunning blows: the murder of my linguistic informant, a flood which totally destroyed the station on which my fiancé had been working, and the theft of all the Colorado language material which I had amassed. Was I still in the hands of divine providence? Was the Lord whose eye is on the sparrow and the terrified mouse not watching when the murder, the flood, and the theft took place?

We know that to those who love God who are called according to His plan, everything that happens fits into a pattern for good. Either God means what He says, or He doesn't. Either He is God, or He isn't. Those were the alternatives, and so far as I could see, the only alternatives. As I gazed into the abyss, I knew that the truth was one thing *or* the other. It could not possibly lie somewhere in the middle. Was God still in charge? It did not *appear* that He was. Was He still God? Yes or no. Were the murder, the flood, and the theft mere accidents with which He had nothing to do? Yes or no?

In family prayers at home, we had often sung that gospel hymn "Trust and Obey": two simple words—simple to understand, hard to carry out. But those two words are loaded. They are the essence of what it means to love God. Those three hammer blows to my faith which I experienced in that first year in the jungle were only the grade school lessons, but I had to choose: it was God or nothing. If God was still God, He was worthy of my worship and my service. If He was not God, I could pack my bags and forget about my mission to the Indians.

Either God means what He says or He doesn't.

You know which I chose or I would not be standing at this podium today. I guess you might say I was precipitated to the next level of the school of faith less than three years later. Jim Elliot and I were by this time married after a long, long wait. One morning in 1956, I learned that he was missing. He and four colleagues had gone into the territory of a tribe thought to be savages. As the chilling message crackled over my short wave, I felt that terrible rush of adrenaline. But then the Spirit of God brought to my mind His own message, "When you pass through the waters, I will be with you. When you walk through the fire, you will not be burned. For I AM the Lord your God, the Holy One of Israel, your Savior."

Was I afraid? Yes. But so was the psalmist who said, "What time I *am* afraid, I *will* trust." Five days later, we knew that all five of the men were dead, speared by the people to whom they had taken the gospel. And once again I looked into that dark abyss . . . and once again I pondered the depth of the mystery of faith.

Those men had sung a hymn just before they left for Auca territory: "We Rest on Thee our Shield and our Defender." Does your faith topple when you consider that prayer and its strange outcome? A God who leads men to trust Him as a shield and then permits them to be speared to death? Do not forget, dear men and women of the class of '94. Jesus Christ is the same yesterday, today, and forever. I'm sure about that.

Two thousand years ago, Jesus Himself was silent as His most faithful servant, John the Baptist, was beheaded because John the Baptist had not only trusted but obeyed. It was that obedience that cost him his head. Then there was Stephen, a powerful orator, full of the Holy Ghost, stoned to death. And there was our Savior, the Lord Jesus, whose hands made all the universes—astronomers now tell us there are perhaps 200 billion universes—those hands were firmly and helplessly nailed to a wooden cross, the instrument of torture designed for criminals. Never forget that cross.

And if you mean to take up the cross and follow, do not be surprised if the Lord leads you into a storm. He did just that with His disciples: He led them into a storm and was so totally at peace Himself that He fell asleep with His head on a pillow. When the sailors woke Him in a panic, His quiet word to them was, "Why are you so afraid? Why is it that you have no faith?"

> **. . . do not be surprised if the Lord leads you into a storm.**

I asked you two questions. The first was what are you afraid of? The disciples feared that the next wave would send them to the bottom and what a way to go. But it did not happen to be their time to die. It was their time to recognize who held supreme authority. Over life and death, over wind and waves, Jesus simply spoke, and there was a calm. To have faith is to make a deliberate decision—I *will* trust. When I *am* afraid, I *will* trust.

Human existence was designed to rest not only on divine creation and God's perfect control of all things, but also upon human decision precisely because God's omnipotence is crowned in the freedom of the individual, to trust or not to trust. To obey or not to obey, to accept or reject Him.

When things fall apart, when your "wee bit housy" is demolished, when the Lord leads you straight into a storm, think of the second question I asked: what are you sure of? This is the fulcrum on which the whole moral and spiritual structure of your life rests. Hear the words of Queen Esther: "If I perish, I perish." Of the apostle Paul: "I'm ready not only to be imprisoned but even to die at Jerusalem for the name of the Lord Jesus." Of Martin Luther: "Though every tile on every roof in Vermes be a demon, yet will I go there." Of David Livingston: "Who am I that I should fear? Nay, verily, I will take my bearings tonight, though they be my last." And of an unsung housemaid named Mary Reece who went to a hostile tribe in Africa. The chief drew a line in the sand and said, "If you step over that line, I'll kill you."

Her response, "Over the line I went in the name of the Lord."

And of Jim Elliot, "Father, take my life. Yeah, my blood, if thou wilt, it's not mine to save. Have it Lord, have it all. Pour out my life as an oblation for the world."

Be afraid. Yes, of Him who holds life and death in His wounded hands. Don't be afraid of *any*thing else. You and I can never be sure of what will happen or not happen in this world, but we can be absolutely sure of the utter faithfulness of the One who made it and engineers all things according to His glorious promises. We cannot search out the hows and the whys and the wherefores, but we can declare with ringing certainty, "I know whom I have believed. And I am absolutely sure that He is able to keep whatever I have committed to Him."

AS A DYING MAN TO THE DYING

Introduction by Dr. John MacArthur

It's really hard to put into words what this particular occasion means to him and to all of us who know and love him. He just leaned over to me and said, "I just thank the Lord I'm feeling very well . . . the only problem is I have terminal cancer." This is a very special day for all of us because I'm sure Dr. Smith didn't know if the Lord was going to allow him to reach this wonderful milestone. But we were confident the Lord would because we need to hear what's on his heart as he has readied himself to enter into his eternal reward. . . .

> DR. CHARLES W. SMITH
> *Masters College*
> *May 11, 2002*

Especially to this graduation class, I wish to extend my congratulation. You have worked hard and completed the requirements for your degree and from the various insignia on your gowns, I see that many of you are graduating summa cum laude, and others are graduating magna cum laude, a few are graduating cum laude, and some are just graduating "thank the laude." But you made it! You made it!

I've learned much from you. This class especially has given me support far beyond what I could ever have hoped for. You've demonstrated your love by your prayers, your notes, your letters, many hugs and expressions of affection; and for that I thank you. I congratulate you parents for having produced children with the character and determination to finish the difficult task of completing your college degree. Thank you for your support and encouragement you have given them. Certainly this is a day of joy, of satisfaction and pride for you, and for some of you, a great surprise. . . .

I must give special greetings to my wonderful family. They have always given me unflagging, untiring support. All three of my children are here today. . . . I'm so glad they could be here. Now, my wife would love to have been here today; but she and the Lord had business to conduct in heaven, and she just couldn't make it.

Today marks a culmination of a journey begun fifty years ago. In that spring I sat where you sit now, having completed the requirements for graduation and anticipating the future. Now, I stand before you at what appears

> **I was taught that a preacher should preach as a dying man to dying men. Today in a very real sense I AM that dying man.**

to be the end of that journey to share with you some of the lessons from life that might help you as you begin your journey. . . .

One year ago, I was diagnosed with meta static prostratic cancer . . . I had 18-24 months before the cancer would work its inexorable, final end of death. So, perhaps today is a very appropriate time for me to bid an official farewell to my wonderful college family. I have no idea before the Lord says, "NOW." It may be soon, and it may be much later; but we cannot presume upon His graces, so I'll take advantage of this opportunity for saying an official farewell.

In my youth, I was taught that a preacher should preach as a dying man to dying men. Today in a very real sense I AM that dying man. I may not have the opportunity of speaking to you again, so I ask you to listen carefully to what I have to say. . . . I want you to take the precepts I am now teaching you and put them into practice in your lives.

The first thing I want to emphasize is to learn to live in the sovereignty of God. One of the main forces in my life was derived from the study of the Psalms, especially Psalm 100, verses 3 and 5. "Know ye that the Lord, He is God. . . For the LORD is good." God is God, God is good. I have been consumed with the sovereignty of God. I have lived in His sovereignty. I have rested in His sovereignty. I have rejoiced in His sovereignty. I have reveled in His sovereignty. There is nothing that has given me more stability in my life than the sovereignty of God. There is nothing that has given me more peace than to know that God is sovereign. Oh, the great freeing power that the sovereignty of God has given me. . . .

Remember, if God is sovereign, nothing can possibly enter your life that is beyond His knowledge and His will. If God is good, then everything that comes into your life is designed ultimately to bring good for you. Everything? Yes, everything. I consciously taught these great truths to my children as well as to my college students. But as you parents know, there is a great problem in teaching lessons to your children. They expect YOU to live by them.

One day I was grumbling and grousing and complaining about my car troubles and the poor timing of my troubles when one of my daughters spoke up, . . . "Dad, is God still sovereign? Did He know about your car problems? Is God still good?

"Shut up, kid, I'm having a pity party!" . . .

I challenge you to learn to love and live and trust the sovereignty of God. And then you will learn to rest in the grace of God. The more I became absorbed in the awareness of the sovereignty of God, the more I realized the grace of God . . .

I have seen God's grace operate in my life. Why would the Almighty God, Maker of heaven and earth, reach down into a poverty-stricken family in Alabama and say to a young boy, "I want you to be my child and preach my Word to others" and then give him opportunities far beyond his imagination? Only God's sovereignty and God's grace. Trust His sovereignty, experience His grace.

Learn to stay close to the Word of God. . . . Learn to READ the Bible. Put the Word of God in your mind. Meditate upon it. But meditation demands knowledge of the words of Scripture. . . . Learn to read the WORDS of the Bible before you try to say the meaning of the Scriptures.

On a more practical note, learn the power of the church. . . . We forget sometimes 1 Corinthians 12:13 for "by one Spirit we are all baptized into one body." . . . The life of the church, the body of Christ, is lived visibly in the local church . . .Your connection with the local church says much about your relationship to the Lord of the Church. . . . There is no substitute for the fellowship of my brothers and sisters in the church. We are one in Christ.

When a man is born again, he becomes a partaker of the nature of GOD. God's nature resides in him.

In your own personal life, develop a passion for holiness. . . .When a man is born again, he becomes a partaker of the nature of GOD. God's nature resides in him. . . . God's nature is holy and therefore, He expects His people to be holy; and they WILL be holy if they have His nature in them. . . Develop a passion for holiness.

And you cannot live a life for God without making much of prayer. . . . [Paul] says, "Unceasingly I make mention of you in my prayers. . . . Always offering prayer.". . . But how can we do this? Well, we can worry without ceasing. . . . What is a legitimate object of worry? Nothing. What is a legitimate object of prayer? Everything. . . . Turn everything into a prayer thought. A problem arises, instead of worrying, pray about it. A situation in life, pray about it. A test is coming up, study, and pray about it. . . . We turn everything into a prayer thought. Give much to prayer. These are some of the lessons that have held me through my life. . . .

And now, it is time for me to teach you how to die. . . . I have only so many days left. What is of life and death importance for me to do? . . .

Soon, God soon, . . . I will be passing through the valley of the shadow of death to go to be with the Lord. . . . Can you even begin to imagine what it would mean as you are slipping from life while you are looking into the faces of the ones you hold most dear on earth to suddenly find yourself looking into the face of the One who is most loved? And to find yourself

For the first time, we'll be able to fully experience the breadth of His love, the depth of His grace, the scope of His wisdom, the extent of His power, the brilliance of His glory

instantly transported into heaven? What a trip! Better and faster than more exciting than any roller coast ride at Magic Mountain, better than a rocket ride from Cape Canaveral. But the thing that excites me most about going to be with the Lord is that at the moment I'll leave this body of corruption, I'll be purged of sin and will forever be perfectly holy. "When we shall see Him, we shall be like Him for we shall see Him as He is." . . .

Soon I will no longer roam the campus creating my kind of chaos wherever I go. . . . [But] our parting is but for a short period of time. We look forward to that day of reunion when all the people of God will be brought together into the presence of the Lord. . . . We will see the Lamb of God . . . for the first time. For the first time, we'll realize the full meaning of His sacrificial death, the suffering He endured for us. For the first time, we'll be able to fully experience the breadth of His love, the depth of His grace, the scope of His wisdom, the extent of His power, the brilliance of His glory. . . . What a reunion that will be. Now THAT is an experience to die for.

FAITH, HOPE, LOVE

Serving as the seventh president of Biola University, Dr. Clyde Cook has served as an administrator, educator, and fourth-generation missionary throughout his life. Early in his life, the Cook family was imprisoned in three different concentration camps during World War II, later reunited in South Africa. Dr. Cook encourages the graduates to be men and women of faith and though they will face challenges in the future, they must remain strong in faith and in love, "with an unshakeable trust in the God of all creation and His beautiful inerrant Word."

CLYDE COOK
Biola University
May 2002

I received a telephone call two years ago in the latter part of April. It was from a fellow president. He said, "Clyde, you're going to have to help me out. I need you to speak at our commencement. . . . Clyde, you'll have to do this for me. We'll fly you up in the morning, you fly right back as soon as you've finished."

I said, "Ed, I don't do commencements."

He said, "Why not?"

I said, "Because nobody listens. Everybody is here for graduation, to cheer for their graduate. Not only that, college and university commencements are no longer dignified services but have deteriorated so they're now like junior high commencements: beach balls, bubbles, air horns and other distractions." I said, "It's okay when they pass out the diplomas, but now it's starting right at the beginning."

He said, "I know what you mean, but you have to do it anyways."

So, as an obedient Christian brother, I flew to the campus for the commencement. When I met Ed, I said, "Ed, who was last year's speaker?" "Sorry, I can't remember."

"How about the year before?"

Same puzzled look. Again, I said, "Ed, how about any speaker in the last five years?" Again a blank. I said, "Ed, that's my point. If YOU can't remember who they were, how can anybody else? Let's just skip the message." He said, "Just DO it."

There [is one] . . . commencement speech that will not be forgotten: Josh McDowell's forty-five second speech in 1998. "Graduating class, my commencement address to you is this: If your life is going to have an impact for Christ after Biola, never stop pursuing an intimate love relationship with your future spouse and spend time with your children." This was repeated twice and he ended with "God bless." Not only has his speech not been forgotten, but it saved us some money, as I paid him by the word. . . .

So why am I here? Three reasons. One, I tried to get two excellent speakers but they were unavailable. . . . Two, I'm saving Biola five hundred bucks on the . . . cost of traveling expenses and three, as I'm completing twenty years as president of Biola University and [since] this year we're celebrating Biola's fiftieth anniversary . . . someone suggested it might be appropriate for me to speak.

> **And how does God turn a no way situation into not absolutely no way?**

So let me share three words with you before we get to the real reason why we're here. These three words are found in 1 Corinthians 13. "In the Word there are three things that last forever: faith, hope, and love. But the greatest of them all is love."

We start with faith because that's where we began. We entered into this new life by faith in the Lord Jesus Christ. "By grace you are saved through faith." There's a mysterious joining of your faith and the Word of God that brought about the miraculous new birth. We believed God and rejected Satan's attempt to cause us to doubt. In the beginning that was his weapon. God said, "Dying, thou shalt die." And Satan countered, "You shall not surely die."

And so, Adam and Eve had a choice to believe God or to believe the Father of lies. They chose the latter and thus eternal death and separation from God came upon them. And thousands of years later, God again speaks and says, "You received eternal death and separation from me because you did not believe. Now in order to be reconciled and receive eternal life, you must believe. Believe in the Lord Jesus Christ and thou shall be saved."

And so we did. And we entered into this new life. A life that is supernatural, a life that has its treasure in an earthen vessel that the excellency of the power may be of God and not of us. A life that when trouble on every side is not distressed, a life that can be "perplexed but not in despair, persecuted but not forsaken, cast down but not destroyed."

Those of you who have been around Biola awhile have heard me talk about what it means to be perplexed and not in despair. . . . I'm sure that in getting through one of your demanding academic programs, that verse has been put to the test many times. You thought that there was no way, no way that you were going to get that paper written, no way that you were going to be able to pass that science exam, no way you were going to be able to continue on because of finances or a THOUSAND no ways— and yet— there was not absolutely no way, because here you are.

And how does God turn a no way situation into not absolutely no way? How is the supernatural life lived? It is lived by faith. The Bible says, "The just shall live by faith." We're to attempt great things for God through faith. Howard Hendricks has written, "We're all faced with a series of great opportunities brilliantly disguised as unsolvable problems."

And Sir Edmund Hillary, who along with Tenzing Norgay was the first to conquer Mt. Everest, echoed this thought when he said, "A challenge you're confident of overcoming is hardly worth starting. Why bother if you are quite confident that you're going to overcome it? The real challenges are the ones that extend you to the utmost. It is more impressive to fail on a difficult objective than to succeed on a modest one."

In the excellent training you've been receiving at Biola University, you've been given the wonderful Word of God and His marvelous world. . . . Hopefully, we have taught you not just how to make a living, but how to live and how to live for the glory of God. I trust that we have equipped you in mind and character to make an impact in the world for the Lord Jesus Christ.

As you move into this next chapter of your life, I trust you'll be men and women of faith. There will be times in your life when you'll be sorely tested in this point. Our Lord said to Peter, "I pray for you that your faith fail not." I used to have a great deal of trouble with this verse. The reason was that just twenty-five verses later, Peter was denying the Lord. So I thought, "Wow, great prayer, Lord. It really worked, didn't it?" If the Lord of all heaven had a prayer that in my opinion was so ineffective, what use is it for me to pray or to have Him praying for me?

Now I know that wasn't the case. I know our Lord's prayers are effective, and yet I couldn't reconcile His prayer with why Peter denied Him so quickly. I went to every commentary I could to see if I could get some help but found nothing to help me. In my struggle, I took this to the Lord and asked Him to show me how to reconcile this and all of a sudden, the answer came. I was interpreting the Lord's prayer to be that Peter sin not. That is not what the Lord prayed, and this is why perhaps the commentators did not mention it because it was so obvious. But to me it was a revelation.

We're to attempt great things for God through faith. Howard Hendricks has written, "We're all faced with a series of great opportunities brilliantly disguised as unsolvable problems."

He prayed that Peter's faith fail not. And although Peter sinned, his faith did not fail. I have met people caught up in sin, and their faith failed; they denied the presence of God and from all outward appearance lost their faith; however, I've known others who have sinned, and during the time of sinning, they were miserable. They had a conflict going along inside them, and their faith did not fail; eventually they repented and turned from their sin and once again lived by faith.

So my prayer for you this day is even as our Lord's that your faith fail not. The Scriptures tell us that we are not to be ignorant of Satan's devices and surely doubt is one of his principal weapons. He used it in the garden, and he uses it now. Your faith will be sorely tested in whatever area of service the Lord places you. May it not fail.

The second quality which lasts forever is hope. Dante said that over the gates of hell it is written, "Abandon hope all ye who enter here." I think of two of the saddest words in all the world are "no hope." Alexander Pope wrote, "Hope springs eternal in the human breast, without hope we despair."

In my office, I have a little poem that says, "Let those who must despair, Let those who will begin again." Only if there is hope will a person attempt to begin again.

To the apostle Paul, hope is a great thing. He speaks about looking for that blessed hope and glorious appearing of the great God and our Savior Jesus Christ. However, he's not talking about using hope to escape from the present realities. I once heard about one of our Talbot students who on the night before every Hebrew exam would go out on his old balcony and look up longingly at the sky and pray, "Oh, Lord, please come back tonight. I don't want to take that exam." This continued throughout his Hebrew studies. In the meantime, he fell in love and was to be married the day after his final Hebrew exam. On the eve of his marriage and the day before his last exam, he went out on the balcony for one last time, looked up at the sky, and said, "Not tonight, Lord, not tonight." . . .

What hope you have is an anchor of the soul, both sure and steadfast.

I can guarantee that every one of you here is going to be put in situations in your life where darkness comes upon you, and you're wondering how you are ever going to get through it, how you're going to endure. You're going to feel the rapture of death is your only escape. May God grant you hope in those dark hours; . . . you have a strong consolation those of you who have fled for refuge to lay hold upon the hope set before you. What hope you have is an anchor of the soul, both sure and steadfast.

The third quality that Paul mentions is love, the greatest of all. . . . If you graduate from our school of business, you start a company that quickly makes the Fortune 500 list, but you have not love, you're nothing. If you're teacher of the year or nurse of the year or a fabulous homemaker, but have not love, you'll be nothing. You're to love God, love the Bible, love the family. Nowhere in Scripture have I been told to be president of Biola University or be elected to prestigious educational boards or invited to speak at important events. I've been told to love my wife, even as Christ loved the church. I've been told to love God's people and to love those for whom Jesus Christ died. . . . The world needs love, not a superficial love which focuses on ourselves, but a God-given agape love which makes a difference in our lives. We need to love those for whom Christ died: people who need a touch from God, people who hurt, people who need someone to love them. . . .

And so, dear graduates, you've been given some of the finest training in the world by our great professors. . . . You're excited about attempting great things for God. You're enthusiastic about a life full of potential to touch men and women around the world. With all your knowledge, with all your understanding, with all your enthusiasm, go as men and women of faith and with an unshakeable trust in the God of all creation and His beautiful inerrant Word.

Go with great hope in your heart, hope that will enable you to endure, that will provide an anchor for you. And above all, go as men and women of love for by this shall all men and women know that you are disciples of the Lord Jesus Christ, the One that called you out of darkness into His marvelous light that you might show forth His praises. . . .

> **The world needs love, not a superficial love which focuses on ourselves, but a God-given agape love which makes a difference in our lives.**

IS YOUR CHRISTIANITY INTELLECTUAL OR IS IT REALITY?

Founder of Campus Crusade for Christ, William R. "Bill" Bright has been one of the most influential leaders of the American evangelical movement within the past 50 years. Mr. Bright created the Four Spiritual Laws pamphlet as well as the famous Jesus film, a film that has been translated into 812 languages and has been viewed by more than 5.6 billion people around the world. After Bright was diagnosed with pulmonary fibrosis in 1999, his remark was, "I can't lose. If I die, I go to be with the Lord, and that is wonderful, glorious." Here he tells the graduates of Liberty University the importance of loving a sovereign God, trusting Him in every way, and obeying Him. But above all, you must die to self and tell others of the love of Jesus Christ. Mr. Bright died on July 19, 2003.

BILL BRIGHT
Liberty University
2002

Graduating class, members of your family, faculty, distinguished guests, it is a great honor and marvelous privilege for my beloved wife, Vonette, and me to be with you today. I've been sitting here just bursting with praise to our great God and Savior for what He has done here. . . . To Him be all the glory. . . .

That introduction . . . reminds me of the man who was introduced as a great orator, a great scholar, a great man of integrity and statesmanship—and he believed it. He was so impressed with himself that he could hardly wait to hear what he was going to say. He meditated on his greatness for days and one day he broke the silence by saying to his wife, "I wonder how many *really* great people there are in the world anyway?" She said, "I don't know, but there's one less than you think."

There is one who is great. His name is Jesus. I was a happy pagan going my own self-centered way, building my own business with great American dreams for my own little empire when I met the Creator of the universe—the One who spoke and the worlds were framed, who came to this little speck of sand, planet earth, died on the cross for me and for all people and then the third day was raised from the dead and came to live within me. If I weren't a Presbyterian, I'd say hallelujah. What an exciting truth—Christ in you, the Hope of glory. There is no truth more important than this: that God, the great Creator God and Savior, Father, Son, Holy Spirit lives within us, and He came for one purpose. He came not to be the greatest teacher the world has ever known, and He was that; not to be the greatest moral example and He was that; He didn't come for many other reasons. He came for one purpose: He came to die for our sins. He came to seek and to save the lost.

Ever since I fell in love with Him, that has been my one goal. Every day I try to evaluate everything I do in light of the great commission. That's why He came—to seek and save the lost; and if I'm really truly committed to Him, then my number one consuming burden is to help fulfill what He came to the world to do 2,000 years ago. Seek and save the lost. . . .

You don't need another sermon from someone like myself. But I do have some things I'd like to share with you in way of personal journey. I've had a great journey. As a pagan, I was introduced to Christ as a result of my mother's prayers and. . . others helped me in my growth, in my commitment. Then Vonette and I were married in 1948. She was twenty-five years old. After we had been married a couple of years, our love for Christ was such that we decided to sign a contract, with Jesus. I'm a businessman; I was in business at that time and in business with Hollywood before I became a believer, and I had written many contracts, but this was to be the most important of my life. If you've never done anything like this, I'd encourage you to do so. We wrote out and surrendered the total title deed of our lives without reservation, irrevocably to this One who died for us. We said, "Lord, from now on we'll do whatever You want us to do, we'll go wherever You want us to go."

We put all our material wealth on the altar so that in 1996 when God by His grace honored me with the Templeton prize of over one million dollars, people asked me, "What are you going to do with that? Are you going to buy a home?" I've never had a home. "Are you going to buy cars?" We don't have cars. We've always lived like kings, but we don't own anything. God takes care of those things. He takes care of His slaves. So, people said, "What are you going to do with all that money?" I said, "I gave it away in 1951 when we signed the contract." Jesus has been our Lord ever since.

There are three things I'd like to share with you this morning to encourage you young graduates and your families as well, lessons I've

> **We wrote out and surrendered the total title deed of our lives without reservation, irrevocably to this One who died for us. We said, "Lord, from now on we'll do whatever You want us to do, we'll go wherever You want us to go."**

learned over these years that are very simple. The Christian life is not complicated. Oh, I had five years of theological study and two fine seminaries. I believe in the inspired, inerrant Word of God, I believe all the basic doctrines of the faith. No one could be more fundamental, more basic in their beliefs than I, but there are three things that stand out among all the other things that I have learned and they're simple. If you want to know an exciting life, if you want to know of fruitful life, love God with all your heart, soul, mind, and strength. Seek first His kingdom. Obey His commandments and trust His promises. And you know what? What you've learned intellectually will become reality in your hearts and wills.

I've learned some lessons in my work with students, even graduates of Christian schools where you've heard the Gospel day after day, class after class, and you've prayed together with your professors. For some of you, the reality of the resurrection, Jesus Christ living in you is intellectual. When you go out into the world tomorrow, you will not know how to handle the challenges greater than any other generation has ever faced in my opinion. Terrorism will be with us as long as we live and beyond until our Lord returns. Every day will be a day of uncertainty. Oh, what a glorious moment it is for us who believe because all around us men and women who are filled with fear and insecurity we can say, "We know the reality of the living Christ in us." We do not need to be afraid, but we have a good message to the world, the most joyful news ever announced

> **As you walk in the light as God is the light, you will out of the overflow of your life, not only fulfill His command to love but His great commission to go.**

It was on the night of our Lord's birth when the angels said to the shepherds who were fearful as they viewed that dazzling star and heard the angelic choir, "Don't be afraid. I bring you the most joyful news ever announced. The Savior, the Messiah, the Lord was born tonight in Bethlehem." Two thousand years have passed. It is still the most joyful news ever announced. Oh, how we need to proclaim this. As you walk in the light as God is the light, you will out of the overflow of your life, not only fulfill His great command to love but His great commission to go. . . .

In Matthew 22, a lawyer asked Jesus what is the greatest of all the commandments, and He responded by saying, "Love God with all your heart, with all your soul, mind, and strength. This is the first and greatest commandment. The second most important is similar. Love your neighbor as yourself. All the other commandments, all the other demands of the prophets, stem from these two laws. Love God, love your neighbors."

In Matthew 5, He admonishes us to love our enemies. Keep only these, and you'll find that you are obeying all the others. God places a very, very high premium on love. There is no truth in the Word of God that captivates me more. I came to Christ because of His love for me. I was living in spiritual ignorance. I didn't know any better. My saintly mother knew, but she had not been taught how to share her faith. My father was not a believer; and I was never introduced to anyone, any man whom I admired, who was a believer. Oh, I'm sure I was, [introduced] but I just didn't recognize it. I didn't recognize them as believers. But when I heard the Gospel, really heard it, I responded.

I believe that if over half the world today, non-believers, were properly approached by Spirit-filled people who know what they're saying, know how to say it, they would receive Christ. Now that may sound like an exaggeration but in meeting after meeting around the world where the *Jesus* film is shown, where I have the privilege of speaking to academia, college students and faculty, people in their board rooms, business executives of the world, I can tell you that is true. Where people hear the most joyful news ever announced something within them says, "This is true. I want to know this great God." And it's not just simply a matter of intellectual approach. It's the Holy Spirit who does His mighty work. . . .

Paul writes . . . "If I gave everything I have to poor people and if I were burned alive for preaching the gospel but didn't love others, it would be of no value whatever." I cannot overemphasize God's priority for love. . . . Love is an act of the will. You and I don't wait for some great emotional moment. We are to love by faith as an act of the will. "Love is patient and kind, never jealous or envious or boastful or proud or haughty or selfish or rude. Love does not demand its own way. It is not irritable or touchy, it does not hold grudges but hardly even notices when others do it wrong."

In Revelation 2, . . . God commended the church at Ephesus for their faithfulness, their hard work; they wouldn't tolerate sin among their members but God said, "I have something against you. You have left (not lost) your first love unless you return, I'll remove your candlestick from this place among the churches." I have asked that one of my books *First Love* be given to each of the graduates today along with a laminated card on the attributes of God because: unless we really understand who God is—holy and righteous, sovereign, omnipotent, all wise, compassionate and faithful—unless

> **God places a very, very high premium on love. There is no truth in the Word of God that captivates me more. I came to Christ because of His love for me. I was living in spiritual ignorance. I didn't know any better.**

we understand who God is, we can't really love Him. You can't be in love with love. You can't trust God whom you don't know, and you can't obey God whom you don't really know. He's not a cosmic policeman, He's not a glorified Santa Claus, He is God. And every morning I bow in reverence before Him. He is my Lord, my Master, my Savior, my King.

My wife and I practiced this even before we were married. We would always pray together on our dates, not a bad idea. We began our days and ended our days wherever possible when we were together in prayer. We are slaves of Jesus and we acknowledge that gladly, joyfully. He is our example. Philippians 2:7 refers to God Himself, Jesus of Nazareth, as a slave. . . .

The greatest thing that ever happened to Vonette and me apart from salvation was the day we signed over the title deed and said "no" to self and "yes" to Christ.

There are three things: first love God with all your heart, soul, and mind. Be sure you understand who the God is you're loving . . . and then trust God. One college student came to me and said, "I want to become a believer, but I have great plans for my life and I'm afraid if I become a Christian, God will change my plans." And I said, "I hope so." He said, "What do you mean?" And I said, "Can you imagine this great Creator who flung a hundred billion or more galaxies into space, who holds it all together with a word of His command having an inferior plan for your life to yours? I'd be scared to death to go back under the old control of Bill Bright.

In Galatians 5 we're told, "The flesh wars against the spirit and the spirit against the flesh." That will go on as long as you live; if it's of any interest to you, at eighty, I still understand that. God knows who we are and who we were and the conflicts that wage in our hearts, but Paul writes to the church in Galatia, "I advise you to obey the Holy Spirit's instruction. Then you won't be doing what your sinful nature craves. The old sinful nature loves to do evil, which is just opposite from what the Holy Spirit wants. And the Spirit gives us desires that are opposite from what the sinful nature desires. These two forces are constantly fighting each other and your choices are never free from this conflict. But when you are directed by the Holy Spirit, you are no longer subject to the law."

> He's not a cosmic policeman, He's not a glorified Santa Claus, He is God. And every morning I bow in reverence before Him. He is my Lord, my Master, my Savior, my King.

Young men and women, parents, friends, faculty, the Christian life is an incredible adventure. Jesus said, "I am come that they may have life and have it abundantly." And I can speak of the reality of that abundant life but that abundant life comes from really loving Him and trusting Him and obeying Him. Jesus said in John 14, "The one who obeys me is the one who loves me and because he loves me, my Father will love him and I will love him too and I will reveal myself to him." I will reveal myself, I will make known myself.

Do you know the reality of Christ in your life? Is your Christianity intellectual or is it reality? He goes on to say, "I will only reveal myself to those who love me. The Father will love them too and we will come to them and live with them. Anyone who doesn't obey me, doesn't love me." Oh, dear friends, I want to tell you that by the enabling of God's Holy Spirit alone can we obey Him. In Psalm 21 we read, "When we obey God, every path He guides us on is fragrant with His lovingkindness and His truth." Friendship with God is reserved for those who revere Him, with them alone He shares the secrets of His promises. To love God, to trust God is the most reasonable, possible way to live. No wonder Paul would write to the church in Rome, "I beseech you therefore, brethren, by the mercies of God, that you present your bodies a living sacrifice, holy, acceptable unto God which is your reasonable service."

Can you imagine this great Creator who flung a hundred billion or more galaxies into space, who holds it all together with a word of His command having an inferior plan for your life . . .

There's nothing more reasonable than saying to Jesus Christ, "I surrender all." You've sung that song dozens of times in the various gatherings in the four years or more that you've been here, but I'm going to ask you in a moment to do something you may have never been asked to do. I'm going to ask you as graduates if you will, in the quiet of today or soon, go along and do business with God in a way perhaps that you have never done. . . . On your knees in the quiet and reverence of the moment, say to God, "I can't really love you with all my heart, soul, and mind." When I read that passage as a young Christian, it scared me to death. I could never do that. I don't have the ability to do that. And to trust God with my life? Impossible. And to obey His commands? I could never do that. And then God showed me there are two ways—I can love and I can trust and obey—and [the latter] is to say total absolute irrevocable death to self.

I've never known anyone to be used of God in any significant way who does not experience the reality of Galatians 2:20. "I am crucified with Christ; nevertheless, I live yet not I but Christ lives in me and the life which I now in the flesh I live with the faith of the Son of God who loved me and gave Himself for me." It is not enough to say "no" to self; it's not enough to make partial commitment. If you want to know life in all of its fullness, if you want to know the kind of adventure that . . . Vonette and I have known all these more than 50 years, love God, trust God, obey God, but that is possible only when you say death to self." Not a 75 percent death, not a 95 percent death, but a daily dying as Jesus says in Mark 8, "If any man come after me, let him deny himself, take up his cross daily, and follow me." Death to self.

This morning I was meditating on Romans 6 and 7 . . . I would encourage you . . . to go back and on your knees, read the first eight chapters of Romans. Dear ones, if you want to know the reality of what I speak this morning, there must first be death to the old person, and that's a matter of dying daily. Each morning when I awaken, when Vonette and I pray, I continue in prayer and in the Word. In so many words I pray this prayer, "Lord Jesus, I'm your slave." Now, I realize I'm a friend of God, I'm an heir of God, I'm a son of God, I'm a joint heir with Christ, I'm seated with Him in the heavens, but by choice like God Himself, I became a slave like Paul and Peter and the rest . . . chose to be slaves of Jesus whether they signed a contract or not. Nobody is going to ever be used of God who does not make that kind of commitment. Their first means needs to be daily dying, not in part but whole. . . .

I know that here among us are men and women who know it [intellectually]. Your family members are waiting to applaud you and to embrace you, but unless you truly understand the importance of dying daily and living in the power of the Holy Spirit, you'll never be God's maximum person. Death to self. So I pray, "Lord Jesus, walk around in my body today," for your body is a temple of God. We're not alone; we've been bought with a price, the precious blood of Jesus. I ask Him to walk around in my body, think with my mind, love with my heart, speak with my lips, be at home in me, do anything You want through me, and I know You came to seek and to save the lost. So my number one priority is to do what you gave the world to do—guide me in helping to seek and save the lost. And with the apostle Paul ,wherever I go, I try to remember as he said, "Christ in you the hope of glory." So, everywhere we go, we tell everyone who will listen about Christ. . . .

> **Do you know the reality of Christ in your life? Is your Christianity intellectual or is it reality?**

In your final session as a graduate of this university, I'm going to ask you, will you make a concerted effort whether you're called to be a businessperson, a missionary, a minister, whatever your calling, that you will indeed daily die to your old self and in the power of the Holy Spirit live for the glory of God? . . . When we exalt Jesus Christ to all men, life in all of its fullness becomes our heritage, our privilege. . . . At your graduation, the final word, say to Christ, "I'm going forth [in my career] but I am not going to that particular calling in the energy of the flesh—I go in the power of the Spirit, and I depend upon Him to take what I've learned all these years, translate it from my mind to my heart to my will so that I'll be a vibrant, dynamic witness to the rest of the [world]." . . .

Holy, holy Father in the name of your risen Son whom we adore, who is unique in all of history, is God, the visible expression of the invisible God, in Him dwells all the fullness of the Godhead body, we're complete in Him, I hold before you these dear graduates and families and faculty and say mighty Savior, King of the universe, do something unique in each life, beyond anything they've ever known. . . . For your glory and praise and for their blessings beyond words. Hallelujah. Amen.

> . . . but unless you truly understand the importance of dying daily and living in the power of the Holy Spirit, you'll never be God's maximum person.

LEARN TO LAUGH
Keep Your Perspective

A time to weep, And a time to laugh; A time to mourn,
And a time to dance.

ECCLESIASTES 3:4 NKJV

INSIGHTS *for* LIVING

Then our mouth was filled with laughter, and our tongue with singing. Then they said among the nations, 'The Lord has done great things for them.' The Lord has done great things for us, and we are glad.

PSALMS 126:2-3 NKJV

A GOOD SENSE OF HUMOR IS AN ESSENTIAL INGREDIENT OF
FAITH ITSELF.

—CHARLES HENDERSON

As I was downstairs putting the robe on, surrounded by this fine faculty and all of these people who are into academia, I felt a little like the man who entered the Kentucky Derby. He said, "I don't expect him to win but I hope that the association will do him some good."

—ERWIN LUTZER

LAUGHTER ADDS RICHNESS, TEXTURE, AND COLOR TO
OTHERWISE ORDINARY DAYS. IT IS A GIFT, A CHOICE, A
DISCIPLINE, AND AN ART.

—TIM HANSEL

I want what God wants; that's why I am so merry.

—FRANCIS OF ASSISI

GREEN IN MY MEMORY

Address delivered June 4, 1902, at Columbia, Mo. When the name of Samuel
L. Clemens was called the humorist stepped forward, put his hand to his hair
and apparently hesitated. There was a dead silence for a moment. Suddenly
the entire audience rose and stood in silence. Some one began to spell out
the word Missouri with an interval between the letters. All joined in. Then
the house again became silent. Mr. Clemens broke the spell.

MARK TWAIN
June 4, 1902
Missouri University

As you are all standing [he drawled in his characteristic voice], I guess, I suppose I had better stand too.

[Then came a laugh and loud cries for a speech. As the great humorist spoke of his recent visit to Hannibal, his old home, his voice trembled.]

You cannot know what a strain it was on my emotions. In fact, when I found myself shaking hands with persons I had not seen for fifty years and looking into wrinkled faces that were so young and joyous when I last saw them, I experienced emotions that I had never expected, and did not know were in me. I was profoundly moved and saddened to think that this was the last time, perhaps, that I would ever behold those kind old faces and dear old scenes of childhood.

[The humorist then changed to a lighter mood, and for a time the audience was in a continual roar of laughter. He was particularly amused at the eulogy on himself read by Gardiner Lathrop in conferring the degree.] He has a fine opportunity to distinguish himself [said Mr. Clemens] by telling the truth about me.

I have seen it stated in print that as a boy I had been guilty of stealing peaches, apples, and watermelons. I read a story to this effect very

> **. . . when I found myself shaking hands with persons I had not seen for fifty years and looking into wrinkled faces that were so young and joyous when I last saw them, I experienced emotions that I had never expected, and did not know were in me.**

closely not long ago, and I was convinced of one thing, which was that the man who wrote it was of the opinion that it was wrong to steal, and that I had not acted right in doing so. I wish now, however, to make an honest statement, which is that I do not believe, in all my checkered career, I stole a ton of peaches.

One night I stole—I mean I removed—a watermelon from a wagon while the owner was attending to another customer. I crawled off to a secluded spot, where I found that it was green. It was the greenest melon in the Mississippi Valley. Then I began to reflect. I began to be sorry. I wondered what George Washington would have done had he been in my place. I thought a long time, and then suddenly felt that strange feeling which comes to a man with a good resolution, and took up that watermelon and took it back to its owner. I handed him the watermelon and told him to reform. He took my lecture much to heart, and, when he gave me a good one in place of the green melon, I forgave him.

I told him that I would still be a customer of his, and that I cherished no ill-feeling because of the incident—that would remain green in my memory.

INSIGHTS *for* LIVING

Joy (in my sense) has indeed one characteristic, and one only, in common with them; the fact that anyone who has experienced it will want it again. . . . It is a kind we want. I doubt whether anyone who has tasted it would ever, if both were in his power, exchange it for all the pleasures in the world. But then joy is never in our power and pleasure often is.

—C.S. LEWIS

I HAVE ALWAYS BEEN DELIGHTED AT THE PROSPECT OF A NEW DAY, A FRESH TRY, ONE MORE START, WITH PERHAPS A BIT OF [BEAUTY] WAITING SOMEWHERE BEHIND THE MORNING.

—J.B. PRIESTLEY

Start living now. Stop saving the good china for that special occasion. . . . Every day you are alive is a special occasion. Every minute, every breath is a gift from God.

—MARY MANIN MORRISSEY

LAUGHTER AND WEEPING ARE THE TWO INTENSEST FORMS OF HUMAN EMOTION, AND THESE PROFOUND WELLS OF HUMAN EMOTION ARE TO BE CONSECRATED TO GOD.

—OSWALD CHAMBERS

A PLACE FOR MERMAIDS

Barbara Bush, First Lady from 1989-1993, married George Bush in 1945 when George was on leave from the Navy during World War II. The Bushes had six children, one of whom died from leukemia as a child. "Because of Robin, George and I love every living human more," Mrs. Bush says of the death of her child. A popular First Lady, Barbara Bush was particularly interested in promoting faith in God, spending time with family and friends, and the importance of literacy. "Find the joy in life," she says to the graduates. Learn to appreciate every moment you have with family and learn to laugh.

> Barbara Bush
> *Wellesley College*
> *June 1, 1990*

The essence of [your] spirit was captured in a moving speech about tolerance given last year by the student body president of one of your sister colleges. She related the story by Robert Fulghum about a young pastor who, finding himself in charge of some very energetic children, hits upon a game called "Giants, Wizards, and Dwarfs." "You have to decide now," the pastor instructed the children, "which you are ... a giant, a wizard or a dwarf?" At that, a small girl tugging at his pants leg, asked, "But where do the mermaids stand?"

The pastor told here there are no mermaids, and she says, "Oh yes, there are," she said. "I am a mermaid."

Now this little girl knew what she was, and she was not about to give up on either her identity or the game. She intended to take her place wherever mermaids fit into the scheme of things. Where do the mermaids stand. . . . All those who are different, those who do not fit the boxes and pigeonholes? "Answer that question," wrote Fulghum, "and you can build a school, a nation, or a whole world."

As that very wise young woman said . . . "Diversity . . . like anything worth having . . . requires effort." Effort to learn about and respect difference, to be compassionate with one another, to cherish our own identity . . . and to accept unconditionally the same in others.

You should all be very proud that this is the Wellesley spirit. Now I know your first choice today was Alice Walker, known for the *The Color Purple.* And guess how I know?

Instead you got me—known for—the color of my hair! Alice Walker's book has a special resonance here. At Wellesley, each class is known by a special color . . . for four years the Class of '90 has worn the color purple. Today you meet on Severance Green to say goodbye to all of that . . . to begin a new and very personal journey . . . to search for your own true colors.

In the world that awaits you beyond the shores of Lake Waban, no one can say what your true colors will be. But this I do know: You have a first class education from a first class school. And so you need not, probably cannot, live a "paint-by-numbers" life. Decisions are not irrevocable. Choices do come back. As you set off from Wellesley, I hope that many of you will consider making three very special choices

The first is to believe in something larger than yourself . . . To get involved in some of the big ideas of your time. I chose literacy because I honestly believe that if more people could read, write, and comprehend, we would be that much closer to solving so many of the problems plaguing our society.

Early on I made another choice which I hope you will make as well. Whether you are talking about education, career or service, you are talking about life . . . and life must have joy. It's supposed to be fun!

One of the reasons I made the most important decision of my life . . . to marry George Bush . . . is because he made me laugh. It's true, sometimes we've laughed through our tears . . . but that shared laughter has been one of our strongest bonds. Find the joy in life, because as Ferris Bueller said on his day off . . . "Life moves pretty fast. Ya don't stop and look around once in a while, ya gonna miss it!"

> **One of the reasons I made the most important decision of my life . . . to marry George Bush . . . is because he made me laugh. . . . that shared laughter has been one of our strongest bonds.**

I won't tell George that you applauded Ferris more than you applauded him!

The third choice that must not be missed is to cherish your human connections: your relationships with friends and family. For several years, you've had impressed upon you the importance to your career of dedication and hard work. This is true, but as important as your obligations as a doctor, lawyer, or business leader will be, you are a human being first and those human connections—with spouses, with children, with friends—are the most important investments you will ever make.

At the end of your life, you will never regret not having passed one more test, not winning one more verdict or not closing one more deal. You will

Who knows? Somewhere out in this audience may even be someone who will one day follow in my footsteps, and preside over the White House as the president's spouse. I wish him well!

regret time not spent with a husband, a friend, a child, or a parent.

We are in a transitional period right now . . . fascinating and exhilarating times . . . learning to adjust to the changes and the choices we . . . men and women . . . are facing.

As an example, I remember what a friend said, on hearing her husband complain to his buddies that he had to babysit. Quickly setting him straight . . . my friend told her husband that when it's your own kids . . . it's not called babysitting!

Maybe we should adjust faster, maybe slower. But whatever the era . . . whatever the times, one thing will never change: Fathers and mothers, if you have children . . . they must come first. You must read to your children, you must hug your children, you must love your children.

Your success as a family . . . our success as a society . . . depends not on what happens at the White House, but on what happens inside your house.

For over 50 years, it was said that the winner of Wellesley's annual hoop race would be the first to get married. Now they say the winner will be the first to become a C.E.O. Both of those stereotypes show too little tolerance for those who want to know where the mermaids stand. So I want to offer you today a new legend: The winner of the hoop race will be the first to realize her dream . . . not society's dream . . . her own personal dream. Who knows? Somewhere out in this audience may even be someone who will one day follow in my footsteps, and preside over the White House as the president's spouse. I wish him well!

. . . Thank you. God bless you. And may your future be worthy of your dreams.

INSIGHTS *for* LIVING

"The foolish man seeks happiness in the distance;
The wise grows it under his feet."

—James Oppenheim

Where your pleasure is, there is your treasure.
Where your treasure is, there is your heart.
Where your heart is, there is your happiness.

—Augustine of Hippo

Mirth is God's medicine.

—Henry Ward Beecher

Joy is the echo of God's life within us.

—Joseph Columba Marmion

Joy is sorrow inside out;

—Hannah Hurnard

This is the secret of joy. We shall no longer strive for our own
way, but commit ourselves, easily and simply, to God's way,
acquiesce in; his will, and in so doing find our peace.

—Evelyn Underhill

WHAT YOU LEARNED IN KINDERGARTEN

Founding Dean of the College of Business and Associate Provost of the University of Dallas, Dr. Robert Lynch shares some of Robert Fulghum's simple advice with the graduates—much of what they need to know they probably learned in kindergarten.

Dr. Robert G. Lynch
The University of Dallas
August 2, 2002

In most cases what you need to know about living your life you learned in kindergarten. I've discovered there's a lot of truth in what Robert Fulghum wrote in his book with that title. You say you don't remember kindergarten? Well let me take a moment to read a short paragraph from Fulghum's book, and then you're on your own: "Most of what I really need to know about how to live and what to do and how to be I learned in kindergarten. Wisdom was not at the top of the graduate school mountain. [That's what *he* said, anyway.] Wisdom was in the sand pile at Sunday School." Here are some of the things you should have learned:

- Share everything.
- Play fair.
- Don't hit people.
- Put things back where you found them.
- Clean up your own mess.
- Don't take things that aren't yours.
- Say you're sorry when you hurt somebody.
- Wash your hands before your eat.
- Flush.
- Warm cookies and cold milk are good for you.
- Take a nap every afternoon.
- And when you go out in the world, watch out for traffic, hold hands, and stick together.

LOOKING FOR TREASURE

*Dr. Scott Hafemann, professor at Wheaton College and Gerald F.
Hawthorne Chair of New Testament Greek and Exegesis, has authored
several books and speaks throughout the country. At this high school
commencement, Dr. Hafemann tells the graduates that this is a "pivotal
time" in their lives: they will ask important questions about the
importance of life and the ways to happiness. But only one treasure is
worth seeking, he says; and that treasure will bring inner joy and peace.*

Scott Hafemann
Masconomet High School
Topsfield, MA
May 27, 199

In four days you will graduate! I want to warn you tonight about what to
expect from your parents, grandparents, uncles and aunts, this coming
Friday when it happens. First, there will be the big question, "How does it
feel to be a graduate?" to which you answer, "great!" (Like the quarterback
who has just won the super bowl by throwing an unbelievable touchdown
pass in the closing seconds of the game, after which the sports announcer
inevitably asks, "Tell us, how does it feel to win the super bowl?") Did you
ever say to yourself, what a stupid question; or wish just once that the ath-
lete would say, I feel terrible, I wish the other quarterback had thrown the
pass, and they had won the game."

But in your case, I hope this question won't be a stupid question because
you will understand what is really going on. What those who love you really
want to know, but aren't sure how to ask it, is whether or not you sense what
a big day this really is. But as I said, most of us don't know how important
this time really is until much later in our lives, and so we miss the importance of the big question. At least I missed it. When my parents asked me in
their own way the big question, I simply said "great" and then hit the road
for the evening to celebrate with my friends.

What a tragedy that was. Graduation is the first of those pivotal times in
our lives when we look back at our past, turn consciously away from it, and
begin to stare our future straight in the face. It is a time in which many of us
begin to ask seriously, maybe for the very first time, the really big questions
like, What will I do with my life? Who will I be? What will my life be like?
What is worth living for? These are mature questions. These are the questions

that, when all is said and done, really make a difference and matter.

The answers to these questions, of course, are by no means clear for you now, and in fact you will work on answering them the rest of your life. But at graduation you begin to notice that school and being a kid are really over and that these questions are your questions too—and not just the questions that adults ask. Life is suddenly becoming more serious. The stakes are higher. Your decisions are becoming more and more important. And those who are older than you and love you know this—and so, not knowing any better way to ask it, they want to know how you feel.

So my purpose tonight, as you approach graduation this Friday, is to remind you of the advice that Jesus gives to those who are asking the big questions of life, as if he were asking you how it feels to graduate. Listen again to his advice:

Do not lay up for yourselves treasures on earth, where moth and rust consume and where thieves break in and steal, but lay up for yourselves treasures in heaven, where neither moth nor rust consumes and where thieves do not break in and steal. For where your treasure is, there will your heart be also (Matt. 6:19-21).

> **Graduation is the first of those pivotal times in our lives when we look back at our past, turn consciously away from it, and begin to stare our future straight in the face.**

First, notice that Jesus understands who we are and what makes us tick. His advice is about looking for treasure. He knows that we are all treasure hunters who are on a safari through life in search of what will make us happy. Everyone wants to be happy, really happy, and everyone tries to do those things which they think will make them happy. There are just two problems. The vast majority of people don't know what real happiness is, and so they don't know how to find it. They are on a treasure hunt in search of something they don't know and thus spend their lives driving right past it looking for something else. Believe me, I know. I am a baby boomer. I was born in 1954, right in the middle of the baby boomer generation. This year 69 percent of baby boomers said that if they could change their lives they would slow them down, because they are peddling so fast in search of happiness they feel like they have zoomed passed it. 61 percent said that they are so busy earning a living that they can't enjoy it.

And what is worse is that we have come up with a group of national experts whose sole purpose in life is to convince you that they know what will make you happy and solve your problems, so that they can sell it to you. These folks are called "advertisers" and their advice is called "advertisements." When I was graduating, the big advice was given to us by a beer company, who told us "to grab all the gusto we can, because we only go around once in life;" and of course, their beer would help us grab this gusto the best. That was 1972. Things haven't changed much. Last month on the radio I heard a car company tell me that their car had 100 ways to make me happy. And on and on it goes.

. . . 69 percent of baby boomers said that if they could change their lives they would slow them down, because they are peddling so fast in search of happiness they feel like they have zoomed passed it.

But then there is Jesus, the Son of God and Savior of the world. And His advice is straightforward and right to the point—He knows that life is no game. He knows that the stakes are high. He knows that the beer commercial was right, we do only go round once in life, and that, as the car company knows, we all do want 100 ways to make us happy. But He also knows, as the one who made us, after whose image we have been created, that the beer company and the car company are both wrong—nothing in this world can be a treasure valuable enough or a substance potent enough to satisfy the deepest longings of our hearts and make us happy, really and deeply, profoundly satisfied. Because none of the treasures of this world, no matter how shiny they are, no matter how much fame and fortune they might bring, no matter how good they might make us feel for the moment, last forever. They all rust and corrode or can be taken away by others, either directly, or indirectly through their accomplishments and possessions. Envy is never satisfied, and those who get their sense of worth and happiness by comparing themselves to others can never win; there will always be someone prettier, smarter, richer, more popular, more athletic, and more successful.

So Jesus is honest with us. Don't spend your lives trying to lay up treasures on earth in your search for happiness. You will be doomed for failure and disappointment. Resist the temptations and lies of this world, which tell you otherwise. You do not just go around once in life; and things, like cars, can never bring you happiness and peace.

Instead, Jesus said, "Lay up for yourselves treasures in heaven." Why? It's simple. As Jesus put it, when it comes to the treasures in heaven, neither moth nor rust consumes and thieves do not break in and steal. In other words, the treasures of heaven last forever and can never be taken from you. Therefore, they are the only things which can really satisfy a treasure hunter who, unlike Indiana Jones, is after the thing that really counts.

What is this treasure? As you know, the answers to this are many these days. But I would be less then honest with you if I did not tell you that I again think and am convinced that Jesus was right. The treasure of heaven is knowing the one and true sovereign creator and sustainer of the universe, God himself, as the only true source and meaning in life; and developing a relationship with him through his Son and our Lord and Messiah, Jesus himself, so that one lives his or her life according to his will and seeks to do His bidding in this world, even as God's will is done in heaven. This is the treasure of heaven, because this life is not all there is to live for, and heaven is nothing less than the dwelling place of God forever.

> **The treasure of heaven is knowing the one and true sovereign creator and sustainer of the universe, God himself, as the only true source and meaning in life; and developing a relationship with him through his Son and our Lord and Messiah, Jesus himself,**

Finally, then, why is Jesus so concerned about what treasure in life we set out to discover in the first place? For the same reason that graduation is so important. Jesus never graduated from high school— He got his education in the school room attached to the synagogue— but he knows the importance of days like graduation, when one turns from the past and begins to look to the future. Jesus knows that "where your treasure is, there will your heart be also." In other words, he knows that whatever it is that you decide is your treasure in this life, this career, that car, that vacation, this home, that college, this set of clothes, that music, these friends, that boyfriend or girlfriend, or knowing God in Christ and living for Him and what he thinks is valuable, whatever it is, it will capture your heart. And whatever captures your heart, will determine how you live. Our treasure, that is, whatever we think will make us happy, determines how we live. And Jesus cares about your life. After all, it was Jesus who said in John 6:47-48, "Truly, truly, I say to you, he who believes has eternal life. I am the bread of life."

Jesus is the treasure that really satisfies and in John 10:10-12, "The thief comes only to steal and kill and destroy; I came that they may have life, and have it abundantly. I am the good shepherd."

Jesus is the treasure that can lead and guide you in this life and into the life to come, because He is the one who lay down His life for us. And finally, in John 14:6, "I am the way, and the truth, and the life; no one comes to the Father, but by me," so that, as we read in John 17:3, "This is eternal life, that they know thee the only true God, and Jesus Christ whom thou hast sent."

The big question is coming this Friday: "How do you feel, now that you have graduated?" I hope your answer will be "great," not only because you are now done with school, but because as you look to the future, you know what treasures are worth pursuing in your life, because you know that only the treasures of heaven can make you truly happy in the way in which the God who created you has intended you to be happy, so that you won't settle for second best when you can have the joy that comes from knowing and experiencing the presence and love of God.

> . . . whatever captures your heart, will determine how you live.

LOVE UNTIL IT HURTS

When an eighteen-year-old girl entered a convent, her name was changed from Agnes Gonxha Bejaxhiu to Teresa. Later, this young woman experienced what she describes as a "call within a call": she was to minister to the poorest of the poor in India. Mother Teresa, founder of the Missionaries of Charity, served thousands of the hopelessly poor in India. She received the Nobel Peace Prize in 1979 and died the day of Princess Diana's funeral, September 5, 1997. She speaks to graduates of the joy and love that can be found in Jesus Christ. "Go out with the conviction that nothing and nobody will separate you from the love of God."

MOTHER TERESA
May 30, 1982
Georgetown University

I am most unworthy of this great honor and the joy of sharing with you this great day. But I accept it for the glory of God and also in the name and for the glory of our poor people throughout the world—our brothers and sisters.

It is wonderful to think on a feast day like this—and the feast of the Holy Spirit, the spirit of love—that you young people have been sent . . . like Jesus came on earth to proclaim the good news that God is love. That God loves us. That we are somebody special to Him. That He knows us by our name. That He has us in His hand. That He loves us tenderly. And on a day like this, now you, too—you, filled with your gift that you have received from this university—you are also being sent to proclaim the good news.

> **What you have received is not for you only. For the less you have, the more you can give; and the more you have, the less you can give.**

What you have received is not for you only. For the less you have, the more you can give; and the more you have, the less you can give. But I am sure you'll go out to proclaim that God loves—by your presence, by your actions, by the life you live, by the joy you share, by the peace you bring. So that people who come in touch with you; they feel the joy of sharing, the joy of loving Jesus in your hearts with all you meet.

You have received much, but especially you have learned to pray. Pray. For the fruit of prayer is always deepening of faith. And the fruit of faith is always love. And the fruit of love is service. Jesus proved that love. When we look at the cross, when we look at the Eucharist, we know how He loved us. And this is what He kept on saying—love as I have loved you. And who to love—whom to love?

Love begins at home—right here. And we must love until it hurts. To be able to love, we must pray; for the fruit of prayer is a clean heart. Prayer always gives a clean heart. And how do we begin to pray? God speaks in the silence of the heart. Listening is the beginning of prayer. And then we speak from the fullness of our heart, and then God listens, and that listening and that speaking is prayer. And this prayer gives us a clean heart. And [one with] a clean heart can see God. And if we see God in each other, we will love one another.

> **You are being sent to proclaim that good news of love, of peace, of joy. And we have never needed this proclamation more than today—the whole world.**

And this is what Jesus came to teach us. Whatever you do to each other, do it to Me. And to make us understand, He says that in the hour of debt we are going to be judged on what we have been to the poor, to the hungry, to the naked, to the homeless, to the lonely, to the unwanted, to the unloved, to the rejected, to the lepers, to the dying. Whatever, you did it to Me. And because you did it to Me, come, come, the blessed of my Father.

It's a beautiful day for you to be sent out. You are being sent to proclaim that good news of love, of peace, of joy. And we have never needed this proclamation more than today—the whole world. And yet the young ones are hungry for God. I'm sure deep down in your hearts you have that hunger for God. You want to give Him to others as He has given Himself to you. Do not be afraid; He loves you. You are precious to Him. . . . I called you by your name. You are mine. Water cannot drown you. Fire will not burn you. I will give up nations for you. You are precious to me. I love you. This is the talk God speaks. And even, even if a mother could forget her child, something impossible, I will not forget you. I love you. I have you in the palm of my hand—wonderful thing.

Just think, each time God looks at His hand, you are there. . . . Suffering, pain, trouble, humiliation, failure, success, joy, sorrow—these are part of our lives. That's why Jesus told us if you really want to follow me, take joy. Take up the cross.

Today when you leave this university, this beautiful place where you have received so much love, so much care, so much tenderness, so much friendship from your teachers, remember, because you are precious to him. You are somebody. And that's why it is wonderful that you keep your heart clean. You will be in love with a young girl . . . or a young girl will be in love

Just think, each time God looks at His hand, you are there . . .

with a young man. This is beautiful. This is God's gift to you. But love each other with a clean heart. And make sure that . . . you [remind] yourself as we have [heard] in the Gospel. You will cleave to each other and become one. Remember that day you give your-selves to each other a virgin heart, a virgin heart that is full of love so that you can make your heart and her heart . . . one in the heart of God.

And this is . . . my prayer for you. That you go out with that conviction. I belong to Him. I will proclaim His love—His presence. Become a carrier of God's love—a carrier of the joy of loving and sharing that joy with others—especially with your family, because you know that a family that prays together stays together. And if you stay together, you will love one another as God loves each one of you. This is my prayer for you.

And another thing, make sure that you come to know the poor in the place where you are. They are the greatest gift of God to each one of us. They are the most lovable people, great people. Right here we have our sisters in Washington. We have them in ten, eight places here in the United States and all over the world. And you would be surprised. They are not hungry for bread. But they are hungry for love—lonely, unwanted, frightened. Do we know them? They are not naked for a piece of cloth like . . . people in Africa and India. But they are naked for human dignity, the respect which we have taken away from them. They are not homeless for a house made of brick. They are carriers of God's tenderness. Go out with the conviction that nothing and nobody will separate you from the love of God. . . . you will be His love and His compassion where you go—especially amongst the poor. Look for them. Maybe [give them] only a little smile. But that smile is the beginning of love. Maybe just a little concern . . . but that is the beginning of love. So let us thank God for his great love.

INSIGHTS *for* LIVING

BEYOND A WHOLESOME DISCIPLINE, BE GENTLE WITH YOURSELF. HOLD
ON TO WHAT IT WAS THAT BROUGHT YOU HERE, AND ALL THAT YOU HAVE
ADDED TO IT. LAUGH AS OFTEN AND CRY AS LITTLE AS POSSIBLE. AND
KNOW, ALWAYS, THAT WE CARE ABOUT YOU.

—JUANITA KREPS

COMMENCEMENT PRAYER
JILL BRISCOE
WHEATON COLLEGE
MAY 2003

Oh God,
As I commence to commence, I ask three things—
Firstly, that my knowledge of Thee far exceed
my knowledge of all other things!
Make me a walking statement of Thy Word,
that those that won't read, must read, and reading, learn
the old, old story—purely told till I am old,
and come to Heaven to read Thee there
without a book or page between us then but face to face.
Oh, joy! And then, I ask my service for thee far exceed
my service of all other things through the life
You have planned for me, that only can spell full fulfillment.
Amen

Jill Briscoe

ONE OF THOSE COME-BACK DAYS

Bob Hope, comedian, actor, and entertainer for thousands of soldiers, gave this speech in 1962 upon receiving an honorary degree as "a man of upright life, of great wit and great heart." It was a momentous occasion for Mr. Hope, particularly as his son also received a degree with honors from the same university.

BOB HOPE
June 4, 1962
Georgetown University

This is just wonderful, ladies and gentlemen. I don't have to tell you; you can tell by just looking at me up here. You've never seen this kind of an expression on my face, I'm sure. I'm just thrilled about this, and I can't wait until I get home and have my son read it to me.

I just recognized one little word in the Latin, something about "negligence." It sounded like that, anyway. I guess it has to do with my education.

But I'm just thrilled about this; and especially, getting a degree here at Georgetown University is the end for me. But then, you do specialize in miracles, don't you?

I haven't been so thrilled about anything since the government let me declare Bing [Crosby] as a dependent. Last year I received the Humanitarian Award from the Academy of Motion Picture Arts and Sciences and this year, I get this Doctor of Humane Letters. If I can remain a human for about a year more, I get to keep them, I guess.

But there's a dangerous side to these honorary doctorates. The last time I was sick, I took two aspirins and called myself in the morning. . . . But I don't want you to think that I'm making light of this honor. As I stand before you here in this shrine of knowledge before you educators and educated, I'm in awe. I feel as out of place as President Kennedy at a meeting of the American Medical Association.

I'm very proud of my son Tony. He has done more with his twenty-two years than I've done with my forty-nine; and I've had my forty-nine years longer than anybody. You know, Tony has learned a lot here. He can write home for money in five languages. The other day he wrote me a letter in Latin, and I took it to my drug store and had it filled.

I'm thrilled to be here for this great occasion. I know it's a very important day in your life and very important to the nation, too. After today, you can all go to work and help support your government. You are the future of our nation, you graduates; our future senators, congressmen, presidents. Of course, a few of you may be Republicans, but I suppose there's a place for you.

I know you're going to do great. And remember: "Ask not what your country can do for you, but what you can do for country." That's a line I picked up from Billie Sol Estes.

I've only been here a couple of times to Georgetown, and I'm surprised to find this campus so close to the nation's capitol. Judging from the Cabinet, I thought Harvard was the nearest school.

I may give it back, but I'd like to offer a couple of words of advice to you young people about to go out into the world: Don't go.

I was out there last week, took one look at the stock market, and came right back in. Steel went down so low President Kennedy bought some. AT&T went way down. I didn't realize how bad things were until I put a dime in the phone this morning, and a voice said, "God bless you."

I wish my mother could be here at this ceremony. She was a realist and a wise one. I remember her saying, "Leslie,"—that's British for Robert—she said, "It's not so important that you go to college. What's important is that you get an education." She felt that a person does not become educated because he is taught but because he is given a desire to learn.

> . . . a person does not become educated because he is taught but because he is given a desire to learn.

And then she hit me with another bit of old-fashioned wisdom: that every young man receives two educations—the first from his teachers; the second, more personal and important, from himself. But Mom was only a mother. I didn't pay too much attention.

A good many years later, a couple of wars later, thousands of moments later of seeing how much a few laughs can do for men on the thin edge of dying for their country, I discovered what she meant by "more personal and important." I discovered that the most gratifying kind of education is that which makes a man happy in the knowledge that he's a little bit useful to others.

For the last twenty years, I've been running around this earth entertaining fellows your age in jungles, stuck away on sand bars in the oceans, cooped up in nature's ice boxes, and I've learned that if you give a little of yourself to others that it will come back in carloads.

Today is one of those come-back days. This is one of the greatest memories of my life.

Thank you, good luck, and God bless you.

HONOR

Gary Smalley, one of the country's best-known authors and speakers on family relationships, is the author or coauthor of sixteen books including Love is a Decision *and* If Only He Knew, *as well as several popular films and videos. Dr. Smalley challenges the graduates to apply honor to their lives in every possible relationship they will encounter. "Watch it be a lighthouse to you that keeps your relationships strong," he says.*

Dr. Gary Smalley
Biola University
December 1999

This is a very exciting night that you are sensing and it's going to go really fast in the future. I know you're thinking I'm at the age I am, I've graduated in whatever field you've graduated in, and you're thinking oh, it's going to be a long time. It does seem like yesterday for me that I was where you are. These years pass really, really fast. You can tell that I'm getting on in age—the color of my hair, in fact, the lack of hair is another sign that I'm getting on in years. There are a few signs that you become aware of when you're aging.

A few months ago, I asked my barber, "I said, 'Just between you and me, . . . am I going to keep losing my hair at my age?' . . .

He leaned over real close to me and said, 'Naw, not at your age, you're not going to lose any more hair.'

I said, 'Really? How do you know that?'

He said, 'Well, at your age you don't lose any more hair, it's just reapplied in other areas: it comes out of your nose, your ears, your back.' . . .

You can tell you're getting older when you bend over to tie your shoes, and you look for other things to do while you're down there. You know you're getting old when they light all the candles on your birthday cake and a group of Scouts gather around and start singing "Kum Ba Ya" or your wife gives you that look and says, "Sweetheart, do you want to go upstairs and cuddle?" And you realize you can only do *one* of those. That's part of the fun of growing old—finding out these little things.

In these thirty some years that I've been in ministry and in the marriage and family area, . . . if I had just had one thing to say to you tonight, and one thing that would encourage you in the future, I don't care what vocation you're in, I don't care whether you remain single, get married, have a family, become president of your company, whatever you do in the future, from my perspective, from my understanding, from what life in the Lord has taught me, I still believe to this day that the greatest principle of life . . . has one unifying thread: . . . the concept that I call honor.

When we read Romans 12:10, it says, "Be devoted to one another in love, preferring one another in honor." Honor has saved my neck over the years as a husband and a father and as president of my company. Honor has been the very life-giving principle that has permeated everything we have done as a family and in our organization. I can assure you from my perspective that if you understand honor and apply it to your life, [you will] watch the success you experience in all of your relationships and in what you do in business.

The word honor to me means attaching high value to someone, and it's really beautifully defined in Philippians 2: "It's when you consider others as more valuable than you consider yourself." So for us, for me, for my family, for the people I work with, for my ministry, we've been urging people to place more value on the Lord than anything else. Let Him live his life through us, Galatians 2:20. And then secondly, consider others as more valuable than you consider yourself. . . . Don't forget to highly value yourself but [consider] the *others* as more valuable than yourself.

> **I still believe to this day that the greatest principle of life . . . has one unifying thread . . . : the concept that I call honor.**

This was like a compass . . . it kept us as a family in line, and I've been married for thirty-five years. It's like a beacon, like a lighthouse in a storm—I could always see the light and get back to harmony with my loved ones because of the concept of honor. . . .

I want to share three ways to build honor into your life every day. Watch it be a lighthouse to you, a beacon, the compass that keeps your relationships strong.

Number one: . . . make a decision to highly value your loved ones, your friends, your fellow employees, your fellow students, fellow teachers. . . . You make a decision. You do Romans 12:10: "Be devoted to one another in brotherly love preferring one another in honor." That's all you do. You make a decision. You raise their value—just a hair higher than your own. It *so changes* your motivation. Jesus said, "Whatever a man treasures, that's where his affections are," his heart will be there. What you value tonight is where your motivation is, your treasure. That will go with you the rest of your life. It is the *key*. . . .

What if your mate or future mate or children or friends were autographed by God? What would that do to their value? . . . Make sure you're just a little lower than they are. . . . Clap for them. Whistle for them. Have rose petals and a red runner for them . . . .

Part of what you're doing here tonight is expressing your honor towards each graduate. The honor you're giving towards the teachers and professors—this is the spirit of tonight. . . . Your enthusiasm says we're proud of you, we honor you . . . Is that not true? That's what honor is. . . .

> **People are going to be a little surprised when you start telling them how much you appreciate them, how much you honor them.**

The second is for you to make a list of all the things that you admire, appreciate, love and adore [about your loved one]. . . . I have four and a half single spaced pages of all the things that I appreciate about my wife. Anytime I ever get discouraged about our relationship or I'm down a little bit, I can print out that thing in seconds from my computer, and I start reading that list, I get choked up halfway through and realize *aahh*, am I married to an unbelievable person or what. My memories come back of all the things we've done over the years that's a part of our lives. Record that stuff. It's so important. My wife and I are just the opposite. . . . My wife is a detailed person who loves lists and rules. . . . My personality is more relaxed. . . . It's not real detailed. . . . We're so different but guess what? We value each other's differences. . . .

The third thing you do is you tell people the things you're listing. . . . Tell them. Express it. It's like the businessman, a real serious guy, who bought flowers and a gift on his way home as he went through his list of things to tell his wife, things he loves and appreciates about her. He knocked on the door, which he'd never done before, she comes to the door, he puts the gift and the flowers out in front of him, and he says, "Hi, honey, I just wanted you to know how much I love you and how much I appreciate you." She broke down and started sobbing. . . . He said, "What's wrong with you?" She said, "Everything's gone wrong today, the baby's been grouchy and messy all day, the dishwasher clogged up and flowed all over the carpet, and now *you* come home drunk."

People are going to be a little surprised when you start telling them how much you appreciate them, how much you honor them. That's okay, you work through that, and eventually they'll get used to it.

Here's what I want to conclude with. I want to say it again: Romans 12:10.

I don't know what you're going to do in the future. I don't know of any exception when you have a healthy marriage, a healthy family, a healthy friendship, a healthy company that's successful, I don't know of any exception . . . that [they] do not have honor at the center of their relationships and their organizations. So, you want to be successful at all you do? Start with the skill of honor. Make the decision, make the list, and tell them about it. Thank you very much.

> . . . you want to be successful at all you do? Start with the skill of honor.

ACCEPTING THE BATON
Find Purpose in Your Past

Then the LORD answered me and said:
"Write the vision And make it plain on tablets,
That he may run who reads it.

HABBAKUK 2:2 NKJV

INSIGHTS *for* LIVING

You today are smarter than we were. You are better educated and better informed than we were twenty-five years ago. And that is part of your heritage. You enjoy these added benefits because more than 100 years ago near this very spot, a man plunged an ax into a tree and said, 'Here we will build a school for our children.

—Ronald Reagan

The great value of formal education is that it is designed to foreshorten human experience. It endeavors with ease and economy to bring each succeeding generation up to date with respect to the past, and to make it at home in the world. In this sense, it prepares each generation for life.

—Virgil M. Hancher

Be careful to leave your sons well instructed rather than rich, for the hopes of the instructed are better than the wealth of the ignorant.

—Epictetus

Colors fade, temples crumble, empires fall, but wise words endure.

—Edward L. Thorndike

When we honestly ask ourselves which persons in our lives mean the most to us, we often find that it is those who, instead of giving advice, solutions, or cures, have chosen rather to share our pain and touch our wound with a warm and tender hand. The friend who can be silent with us in a moment of despair or confusion, who can stay with us in an hour of grief and bereavement, who can tolerate not knowing, not curing, not healing, and face with us the reality of our powerlessness, that is a friend who cares.

—Henri Nouwen

LIVE IN THE DASH!

Dr. Crawford Loritts, Associate Director of U.S. Ministries for Campus Crusade for Christ, co-founder of Oakcliff Bible Fellowship, and author of Lessons from a Life Coach: You Are Created to Make a Difference, *warns graduates of four barriers that face the Christian marketplace today. But don't sit around, he says. Serve God with excellence and diligence for "God does not deserve leftovers."*

CRAWFORD W. LORITTS, JR.
Moody Bible Institute
1993

It's a joy to be here with you. I have no delusions about my purpose here. You all are not here to listen to some speaker drone on; you're here to see your child graduate, so I'm going to say what I have to say and get on out of the way. . . . I understand how these things work—I sat on that side, too. . . .

Graduation represents both a celebration and a commissioning time. As I have reflected upon what I should share, my heart has been exercised and deeply moved and burdened by the context in which Christianity finds itself in our culture. I'm deeply disturbed by certain trends that are developing in our environment. At this point in your lives, you're about ready to embark upon some meaningful activity in ministry; . . . the focus of your life will be the arena out there in the context of society. As the twentieth century draws to a close, however, and as you leave Moody Bible Institute, the critical question is what is the environment, what is the atmosphere that you're stepping into? What is it that's out there that you will be immersed in? . . . I'm concerned that as we leave institutions, and as we seek to develop significant ministry out there in the marketplace; that we must identify the trends or the barriers that are prominent in our culture and society today.

I would like to suggest to you that there are four dominant barriers that face all of evangelicalism in the Western world right now at the end of the twentieth century. Four things which we must be painfully aware of as we seek to represent Jesus Christ out in the marketplace, that represents the atmosphere.

One is that you will be stepping into the evangelical industry phase of Christianity. Let me explain what I mean by that. Not too long ago, about thirty years or so ago, many of the organizations that you see dominating evangelical institutions were just dreams. They were just getting by. There were great men and women of God who were pioneers, who did not have mailing lists and did not have consultants, and did not have layers of management, did not have positioning in the "Christian" marketplace. All they had was a dream and a vision and a passion, and they believed God to translate into reality what God had placed on their hearts.

I'm a part of the world's largest Christian organization of its kind, Campus Crusade for Christ, and I've heard Dr. Bright say on more than one occasion with tears in his eyes that he is terribly concerned, terribly concerned about the next generation of leadership who do not know what it really means to trust God, to translate something into reality that did not exist. You will have the dastardly tendency and temptation, instead of relying upon God and going to new ventures in the Christian life, to trust in your mailing list, to trust in your ability to raise funds, to trust in the trinkets and the toys and the processes of ministry rather than to trust in the power of God to lead the cause of Christ to new areas and new directions. We're stepping into the industry phase of evangelicalism.

There's another barrier—I hate to even mention this—however, we are stepping into still an old problem, our old nemesis in our society, and that is racism. Statistically speaking, by the year 2010 for the first time in history, the white society in this country will be a minority. . . . That's the good news. But the tragic news is this—evangelicalism is still lagging far behind in modeling what it really means to be the body of Christ. Somehow or another, we're not leading the culture in prophetic witness and prophetic reconciliation, and you're stepping into a world that is painfully aware of that big wart on the body of Christ.

Another barrier that will face you as you leave, that permeates the atmosphere is the dismantling of the family. All around us the structures of our home, that grand incubator of values and direction in our culture and society, is unraveling. The problem is that statistically, and it is a tragedy— a tragedy—that Christian families are no different, statistically, than nonbelievers. The divorce rate is the same among believers as it is out there in the marketplace. Our homes are unraveling; we no longer have the grand pillars in our community that protect us and give us a sense of direction, a sense of hope. . . . We have to face the reality that the family structure as we knew it ten, fifteen, twenty years ago no longer exists.

The fourth barrier that permeates our atmosphere has to do with a general erosion of values. Be very careful of how many of our political leaders . . . popularize the term "family values." That's a warm, fuzzy statement but their definition is not the same as ours. There's been the prostitution of authority, there has been the negation of a sense of accountability and responsibility throughout the culture. I'm forty-three years old, and I'm of that last generation in which what my mother and father taught me at home was affirmed in church and endorsed at school. . . . Today. . . the level of our values are being eroded with every generation. . . .

Well, what do we do? What do we do? I remember reading some time ago the story of Sir Winston Churchill and his famous bunker on the Piccadilly Square. At the end of the war, the reporters couldn't wait to ask him, "Sir Winston, what in the world did you have in that bunker while Great Britain, particularly London, was being bombed during World War II? What was in that bunker, it's a great mystery?"

He kind of smiled and said, "Really, it's quite plain. I had some communication, a simple desk there, and I had a map of the continent."

Then of course the follow-up question was, "What were you doing during England's darkest hour?" Listen to this. Listen to this. Hear me. He said, "I was planning the invasion of Germany." I was planning the invasion of Germany.

What ought our attitude to be in the context of a crumbling culture and society? First Corinthians 15:58: . . . the apostle Paul had in the back of his mind to offer hope to the church at Corinth, for they, too, were living in a hostile society. They were freaks, they were the outcasts, . . . there was no evangelical subculture. . . . He says in verse 58, . . . "Therefore, my beloved brethren, be steadfast, immovable, always abounding in the work of the Lord, knowing that your toil is not in vain in the Lord." . . . .

Paul is saying "Take advantage of your moment, DO SOMETHING! GET ON WITH IT! Don't sit around here discussing things—so what! Be intentional"—"therefore, my beloved brethren, be steadfast, immovable, always abounding in the work of the Lord." Three observations. . . .

> **Take advantage of your moment**
>
> **DO SOMETHING!**
>
> **GET ON WITH IT!**

Number one, serve the Lord with diligence. . . . The Greek word . . . implies focus, courageous action. Stick to the stuff. You know what it's all about. Don't be deterred by the whims and the hassles of society, the different directions, the ambivalence of the culture. Be steadfast, keep moving in the midst of adversity. Serve the Lord with diligence.

Secondly, he says serve Him with perseverance, . . . It is the idea of rock solid steadiness while under attack. . . . Don't allow the situations in society to cause you to give up. . . . Last summer . . . my son pitched his best game— and it wasn't pretty. . . . This one guy took him deep, it was a dogfight. We had no more pitchers, and Bryndan had to finish the game. . . . It was a dramatic situation. We were leading 6-5. The guy who had taken him deep was up at bat. Bryndan was nervous, he had fought him to a full count, 3 and 2 and . . . he looked around . . . he looked for me and he caught my eye; and I said, "Son, from the heart, boy." He bore down. Threw him this beautiful change-up. Strike three! Take a seat. . . . God says to you, when you get out there and there's too much month at the end of the money, there are things you will face that they could never teach you in a classroom. The avalanche of problems . . . the ambivalence and the pressure comes, Jesus stands at the right hand of the God the Father and says, "From the heart."

> You do the very best you can with what you have, and do it in an excellent way. God does not deserve leftovers. He wants us to excel and he wants us to accel—get on with it, do it, do it.

Serve him with diligence, serve Him with perseverance, but finally serve Him with excellence. . . . "Always abounding." . . . [This word] not only means to "excel" but to "accel" in the work of God. . . . There are too many lazy people in Christian work . . . You do the very best you can with what you have and do it in an *excellent* way. God does not deserve leftovers. He wants us to ex-cel and he wants us to accel—get on with it, do it, do it.

I am who I am by the grace of God and because of the love of two men in my life: my dad and an uncle. . . . I was asked to speak at [my uncle's] funeral. . . . and I said, "In these few short minutes, we're going to take his remains and put them in the hearse outside of the church. . . . They will cover his body and in a couple of days, they will put a grave marker there. And on that grave marker will be the date of Henry's birth, there'll be a dash, and then there will be the date of his death. [My uncle] couldn't do anything about the day he was born, neither technically could he do anything about the day he died. But five years ago, my uncle gave his heart and life to Jesus Christ, and he did something about the dash."

Graduates, I want to tell you—live in the dash. *Live in that dash.* You're going to have to translate content to transformation. You're going to have to take truth and infuse it in a godless marketplace. This is not a place for the weak-hearted and the faint. You have to fall on your face before God and ask Him to help you redeem every moment of your life for the glory and honor of our great God and Savior of our Lord Jesus. Congratulations and God bless you.

THIS IS US

Brian Brenberg
University of St. Thomas
Student Speaker
May 18, 2002

B ut our journey does not end here. In fact, these last four years have shed only the first rays of light on the individual paths we will take over the course of our lives. . . .

This is not the book or movie of an old and great generation. We cannot skip to the ending nor turn down the volume. This is us, literally, standing at the foot of a mountain, brought here by a determined effort over the past several years. As we say our farewells and pose for the camera this event will become just one moment frozen in time, as it was for the marines atop Suribachi [in World War II]. They went on to fulfill their duty, and so will we, because in our hands we hold their flag: the flag of our fathers, our mothers, our grandparents and all who came before them. Its fabric the sacrifice of past generations, the hope of future generations. We cling to it now, raise it before us and brace for the climb. It is our reality. It is our duty. Thank you and God bless.

INSIGHTS *for* LIVING

Your parents have given you wings. . . . If you keep exercising them, you're going to do a great thing for your country, and a great thing for yourself. . . . We've got to have rootedness. You can be out trying your wings all day long, but at some point during the day, you've got to coalesce and sink your roots with the group that you live with. . . . Try to give your spouses, your family, your children the same things your family gave you. Try to give them wings. . . .

—PATRICIA SCHROEDER

TREASURE EACH OTHER IN THE RECOGNITION THAT WE DO NOT KNOW HOW LONG WE SHALL HAVE EACH OTHER.

—JOSHUA LOTH LIEBMAN

As we live our lives, we have many accomplishments— some are better remembered by your parents than by you. Do you remember when you first walked? How about the time you first went to school? Got your first bike? Got your first report card? And learned how to drive? How about when you made your first real friend or fell in love?

—CAPTAIN ANDREW GERFIN

HE WHO GOVERNED THE WORLD BEFORE I WAS BORN SHALL TAKE CARE OF IT LIKEWISE WHEN I AM DEAD. MY PART IS TO IMPROVE THE PRESENT MOMENT.

—JOHN WESLEY

PAY DOWN THE DEBT

J.C. Watts, the first African American Republican elected to the House leadership, served as an Oklahoma Representative, the Chairman of the House Republican Conference, and as a member of the House Armed Services Committee before he retired in 2002. "J.C. will leave behind a legacy of compassion and commitment to public service," President George W. Bush said. In Watts' speech, he dares the graduates to dream as he did, to thank their parents, and to serve their community.

J.C. WATTS
June 9, 2000
Ohio State University

This is a great day to be a graduate. This is a great day to be an American. And Lord help me for saying it: This is a great day to be a Buckeye.

As we all know, every commencement is a time of new beginnings—but this year, that is especially true. Imagine: to be new graduates not only in a new century, but a new millennium. . . . And to celebrate this day not just anywhere, but in America—the land where dreams still come true.

As parents, we read our children stories with fairy-tale endings. Well, this story—the story of these graduates here today—is a fairy-tale beginning.

Ladies and gentlemen, I truly believe that. I believe that because I am a child of the American Dream. I learned long ago never to be surprised by what life has in store. Never in a million years did I dream that the fifth of six children born to Helen and Buddy Watts—in a poor black neighborhood, in the rural community of Eufaula, Oklahoma—would someday be called Congressman.

And never in all the years I spent in school did I dream I'd stand one day at a ceremony like this, not to receive a diploma—but to deliver the commencement address.

And never in twenty-three years—not since that Saturday back in 1977 when my Sooner teammates took a one point win away from the

> **. . . the story of these graduates here today is a fairy-tale beginning. Ladies and gentlemen, I truly believe that. I believe that because I am a child of the American Dream.**

immortal Woody Hayes and his Buckeyes—never did I dream I'd be in a situation facing twenty-five thousand Buckeye fans—all by myself.

Now, it seems to me that the typical commencement speech is usually full of advice that's about as disposable as the disposable cameras some of you graduates are carrying today. So let me start with what you won't hear: you won't hear me tell you that I learned everything I needed to know in kindergarten, since I'm still learning each day to live the life marked out for me. And no—I'm not here to remind you always to wear your sunscreen . . . or to give you my "best and final answer" to the million-dollar question of life.

I think we can all see that a self-help society generates a lot of self-help silliness. It all reminds me of the fellow who went into a bookstore and asked the clerk at the information desk, "Where will I find the self-help section?"

And the clerk said, "Well, if I told you, that would defeat the whole purpose, wouldn't it?"

I am here today not simply to celebrate your accomplishment and stroke your egos—but to challenge you. To remind you on this day when you stand in the center spotlight—of all the other people who helped make this moment possible.

And that's a little bit unwelcome—I know that. Particularly on our graduation day, we all like to bask in the glow—we all like to think we are the secret to our own success. I know when I look back on my own graduation day, standing with my friends, getting ready to go forth and to go pro—I know I was pretty pleased with myself, pretty impressed with my accomplishments. I saw myself as a regular self-made man.

And I was—as long as you didn't count my mother and father. or my wife, Frankie . . . or my Grandma Mithe . . . or Coaches Bell or Anderson or Switzer . . . or Max Silverman . . . or Mrs. O'Reilly, my fourth grade teacher who called me out when I was headed wrong and steered me back to the straight and narrow. The truth is, it took more people to make the "self-made me" than you can count.

> **The truth is, it took more people to make the "self-made me" than you can count.**

Well, you see where I'm going: I was no more a self-made man that any man or woman whom God ever set on this earth. None of us are self-made—and all of us owe a debt. And that brings me to my message today.

Now, debt is a four-letter word I am sorry to have to inflict on your ears, whether you're a parent who's still basking in the well-deserved glow of writing that last tuition check—or a graduate with a diversified portfolio of student loans. Today I've got a different kind of debt in mind—and I don't care if the OSU Registrar has stamped your diploma "paid in full:" You may not owe a dollar—but you still owe a debt.

You owe a debt to your parents who gave you life, who gave you love—

who believed in you every step of the way, from the first, faltering baby step, to the step you take today across this stage—and into the next stage of your life.

You owe a debt to your extended family—your brothers and sisters, your aunts and uncles, your grandmoms and granddads for making you a life member in what philosopher Edmund Burke called life's "little platoon"—the community we call family.

And we're not done tallying up because you owe a debt to your friends and fellow students, to your professors and the administrators here who welcomed you into this community of learning. Take it from me: you have no idea today how much the life of your mind—the forward arc of your intellect—will owe to the foundation you have built here: to the ever-expanding universe of learning of which this university is a part.

Now, if you're thinking—that's a lot of debt to be carrying at such a young age. Don't worry: you've got a lifetime to pay it off.

What do you do with the kind of debt I'm talking about? You do what every debtor does: you pay it back—with interest.

So think of that diploma you receive today as a promissory note. And the minute this ceremony is over—the very first second of the rest of your life—find the people who made your education and your graduation possible and start paying down the debt.

Tell them—thank you. Thank you for making this day possible. Tell them the truth: that you couldn't have done it without them.

You owe a debt to your parents who gave you life, who gave you love—who believed in you every step of the way, from the first, faltering baby step, to the step you take today across this stage—and into the next stage of your life.

Now, if you think that's all there is to paying off your debt—I've got news for you. It's not that easy.

There's a saying I've heard—most people offer it as a lesson for living—that life is divided into three phases: you learn, then you earn, then you serve. By that yardstick, as graduates today, you've done your learning, and now it's time to do some earning—to build the career that allows you to give back later. And what better time to indulge your dot-com dreams or your entrepreneurial urges. For young people with skills, it's a seller's market out there—you can go as far and as fast as your dreams and your drive take you.

There's only one problem. It's hard to know when you're done earning and it's time to serve. . . .

Not too long ago, I read a book titled *The New New Thing.* . . . It tells the story of a man named Jim Clark who was the founding genius of Netscape. Clark made an incredible amount of money—and when people asked him when he would retire, his stock answer was, "After I become a billionaire."

Well, when he became a billionaire, he upped the amount to $3 billion dollars. And when he got to $3 billion, he told people, "I just want to have more money than Larry Ellison," the president and CEO of Oracle.

So when Clark passed Ellison he still didn't retire—the goal post moved again. He raised that billion-dollar bar even higher. He told people, "Just for one moment I would like to have the most of anyone—even Bill Gates. Just for one tiny moment."

And that really is a parable for our time—a tale of how the power of money can rule our lives. Maybe we all need to reflect a bit on the fact the highest number—the highest value in the world of numbers—is infinity. No matter how high you stack the bills, there's always another dollar out there. In other words, if you're playing the money game, infinity is a goal line you'll never cross.

Personally, I put my value in another kind of infinity—the eternity of the hereafter—and so do other people I know.

People like Warren. Warren isn't a philanthropist. You'll never find his name on the Forbes 400 or take a TV tour of his house on *Lifestyles of the Rich & Famous*. Warren's a shoeshine man I met one day in Oklahoma City. As we talked, he was telling me about his three grown kids—all college graduates. Three kids he'd put through college shining shoes—at $2 a throw. . . .

Now I know you don't know Warren . . . no matter. Add him to your list.

. . . life is divided into three phases: you learn, then you earn, then you serve. . . . and now it's time to do some earning—to build the career that allows you to give back later.

That's right—you owe him a debt—and everyone like him who takes a little smaller share for themselves so that their children and grandchildren can reach higher, dream bigger, go farther. . . .

The strength of America isn't in agriculture or oil and gas . . . or in the automobile industry or financial services or even today's highest flying IPO. The strength of America is her people. You. Me. Us. Our hopes. Our dreams. Our ambitions—and most important, our goodness. . . .

And so this morning my challenge to you [is] whether you stay on here . . . or start anew in a new city or state far away from here. . . .

Pay down the debt.

Go to a church, a parish, a synagogue, a school, or a shelter; find the person in charge and tell them: "I'm here to do whatever needs doing."

Pay down the debt.

Don't measure your worth by your paycheck or your latest promotion—but by the difference you make to people in need.

Pay down the debt.

Don't think of charity as an envelope you put in the church offering on Sunday. Don't just give of your dollars—give of yourself.

Pay down the debt—honor those who have come before and obligate those who come after.

Pay down the debt. . . . Build on—and build up—this land we love.

Graduates of the Class of 2000. May God bless you—and may God bless America.

> **Pay down the debt—**
>
> **honor those who**
>
> **have come before**
>
> **and obligate those**
>
> **who come after.**

CROSS OVER

Dr. Charles Betters, Senior Minister of Glasgow Reformed Presbyterian Church in Bear, Delaware since 1986, says that the death of his sixteen-year-old son, Mark, "unbolted [he and his wife] from [their] love affair with this world." As a national speaker and co-author of Treasures of Faith *with his wife, Sharon, Dr. Betters also speaks on radio segments entitled* In His Grip *and organized MARK Inc. Ministries, Make Abundant Riches Known in the Name of Christ, a preaching and teaching ministry. Here Dr. Betters reminds graduates that they are the new generation crossing over into the "promised land." But it is because of God's sovereignty that they can raise their heads and look beyond themselves.*

CHARLES BETTERS
Covenant Theological Seminary
May 22, 2000

I thought about what I might want to say to you tonight and I have one word for you graduates—RUN! Run like mad! It's not too late; you can still get out. Take up something safe like testing sky-diving equipment or something like that. . . .

Now the time has come for a new generation to take the first step into the "promised land." . . . The gospel ministry is a journey. For some, it's brief, as in the case of our son. For others, it's long . . . and painful but it's a remarkable journey that ought to cause us to step back in wonder and amazement and look at what the Spirit of God wants to do, desires to do in each of your hearts. Quietly, behind the scenes, leadership is emerging.

It's quite a sight to . . . see this sea of black gowns, knowing that inside each of those black gowns is potential, dynamic potential for expanding the glorious kingdom of Jesus Christ. . . . But the puzzle is not complete, the mosaic is being put together, the picture is not fully painted. Each piece must be put into place.

Somebody needs to step into the water, somebody needs to cross over. The preparations have been made. . . .

A commitment to cross over, graduates, requires a certainty of God's direction and God's call in your life. . . . History is filled with men and women who with great personal costs, at great personal price and sacrifice crossed over into uncharted waters and paved the way for generations to come. Somebody had to step into the water first. . . . Somebody had to say, "It's my turn to cross over, to put my feet in the water." Luther, an Augustinian monk in the sixteenth-century Germany, crossed over. He dipped his toe in the water when he nailed those ninety-five theses to that church door. Wesley and Whitefield and Edwards . . . stepped into the water . . . crossed over.

Our crossing over may not be as dramatic as these men but it's just as significant for the building up of that corporate . . . picture, that glorious mosaic of what God is putting together called the kingdom of God. . . . We need to see God's confirmation of His presence in not only calling us but sending us and challenging us to put our feet in the water. There's a heavy price tag because, graduates, you've not passed this way before. There's more awaiting. The preparations have been made but there's more that awaits you. . . .

Ever seen someone who's ironed a shirt, and they've left that iron on that shirt a little too long; and you have this image of the iron that's burned into that beautiful white shirt? It's there. You can't wash it away—it's there forever. I believe God invades us that way . . . with scorch marks . . . where he impresses upon each of you an urgency of your calling that you are about to enter into uncharted waters. You are about to cross over. You may be heading north. And God invades and says, "No," it's south. . . . Throughout your career and your life, God will invade and He will scorch and you will remember those scorch marks. They're indelible, they don't go away. And they teach us who's in control. . . .

Somebody had to step into the water first. . . .

Thirty-one years ago, . . . I came out of seminary believing I knew it all. I knew more than my professors, [I] knew more than my mentors, and I was going to turn the world upside down and inside out for the kingdom of God. Control. No matter what it was, I felt like I could fix this. No matter what it was. I've identified in my life twelve scorch marks, the last of which is that one where we lost our child in 1993, but there were eleven others before that—each one reminding me of who's in control.

I remember when my wife . . . developed [stage four] cancer . . . But you know, I could fix those problems. There was a part of my heart that said, "I can fix this." But when [my son was killed in a car accident], I held that 6 ft. 3 inch body in my arms . . . [and] from that day forward, He has been teaching me some of the most significant and valuable lessons about crossing over I have ever learned in my thirty some years of marriage. And at the top of my list is [this] . . . it's not about you. It's not about you. It's about the glory of God in you and through you. It's about Him. Crossing

> **It's not about you. It's about the glory of God in you and through you. It's about Him. Crossing over demands that the . . . presence of God goes before us.**

over demands that the . . . presence of God goes before us.

Along the way we are going to be scorched. Along the way God is going to change the course of our ministry . . . but the commitment to cross over requires a personal consecration of one's inner man to the cause of Christ. Joshua told the people, "Consecrate yourself for tomorrow the Lord will do amazing things among you even though you've never been this way before." Amazing things. . . .

God's putting together a wonderful mosaic, He's putting together a wonderful masterpiece and you graduates are a part of it. You're a little piece in that masterpiece. . . .

You see, graduates, it's not about you. It's not about me. It's about the glory of God who called you to step foot in the water, to step over. The Lord Jesus Christ two thousand years ago died on a cross. They put him in a grave. They put a stone up against that grave, and the world thought they were finished. But three days later, the angel came and rolled back the stone, not in order to let him out but to let us in, to see that He had already risen, He was already gone, He had already experienced the glory of resurrection, the power of resurrection. He holds those nail-scarred hands out to you and to me tonight. He says "Come and see, come and see; I am a sovereign God, and I can be trusted. Raise your eyes; lift up your head; look beyond.". . .

Graduates, He's called you to step over, to cross over. . . . See the bigger picture of what God is doing that will count for all eternity. . . . May God receive all the glory. . . .

INSIGHTS *for* LIVING

You're being flung into a world that's running about as smoothly as a car with square wheels. It's okay to be uncertain. . . . If you weren't a little uncertain, I'd be nervous for you. Adulthood has come upon you, and you're not all that sure you're ready for it. I think that sometimes I'm not ready for adulthood either—yours or mine. . . . As I get older, the only thing that speeds up is time. But if time is a thief, time also leaves something in exchange: experience. And with experience, at least in your own work, you will be sure.

—ALAN ALDA

DON'T EVER DARE TO TAKE YOUR COLLEGE AS A MATTER OF COURSE— BECAUSE, LIKE DEMOCRACY AND FREEDOM, MANY PEOPLE YOU'LL NEVER KNOW HAVE BROKEN THEIR HEARTS TO GET IT FOR YOU.

—ALICE DRUE MILLER

I genuinely feel elated at seeing your faces and knowing how happy you are today, and how relieved your parents are. Some of your parents have postponed dental surgery, taken no vacations, worked extra jobs, and will be in debt for a little while longer. But here they are, so you must have done something right.

—ARTHUR ASHE

FINISHING THE FIRST QUARTER

Jerry Falwell, founder of Moral Majority and Liberty University in Lynchburg, Virginia, Falwell has taken an active voice in moral issues within the federal government and public policies. His television channel LIBERTY CHANNEL provides segments on areas such as character building and family entertainment for its viewers. In this speech to high school graduates, Mr. Falwell likens life to a football game with its needed practice and learned pain while at the same time, encouraging the graduates to celebrate their youthfulness and "stir up a heart for God."

JERRY FALWELL
North Raleigh Christian Academy
2003

You are in the process of finishing your first quarter of life. You will be entering the second quarter as you enter college this fall. I am concluding my fourth quarter. You live life looking forward, but you understand life looking backward.

When we're in grade school, we look forward to junior or middle school, and then to high school; and when we're in college we look forward to marriage. When you ask a child his or her age, they always say, "I am going on (whatever their next birthday is)".

Paul said in Philippians 3:13, "This one thing I do, forgetting those things which are behind and looking forward to those things which are before".

At age 20, a man wants to wake up romantically;

Age 30, he wants to wake up married;

Age 40, he wants to wake up successful;

Age 50, he wants to wake up rich;

Age 60, he wants to wake up contented;

Age 70, he wants to wake up healthy;

Age 80, he just wants to wake up.

Your success in the second, third and fourth quarter begins long before the game begins. Your success in the game of life begins on the practice field. You learn the playbook, you practice the plays, you learn how to get along with team members, and you get mentally prepared for the game.

My friend, John Maxwell, says that in life if we "play now, we will pay later." By that he means, if you spend your youth always playing and don't prepare for life, then you will pay for it later. However, John Maxwell says,

"Pay first, you can play later." By that he means, if we pay the price early in life and learn how to live, how to work, how to earn and save money, and how to make our families happy and successful, then, later on, we will enjoy happiness. Proverbs 24:27, "Develop your business first before building your house."

The greatest thing about the third and fourth quarters is still being in the game. Think about all the people who got tired of playing and quit . . . or the coach took them out because they didn't play well . . . or they didn't even get in the game in the second half. When the coach leaves you in during the final minutes of the fourth quarter, it's because the coach (our Lord) believes in you and knows you can get the job done.

I remember Terry Bradshaw coming to Lynchburg to visit me shortly after he trusted Christ. He was in his final years quarterbacking the Pittsburgh Steelers. He spent the night with us. We talked into the wee hours. I asked him to stay several days. He said he dared not do that. He was fearful some young quarterback might take his job if he missed practice. No one bumped him, and he went out with a blaze of glory.

The longer you stay in the game, the more comfortable you get playing the game. During the first play of the game, usually you are a little tense and scared. You don't know if you can block the guy, or if you can catch the pass or [if] you can hit the ball. But the longer you stay in the game, the more comfortable you get. You learn what you can and can't do.

The longer I serve the Lord, the more comfortable I am serving the Lord. I know what my calling is, what I can do, and what I can't. I am Jerry Falwell, I am not a Bible teacher like many I could name. I am not an area-wide evangelist like Billy Graham. I am a pastor. . . .

You are one of a kind. You have a special calling. The longer you exercise your calling under the Holy Spirit, the more comfortable you become doing it.

Even though the game gets more comfortable in the advanced quarters, it never gets any easier. Sin is as divisive as ever, and Satan is as determined to destroy us as ever. I know who my enemy is, and I know that some members of the team are going to get hurt in the fourth quarter. But I also know who my Coach is, and I know who eventually will win the game. Therefore, I can't let up because I know we will eventually win. I've got to protect the others who are playing with me, and I've got to recruit as many to get on the team as

Your success in the game of life begins on the practice field. You learn the playbook, you practice the plays, you learn how to get along with team members and you get mentally prepared for the game.

possible. Last week, author Dr. Tim LaHaye told me the name of his final book in the twelve "Left Behind" novels. It is "Jesus Wins!!".

I'm a better team player in the next quarter. When I first began my ministry over fifty years ago, I wanted everyone to be a preacher, I wanted everyone to be a soul-winner, I wanted everyone to be and do what my heart was burdened to be and to do. But as I grew older, I have learned to respect the differences of the players on the team. Just as a quarterback must respect his blockers, flankers, and running backs, so I respect those who serve God with music, Sunday school teaching, counseling, administration, ushering and many other ways.

> You are one of a kind. You have a special calling. The longer you exercise your calling under the Holy Spirit, the more comfortable you become doing it.

The longer you stay in the game, the better perspective you have of the big picture. Those who are in the final quarter have a larger vision of life than those who are just starting out. When I just started out, all I could see was building a church in our section of Lynchburg, Virginia. However, the more I stayed in the game, the more I realized what God could do through me and Thomas Road Baptist Church in America and around the world. I have over fifty years of ministry experience, over fifty years of viewing the game. Now that I am in the fourth quarter, I see more, I see farther than ever.

In the fourth quarter, you're not as distraught about your past failures. When you miss a play at the beginning of the game, you think you've lost everything. You become discouraged and defeated over your failures. However, now that I am in the fourth quarter, I realize that past failures didn't kill me and put me on the sidelines. Sure, my failures embarrassed me, I began some projects that failed, and I had to start over again. I began some projects that didn't work and had to forget them. And now in the fourth quarter, I am still in the game; and I don't let past failures bother me.

I'm sometimes asked, "What would you do differently if you could live your life over?" That question is hypothetical because no one will get that chance. We are the product of our successes and failures.

In the fourth quarter, you return to your tried and proven methods. You've spent four quarters in the game and you still have to struggle for victory. In the fourth quarter, you've learned what works and what doesn't work for you. You look back on the past experiments you tried and failed. You've tried new twists and been knocked down. So in the fourth quarter, you're not ready to give up on the old "tried and proven" ways. I know what works for me, so I am going to keep on working it as long as I am in the game. I'm not going to try a lot of new things, at least I won't try new things

I know won't work.

The greatest thing about the fourth quarter is the confidence you have developed. When you come into the fourth quarter of the game, you know most everything you need to know. That means that when you started life at age twenty or so, you knew most of the facts, lessons, and principles that you needed to know. But the trouble is, you knew all of this in your head only, and not in your heart.

Young people know much, but don't have the experiences to back up what they know in their head. But as you live life, you learn how to apply principles, you learn timing, you learn the secrets to relationships. You learn through sleepless nights of prayer, you learn through the agony of defeat, you learn through the bitterness of tears, and you learn when friends turn away from Jesus Christ.

So in the last quarter, you don't need to learn much in your head. But in the last quarter you have to rely on your experiences, and they have a deeper meaning to you because they've come from life's learning curve.

There's another experience you've got to be sure you never lose—passion. In the fourth quarter you have learned how to play with pain. You don't pay as much attention to pain in the fourth quarter as you did when you began the game. Now, no one likes to be hurt. However, when you become seventy, as I have, you realize that some things in life are "a trade off" for other things. You take the pain, so you can get the gain. To get to the fourth quarter, you learn to live with your aches, limitations, and you keep on going.

NO PAIN, NO GAIN.

When you're a young man, you pay attention to pain; just like you pay attention to food, and to all the things that please the body or feed the flesh. But when you get older, you learn there are a lot of things more important than pampering the body, protecting the body, and pleasing the body.

Older people have more aches and pains than younger people. So you learn to play through the pain.

Let me summarize three attitudes I have toward pain:

(a) Winning is more important than pain.
(b) Pain may hurt, or even slow you down, but it doesn't need to stop you.
(c) Pain is one of the "trade offs" for making it through the fourth quarter.

Playing in the fourth quarter means understanding your limitations and being thankful to still be in the starting lineup. When you're playing in the fourth quarter, "limitation" is a good friend of yours. You take limitation by the hand every day, and go where it leads you. You

When we were all young, we wanted to be older . . . wiser . . . better . . . we all wanted to be something we were not.

> **I am happy for my teachers and mentors who shared with me what they learned in their fourth quarter, so I can now play well in my fourth quarter.**

look at the strong bodies of young men, and know you cannot do what they do. You ask yourself the question, "Was I ever able to do that?" Now that you're older, you know what you can do; that means, "you play within yourself."

In the fourth quarter, you gain a new appreciation for youth. Dr. B.R. Lakin used to say, "Youth is such a wonderful thing. What a pity to waste it on young people." When we were all young, we wanted to be older . . . wiser . . . better . . . we all wanted to be something we were not. And when we get to be older, we look back at youth and appreciate the "potential of youth."

Aged Paul told young Timothy, "Stir up the gift of God that is within you" (2 Timothy 1:6). A young man is supposed to stir up and grow in his spiritual gifts. "Let no man despise thy youth" (1 Timothy 4:12).

My promise to this young generation rising behind me:

1. I will always believe in youth.
2. I'm going to recruit youth. I am going to let youth stand on my shoulders and reach higher than I ever attained.
3. I'm going to hand the baton of leadership to them. I am going to point them in the way.
4. I am going to be their cheerleader.

I am happy for my teachers and mentors who shared with me what they learned in their fourth quarter, so I can now play well in my fourth quarter. I am happy for their teaching me New Testament church strategy. I am happy for the late Dr. Bill Dowell teaching me local church evangelism. I am happy for the late Dr. B. R. Lakin teaching me to ignore my critics. I am happy for the late Dr. Francis Schaeffer telling me to educate the young. I am happy for Dr. John Rawlings teaching me to be "tough" in my assault against sin and Satanic obstructions.

INSIGHTS *for* LIVING

WE ARE OBLIGATED TO LEAVE AS GOOD A FUTURE AS WE CAN
FOR OUR CHILDREN. THE OTHER SIDE OF THAT COIN IS THAT
THEY WILL INHERIT THE FUTURE AND BE RESPONSIBLE FOR
RUNNING THINGS. WE NEED TO MAKE SURE THEY'RE QUALIFIED.

—HOUSTON MAYOR LEE BROWN

*I shall not exhort you with clichéd challenges to build a
better world, to correct the mistakes we made. In fact, I find
it offensive to deprecate the achievements of previous
generations. It was their efforts that moved this nation and a
large part of the world to a position in which such a large
proportion of us enjoy education and freedom of choice. In
retrospect, many who preceded you would do some things
differently, just as each of you in time will mourn past
mistakes. But know how easy it is to avoid making mistakes:
one has only to do nothing.*

JUANITA KREPS
U.S. Secretary of Commerce
Duke University

IT SURE SEEMS FUNNY—THE OLDER I GET THE SMARTER
MY MOTHER AND FATHER SEEM TO GET.

—WILL ROGERS

"WHO IS GOD?"

*Mrs. Vonette Bright, co-founder of Campus Crusade for Christ
International, has worked side by side with her husband for more than
fifty years. Mrs. Bright began a career as a teacher in the Los Angeles
school system when she was first married and later received the 1973
Churchwoman of the Year by Religious Heritage of America, distinguished
alumna of Texas Woman's University, and many other awards. Mrs.
Bright founded the Great Commission Prayer Crusade in 1972 and later
served as chairwoman of the National Day of Prayer Task Force. She
challenges the graduates to be used by God in great ways, to embrace Him,
and to make themselves available to Him.*

VONETTE ZACHARY BRIGHT
Palm Beach Atlantic College
May 5, 2001

Well, do I remember my graduation day from college. My parents were there—they were so proud of my accomplishment. I had actually made it! I don't remember anything about the words that were delivered, the program, who spoke, or anything else. I just know the biggest decision of my life was before me—a decision I had to make by the end of that commencement! That makes me wonder if you will remember one word I say to you today.

I want to be practical and hopefully give you some principles to apply that will lift you to a leadership role just a little taller, a little more influential, and a greater builder of a stronger future for those who will follow in your footsteps. Recently I've heard that today's youth generation is described as a nameless, faceless generation who are biblically illiterate. The enemy of men's souls is stealing their confidence.

George Barna, president of a company that conducts religious surveys, said in his most recent annual report that "our nation seems to be mired in spiritual complacency. We seem to have become almost inoculated to spiritual events, outreach efforts, and the quest for personal spiritual development. But overall, Christian ministry is stuck in a deep rut." ... Though this is a recent statement, it's not too far from what I was experiencing as a devout church member and a professing Christian fifty-two years ago.

Bill and I had become formally engaged in December. Now, six months later, we were poles apart in our view of God. The decision I had to make on my graduation day was to determine whether I was going to accept a teaching contract in my hometown, or take a trip to California against my parents' wishes to try to salvage a relationship with the man I loved, Bill Bright. My parents felt that since we had announced our plans for a September wedding and we were uncertain, I should take a teaching contract and get on with life.

Bill and I had known each other all of our lives. He was ambitious. Material things meant a lot to him. He had about every honor possible in college—handsome, moral, successful—and became the youngest manufacturer of epicurean food products in the U.S. He wandered into Hollywood Presbyterian Church, where he met the most beautiful and successful young people he had ever met.

It wasn't long until he trusted Christ as his Savior. He was captured by the love of Christ—nothing else really mattered. It was then, my sophomore year of college, that I received my first communication from him. I didn't answer him for several months. Though I was impressed, I wasn't about to let him know I was. When I did answer, it began a daily correspondence and frequent phone calls. After four months, he proposed to me on the first date. . . .

As awesome as Bill was to me, as a person, as much as I had come to love him, suddenly I could not understand why he was so consumed with what it meant to be a follower of Jesus. I concluded he was being unduly influenced by a group of religious fanatics. I was sure that if I were with him, I could convince him not to be so radical.

At the same time, I had three basic questions that plagued me: "Where did I come from? Why am I here? Where am I going?" I believe these questions plague every person until they find the answers in Jesus Christ. They can all be answered by the answer to this question: "Who is God?" I believe this question is the greatest question to be answered today.

I had three basic questions that plagued me: "Where did I come from? Why am I here? Where am I going?"

Our view of God affects every decision we make in life—the profession we will choose; whom we marry; the type of entertainment we enjoy in our homes, the kind of education we provide for our children. Our entire lifestyle is determined largely by the answer to the question, "Who is God?"

We've forgotten that the Bible is God's textbook to mankind. It's this book that tells us how to relate to God, how to relate to each other, man to man, woman to woman, parents to children. It has the answers to questions of life. . . .

While I was considering my point of view toward Bill, he was concluding that I was an active church member but I did not know Christ personally. Bill wanted me to attend a college briefing conference in California. He was sure we could work out our differences.

Finally the commencement speech was over, and I could get that piece of paper that was my degree. My maiden name, Zachary, put me at the end of the line. As I approached the stage, a telegram from Bill was placed in my hand, "Congratulations. I love you. No pressure!"

I then knew my decision. I loved this guy, and I had to try to rescue him. If I didn't go to California, I feared this would be the end of our relationship.

Proud, teary-eyed parents met a confident, determined daughter outside the auditorium. I said to my dad, "Dad I have to go to see if I can salvage this relationship." He reached in his pocket and handed me a roll of bills and said, "You have to do what you have to do." What a dear moment that was. My parents left that day with my possessions in their car, but not their daughter. I was on my way to California!

> **What a dear moment that was. My parents left that day with my possessions in their car, but not their daughter. I was on my way to California!**

When I arrived, I met the most enthusiastic Christians I had ever seen. They were attractive, successful, and they possessed the greatest quality of life I had ever seen. After three days, I concluded it was all new to them. This will wear off. It won't work for me. I have tried it. I told Bill we should break our engagement. I loved him too much to interfere with his life. God was not that much of a reality to me.

Bill suggested we go to talk to Dr. Henrietta Mears. She had taught chemistry in Minneapolis city schools and now was the Christian education director at Hollywood Presbyterian Church. She explained for the first time to my understanding what it is like to know God personally through faith in Jesus Christ. So, alone with Dr. Mears, I received Christ as my personal Savior.

Talk about a transformation! A hot-tempered, cocky, strong-willed, small-town, Southern girl suddenly knew God wanted to change her life, and now I was ready! Now, with our differences resolved, Bill and I began to make plans for a December wedding. Ours is almost an "and they lived happily ever after" story. . . .

A few years ago, an outstanding theologian asked my husband in a radio interview, "What is the most important truth for a person to know?" Bill's answer, quickly without thought, was, "The attributes of God." He was surprised himself and later gave thought to his answer. As a result of years of study, he wrote a book on the attributes of God, which he called *God:*

Discover His Character. I think it's a classic. There are so many attributes of God; it would be impossible for one volume to adequately explain them all. My husband chose thirteen. I think they are so important that every person would benefit from knowing at least these thirteen attributes. I brought you graduates a gift today that may well change your life. They are available on the table as you leave the platform. Let me read them to you.

You graduates are uniquely suited for this time in history when your generation is looking for that which is authentic. Your generation has a new boldness, a willingness to speak the truth, and a heart for community

1. Because God is a personal Spirit . . . I will seek intimate fellowship with Him.
2. Because God is all-powerful . . . He can help me with anything.
3. Because God is ever-present . . . He is always with me.
4. Because God knows everything . . . I will go to Him with all my questions and concerns.
5. Because God is sovereign . . . I will joyfully submit to His will.
6. Because God is holy . . . I will devote myself to Him in purity, worship, and service.
7. Because God is absolute truth . . . I will believe what He says and live accordingly.
8. Because God is righteous . . . I will live by His standards.
9. Because God is just . . . He will always treat me fairly.
10. Because God is love . . . He is unconditionally committed to my well-being.
11. Because God is merciful . . . He forgives me of my sins when I sincerely confess them.
12. Because God is faithful . . . I will trust Him to always keep His promises.
13. Because God never changes . . . my future is secure and eternal . . .

You graduates are uniquely suited for this time in history when your generation is looking for that which is authentic. Your generation has a new boldness, a willingness to speak the truth, and a heart for community. God can use the pain of your generation's brokenness, disillusionment, and skepticism to reach a culture that is experientially based, not believing in absolutes, and embracing tolerance of everything. . . . There is great need for the leadership you personally can give to a world looking for the answer to the question, "Who is God?"

It has been fifty-three years since my graduation day. I've lived enough of life for a dozen people. Life with Bill Bright has been the most exciting, rewarding life we could imagine. Serving our Lord together has been a great

> **If God can use two people from a small Oklahoma town to touch the world, He can and will use you as you embrace Him and make yourself available to Him.**

adventure that continues. Now, we have almost 25,000 full-time staff and over half-a-million trained volunteer staff. Campus Crusade has either full-time staff or a ministry presence in 191 countries, representing 99.6 percent of the world's population. Since the ministry began in 1951, there have been more than 6.1 billion exposures to the gospel worldwide through Crusade and partnership activities. Obviously some of that number has been duplicated. We celebrate fifty years of ministry in July. At that time, we are passing the torch to new leadership who are godly, mature, able and committed people.

If God can use two people from a small Oklahoma town to touch the world, He can and will use you as you embrace Him and make yourself available to Him. We are still calling people to come help change the world. In whatever way God speaks to you, will you answer His call to leadership—to helping others answer the question, "Who is God, and how can I know Him in an intimate and personal way?"

Of course, you and I know that a relationship with God is possible only through faith in our Lord Jesus Christ. I'm in your rooting section. Graduates, go for it!

TAKING THE LONGER VIEW

Living For God and Country

Ask *of Me, and I will give* You *The nations* for *Your inheritance, And the ends of the earth* for *Your possession.*

PSALM 2:8 NKJV

INSIGHTS *for* LIVING

"WHAT DO WE MEAN BY PATRIOTISM IN THE CONTEXT OF OUR TIMES? I VENTURE TO SUGGEST THAT WHAT WE MEAN IS A SENSE OF NATIONAL RESPONSIBILITY . . . A PATRIOTISM WHICH IS NOT SHORT, FRENZIED OUTBURSTS OF EMOTION, BUT THE TRANQUIL AND STEADY DEDICATION OF A LIFETIME."

—ADLAI STEVENSON

Oh, Lord, let me not live to be useless!

—JOHN WESLEY

I WILL CONSIDER MY EARTHLY EXISTENCE TO HAVE BEEN WASTED UNLESS I CAN RECALL A LOVING FAMILY, A CONSISTENT INVESTMENT IN THE LIVES OF PEOPLE, AND AN EARNEST ATTEMPT TO SERVE THE GOD WHO MADE ME.

—JAMES L. DOBSON

"Courage is not simply one of the virtues, but the form of every virtue at the testing point, which means at the point of highest reality. A chastity or honesty or mercy which yields to danger will be chaste or honest or merciful only on conditions. Pilate was merciful until it became risky."

—C.S. LEWIS

PEACE CANNOT BE KEPT BY FORCE. IT CAN ONLY BE ACHIEVED BY UNDERSTANDING.

—ALBERT EINSTEIN

LIVE BY HOPE

Vice President of the United States under President Lyndon Johnson,
Hubert Horatio Humphrey, Jr. was narrowly defeated by Republican
Richard Nixon in 1968. Humphrey died in 1978 of cancer while serving in
the Senate again; his wife was appointed by Minnesota's governor to finish
his term. Here Hubert Humphrey exhorts graduates to remember the
message of America: "all men are created equal... endowed by their
Creator with certain unalienable rights" and "among these are life, liberty,
and the pursuit of happiness."

HUBERT HUMPHREY
U.S. Vice President
University of Pennsylvania
Date unknow

The message of the United States is a spiritual message, a statement of high ideals and perseverance in their achievement. It is the message of human dignity; it is the message of the freedom of ideas, speech, press, the right to assemble, to worship, and the message of freedom of movement of peoples.

It is the message of the Bill of Rights. It is the message of the Declaration of Independence, where we boldly proclaimed to a world dominated by monarchs and tyrants that "all men are created equal . . . endowed by their Creator with certain unalienable rights," and "among these are life, liberty, and the pursuit of happiness."

This is the message of America. This is the source of our power. This is the source of our strength.

Our nation's security lies in the strength of our people—our people at work, in prosperous communities, in sound mental and physical health. This is where our true national security lies. This is the source of our strength—moral, political, and economic. . . .

When our Founding Fathers met here in Philadelphia two hundred years ago, they gave us and the world a set of promises—promises toward a *more* perfect, not *the* perfect, union. America is a promise and a hope in the minds and hearts of all those who cherish liberty, justice, and opportunity.

We live by hope. We do not always get all we want when we want it. But we have to believe that someday, somehow, some way, it will be better and that we can make it so.

INSIGHTS *for* LIVING

*One hopes you will be actively involved in your community
and your country—but not be so totally consumed by your
desire to "settle the world right" that you begin to use people
as instruments of your design, rather than enjoy them for
their own qualities.*

—*Gerald Ford*

THE ENTIRE OCEAN IS AFFECTED BY A PEBBLE.

—BLAISE PASCAL

Your influence is negative or positive, never neutral.

—*Henrietta Mears*

THINGS ARE GETTING BETTER

As President of the United States from 1981-1989, Ronald Reagan felt he had fulfilled his campaign pledge to restore "the great, confident roar of American progress and growth and optimism." He shares this optimism with the graduates of Seton Hall as he tells them, "Don't get discouraged with the situation of the world. Things are getting better. And believe it, we need you."

PRESIDENT RONALD REAGAN
Seton Hall University
May 21, 1983

Something I've noticed in attending graduations over the years is the way time has a habit of catching up with you. First, you start to notice that you're older than the students. And next, you begin to realize that you're older than most of the faculty. But today marks a new first for me. I'm even senior to the Jubilarians who are gathered here today. They graduated in 1933. Well, I'm class of '32—Eureka College. And you immediately say to yourself, 'Where is that?' And if I tell you, you won't know any more than you know now. It's in Eureka, Illinois.

. . . To you members of the class of '83, I'm sure [76 years ago] seems like a long, long time ago, and you're right. The world has seen things happen—great miracles and great tragedies that no one could have dreamt of 51 years ago. Back then, the big breakthrough were propeller aircraft that could fly as far as Paris, movies that could talk, and a thing called radio that had a voice but no picture. I heard a little boy one day come in the house to his mother and say that he'd just been next door with his friend. And he said, 'You know, they've got a box over there that you can listen to, and you don't have to look at anything.'

Yet, if today's technology is more sophisticated than anything we had around in 1932, some things—and some very important things—remain the same. Just to give you one example, I can remember thinking, on my graduation day, that it was a time for me and my friends and my teachers and my family. And the commencement speaker seemed to be an intruder at a private party—an outsider at an intimate celebration of moments shared all leading up to this very special day.

Now, I can't believe that it feels very much different for you today . . . I know there's some of you probably think that my first degree was engraved in a stone tablet. . . .

> . . . these qualities of faith and common sense and dedication, if you can cultivate and keep them, will see you through lifetimes that will not only be rich in meaning for you as individuals but which will also leave behind a better country and a better world.

What I do sense here today—and whenever I visit with young Americans— . . . is the same unquenchable spirit that I remember among my own classmates. Ours, too, was a time of great change and uncertainty. Many of the things that our parents had taught us to take for granted suddenly seemed very fragile or even lost. . . .

We had our share of suffering in America, greater suffering than this country has ever known since. But something held true, something that still lives in the American spirit, your spirit. More than half a century and countless other trials later, some of that spirit is captured, appropriately enough, in the words that the late Cardinal Spellman used to describe Mother Seton herself. 'She was not,' he wrote, 'a mystical person in an unattainable niche. She battled against odds in the trials of life with American stamina and cheerfulness; she worked and succeeded with American efficiency.'

Well these qualities of faith and common sense and dedication, if you can cultivate and keep them, will see you through lifetimes that will not only be rich in meaning for you as individuals but which will also leave behind a better country and a better world. And that'll make all the effort that you've put into your school years and all the sacrifice of parents and other loved ones who've helped to see you through worth many times their cost.

You who are graduating have taken virtually your entire lives to reach this moment. To you it seems like a very long time. But there are others here today, parents and grandparents who share this day with you. And as they look back, it seems as if the journey only started yesterday. As a matter of fact, they can remember when if you took their hand, your hands were so tiny they only could encompass one finger. But you left an imprint on that one finger that they can still feel today. . . .

And possibly that explains the paradox of calling the day "graduation" at the same time that we call it "commencement." For even as you graduate today and commence life's journey in the outside world, you draw closer to the day when you, in your turn, will be the parents of another generation of young Americans. And, not long after that, your children will begin their own schooldays. . . .

Abraham Lincoln is supposed to have said that the best thing about the future is that it comes only one day at a time. In this modern age, it often seems to come a little more quickly than that. Our nation is speeding toward the future at this very moment. We can see it coming, if not in sharp detail at least in broad outline. . . .

Today is your day, graduate, teachers, friends, and family. And it's a day for you to remember, not for anything that I've had to say but for what it will mean to you for the rest of your lives. And I—speaking for those people over there in that particular section—tell you, you'll be amazed a half a century down the road at how clearly and how warmly the memories of these last few years will stay with you and how much they'll mean to you. . . .

You've been given special blessings, special gifts, families that care, that have given you the values of honesty, hard work, and faith that has seen you through the formative years of your lives; teachers who've taught you to think and to learn in preparation for productive careers; and a country that, for all its faults, is still what Lincoln called it more than a century ago: 'the last, best hope of Earth.'

. . . even as you graduate today and commence life's journey in the outside world, you draw closer to the day when you, in your turn, will be the parents of another generation of young Americans.

Now, I know there are certain clichés and things that go with commencements, such as a graduation speaker is supposed to tell you you know more today than you've ever known before or that you'll ever know again. I won't say that. But if I could do something else that probably is all too often done, would you listen for a moment to a little advice and based on personal experience?

Because this graduation year is so similar to that one of fifty and fifty-one years ago, in the depths of that Great Depression, I remember, diploma in hand, going back to my summer job that I'd had for seven years, life guarding on a river beach out there in Illinois. And I remember all—you didn't think of career, listening to those announcements I mentioned a little while ago on the radio—all you thought about was how, how when the beach closes this fall, where do I go? What job is there?

And I was fortunate. A man who had survived the Great Depression until then, and was doing well out in the business world, gave me some advice. He said, "Look, I could tell you that maybe I could speak to someone, and they might give you a job. But," he said, "they'd only do it because of me" And then he said, "They wouldn't have a particular interest in you." He said, "May I tell you that even in the depths of this depression," and so I will say to you even in the depths of this recession, there are people out there who know that the future is going to depend on taking young people into whatever their undertaking is and starting them out so that—whether it's business, industry, or whatever it might be—it will continue on.

> . . . we need you. We need your youth. We need your idealism. We need your strength out there in what we're trying to accomplish today. So, welcome to the world.

"Now," he said, "a salesman has to knock on a lot of doors before he makes a sale. So," he said, "if you will make up your mind what line of work you want to be in, what industry, what business, whatever it is, profession or other," he said, "and then start knocking on doors, eventually you'll come to one of those men or women who feels that way. And all you have to do—don't ask for the particular job you want; tell them you'll take any job in that industry or that business, whatever it may be, because you believe in it and its future and you'll take your chances on progressing from there."

Well, my means of travel in that early era was hitchhiking, and I hitchhiked from one radio station to another. Radio was the most new industry of that time. And he was absolutely right. I came to one one day when I was just about out of shoe leather and didn't know how much further I could go. And I started on a career that led to another career, and that led to some things that are more visible today.

But he was right. And so I say it to you, I pass on his advice to you. Don't get discouraged with the situation of the world. Things are getting better. And believe it, we need you. We need your youth. We need your idealism. We need your strength out there in what we're trying to accomplish today. So, welcome to the world.

The world you inherit today may not always be an easy one, for nothing worth winning is easily gained. But it's a good world, and it's a world that each of you can help to make a better one. What greater gift than that — what nobler heritage could anyone be blessed with?

So, may I add my congratulations to all of you, good fortune to all of you. And above all, God bless you.

Thank you.

NEVER, NEVER . . . GIVE IN!

*Sir Winston Churchill, Prime Minister, Minister of Defense, and Member
of Parliament during the 1940's and 50's, received the dignity of
Knighthood by Queen Elizabeth II and American honorary citizenship by
President Kennedy. Here he speaks at his alma mater in England before
many graduates who will leave their diplomas behind and serve their
country in the throes of World War II.*

WINSTON CHURCHILL
Harrow School
October 29, 1941
*Reproduced with permission of Curtis Browm Ltd, London, on behalf of
Copyright Winston Churchill*

The ten months that have passed have seen very terrible catastrophic
events in the world—ups and down, misfortunes—but can anyone sitting here this afternoon, this October afternoon, not feel deeply thankful for
what has happened in the time that has passed and for the very great
improvement in the position of our country and of our home?

You cannot tell from appearance how things will go. Sometimes imagination makes things out far worse than they are; yet without imagination
not much can be done. Those people who are imaginative see many more
dangers than perhaps exist; certainly many more than will happen; but then
they must also pray to be given that extra courage to carry this far-reaching
imagination. But for everyone, surely, what we have gone through in this
period—I am addressing myself to the school—surely from this period of
ten months this is the lesson: never give in, never give in, never, never, never,
never—in nothing, great or small, large or petty never give in except to convictions of honor and good sense. Never yield to force; never yield to the
apparently overwhelming might of the enemy. We stood all alone a year ago,
and to many countries it seemed that our account was closed, we were finished. All this tradition of ours, our songs, our school history, this part of the
history of this country, were gone and finished and liquidated. . . .

Do not let us speak of darker days: let us speak rather of sterner days.
These are not dark days; these are great days—the greatest days our country
has ever lived; and we must all thank God that we have been allowed, each of
us according to our stations, to play a part in making these days memorable
in the history of our race.

"YOU CANNOT STOP"

During World War II in 1943, Winston Churchill was awarded an honorary degree by the President and Fellows of Harvard University. Churchill traveled to Cambridge, Massachusetts, with his wife and daughter to accept the honor; to ensure Churchill's safety, the visit was shrouded in secrecy with no public announcement made. Here he encourages American youth with a message of responsibility, reminding them that their "conduct is liable to be scrutinized not only by history but by their own descendants."

WINSTON CHURCHILL
Harvard University
1943
Reproduced with permission of Curtis Browm Ltd, London, on behalf of Copyright Winston Churchill

The price of greatness is responsibility. If the people of the United States had continued in a mediocre station, struggling with the wilderness, absorbed in their own affairs, and a factor of no consequence in the movement of the world, they might have remained forgotten and undisturbed beyond their protecting oceans: but one cannot rise to be in many ways the leading community in the civilized world without being involved in its problems, without being convulsed by its agonies and inspired by its causes. . . . But to the youth of America, as to the youth of all the Britains, I say, "You cannot stop." There is no halting-place at this point. We have now reached a stage in the journey where there can be no pause. WE must go on. It must be world anarchy or world order. . . . If we are together nothing is impossible. If we are divided all will fail. . . .

Here let me say how proud we ought to be, young and old alike, to live in this tremendous, thrilling, formative epoch in the human story, and how fortunate it was for the world that when these great trials came upon it, there was a generation that terror could not conquer and brutal violence could not enslave. Let all who are here remember, as the words of the hymn we have just sung suggest, let all of us who are here remember that we are on the stage of history, and that whatever our station may be, and whatever part we have to play, great or small, our conduct is liable to be scrutinized not only by history but by our own descendants.

Let us rise to the full level of our duty and of our opportunity, and let us thank God for the spiritual rewards He has granted for all forms of valiant and faithful service.

A MATTER OF HUMAN RIGHTS

Only three years after his presidential acceptance speech and five months prior to his own assassination, one of the most shocking events of the twentieth century, President John F. Kennedy speaks here to graduates of American University in Washington, D.C., about the necessity of peace and respect toward others. Confident and unafraid we must strive, he says, to create a world of peace rather than annihilation.

JOHN F. KENNEDY
American University
June 10, 1963

It is the responsibility of the executive branch at all levels of governments—local, state, and national—to provide and protect that freedom for all of our citizens by all means within their authority. It is the responsibility of the legislative branch at all levels, wherever that authority is not now adequate, to make it adequate. And it is the responsibility of all citizens in all sections of this country to respect the rights of all others and to respect the law of the land.

All this is not unrelated to world peace. "When a man's ways please the Lord," the Scriptures tell us, "he maketh even his enemies to be at peace with him." And is not peace, in the last analysis, basically a matter of human rights—the right to live out our lives without fear of devastation—the right to breathe air as nature provided it—the right of future generations to a healthy existence? . . .

The United States, as the world knows, will never start a war. We do not want a war. We do not now expect a war. This generation of Americans has already had enough—more than enough—of war and hate and oppression. We shall be prepared if others wish it. We shall be alert to try to stop it. But we shall also do our part to build a world of peace where the weak are safe and the strong are just. We are not helpless before that task or hopeless of its success. Confident and unafraid, we labor on—not toward a strategy of annihilation but toward a strategy of peace.

A NEW WORLD

Jimmy Carter, raised in the farm country of Georgia, graduated from the U.S. Naval Academy in 1946. In 1962, Carter entered local politics, by 1971 was elected Governor of Georgia, and by 1976 had defeated Gerald Ford to become the 39ᵗʰ president of the United States from 1977-1981. Since leaving office, Carter has worked internationally for the disenfranchised, fighting hunger and poverty through a variety of non-profit organizations. In 2002, he was awarded the Nobel Peace Prize for his years of humanitarian work. In the following speech, he encourages the graduates as Americans, a people with policies "designed to serve mankind."

JIMMY CARTER
Notre Dame
May 22, 1977

In less than a generation, we've seen the world change dramatically. The daily lives and aspirations of most human beings have been transformed. Colonialism is nearly gone. A new sense of national identity now exists in almost one hundred new countries that have been formed in the last generation. Knowledge has become more widespread. Aspirations are higher. As more people have been freed from traditional constraints, more have been determined to achieve, for the first time in their lives, social justice.

The world is still divided by ideological disputes, dominated by regional conflicts, and threatened by danger that we will not resolve the differences of race and wealth without violence or without drawing into combat the major military powers. We can no longer separate the traditional issues of war and peace from the new global questions of justice, equity, and human rights.

It is a new world, but America should not fear it. It is a new world, and we should help to shape it. It is a new world that calls for a new American foreign policy—a policy based on constant decency in its values and on optimism in our historical vision.

We can no longer have a policy solely for the industrial nations as the foundation of global stability, but we must respond to the new reality of a politically awakening world.

We can no longer expect that the other 150 nations will follow the dictates of the powerful, but we must continue—confidently—our efforts to inspire, to persuade, and to lead.

Our policy must reflect our belief that the world can hope for more than simple survival and our belief that dignity and freedom are fundamental spiritual requirements. Our policy must shape an international system that will last longer than secret deals. . . .

More than one hundred years ago, Abraham Lincoln said that our Nation could not exist half slave and half free. We know a peaceful world cannot long exist one-third rich and two-thirds hungry.

Most nations share our faith that, in the long run, expanded and equitable trade will best help the developing countries to help themselves. But the immediate problems of hunger, disease, illiteracy, and repression are here now. . . .

It is a new world, but America should not fear it.

We have a special need for cooperation and consultation with other nations in this hemisphere—to the north and to the south. We do not need another slogan. Although these are our close friends and neighbors, our links with them are the same links of equality that we forge for the rest of the world. We will be dealing with them as part of a new, worldwide mosaic of global, regional, and bilateral relations. . . .

Our policy is based on an historical vision of America's role. Our policy is derived from a larger view of global change. Our policy is rooted in our moral values, which never change. Our policy is reinforced by our material wealth and by our military power. Our policy is designed to serve mankind. And it is a policy that I hope will make you proud to be Americans.

GET INVOLVED!

*The first female in modern history to lead a major Native American tribe,
Wilma Mankiller (whose name means "a protector of a village") served as
Principal Chief of the Cherokee Nation of Oklahoma. In this
commencement ceremony, Mankiller encourages students to leave their
stereotypes behind and to all take part in their communities.*

WILMA MANKILLER
Northern Arizona University
December 18, 1992

I am not going to give the standard advice about going out into the world,
because many of you have already been out in the world and worked and
been very involved in your communities. What I would like to do is
encourage you in whatever you pursue or wherever you go from here to get
involved. What I have seen, I think, in the United States, not just in my community or tribal community or rural community but in the United States,
in general, is a trend for all of us to think that somebody else is going to solve
our problems for us. . . .

Even in my own community I have heard people talk about the environment, housing, hopelessness, or any of the problems that we have; "Well,
they're going to solve that problem." I see that also in American society it is
always, "They're going to solve that problem." I don't know who "they" are. I
always tell our own people that I don't know who they are referring to. To me
the only people who are going to solve our problems are ourselves—people
like you and me. . . . We all have to take part. . . . So I would encourage you to
get involved; you will be immensely rewarded by getting into public service
or by doing small things around your community and trying to help others.

The other advice I have to give you is, do not live your life safely. I would
take risks and not do things just because everybody else does them. . . .
Robert Kennedy said, 'Some people see things the way they are and ask why,
and others dream things that never were and ask why not?' I think that is
where I hope many of you will be. . . . I hope you will take some risks, exert
some real leadership on issues, and if you will, dance along the edge of the
roof as you continue your life here. . . .

I think one of the things we have to do as a nation, besides addressing
specific issues like the economy, health care, education, inner cities, and that
sort of thing, is we have to examine the extent to which we continue to have

stereotypes about one another. I think it is very difficult for us to collectively and symbolically join hands and begin to move forward in solving this country's problems if we continue to have these stereotypes about one another. There still exist in this country many negative stereotypes about black people, Latin people, and Asian people. God knows there are terrible stereotypes about Native Americans; these have to be overcome before we can move forward. . . .

. . . do not live your life safely.

I would urge all of you who are here today, both graduates and families, to examine the extent to which we hold those stereotypes about one another. And finally, I would hope my being here and spending just a couple of minutes today would help you to eliminate any stereotypes you might have about what a chief looks like.

SEEK JUSTICE

The son of a Pentecostal minister, a Yale University graduate with honors, a former Missouri governor and senator, John Ashcroft has served as the Attorney General of the United States since December, 2000. President George W. Bush calls him, "a man of great integrity, a man of great judgment and a man who knows the law." In his address, Ashcroft tells the graduates that justice is more than intellectual-it is a calling and it must be a calling of truth for this generation and the next.

ATTORNEY GENERAL JOHN ASHCROFT
The University of Missouri
Columbia School of Law
May 18, 2000

As graduates of the University of Missouri, you have been schooled in a different vision of justice, one that balances contention with consensus, and puts results over retribution. It is a vision of justice deeply rooted in the American tradition of self-government. In order to form a more perfect union, our Founding Fathers set forth a system of justice in which Americans are not passive spectators but active participants; a system that honors equally the rights of all Americans by making justice available and accessible to all.

Our system of justice balances contention with consensus because, in the marketplace of justice, a monopoly on litigation serves to alienate the people from the law—and distances the legal profession from those it serves. As a young lawyer, Abraham Lincoln encouraged his colleagues to seek compromise whenever possible. "As a peacemaker, the lawyer has a superior opportunity to be a good man," said Lincoln. "There will be business enough." . . . Not all disputes will be reconcilable through mediation, and we will not always succeed in achieving justice through consensus. But today, perhaps more than any time in our history, it is vital that we aspire to a deeper understanding of justice. For justice has enemies in the world. Her defense is more than an intellectual exercise or an academic pursuit. It is the calling of our time.

As graduates, . . . your commitment to the examination of justice does not end with this day but has only just begun. The greatest responsibility of a society is the transmission of values—values of freedom, equality, and justice—from one generation to the next. The education you have received is an extraordinary gift, and it confers an extraordinary responsibility.

At a gathering of lawyers in Charleston, South Carolina in 1847, Daniel Webster raised his glass in a toast: "To the law," Webster said. "It has honored us; may we honor it."

May you, graduates, honor the law as it has honored you. The legacy you inherit is now the hope of future generations, so hold it high, and bear it proudly. Act boldly. Pursue truth. Defend freedom. And above all, seek justice.

. . . justice has enemies in the world.

Congratulations, graduates. God bless you, and God bless America.

TOP TEN PIECES OF ADVICE

Donna Shalala, former Secretary of Health and Human Services and presently serving as the fifth president of the University of Miami, offers her "Donna Shalala top ten" pieces of advice. Facing reality, being honest and patient, and serving your country and family are some of the most important principles graduates can take with them, Shalala emphasizes.

DONNA E. SHALALA
University of Maryland, Baltimore
May 21, 1997

I know that all of you will take time today to thank your families for their love and support that made this day possible. You should also thank hard working people all over Maryland—citizens you will never meet—who pay taxes to maintain this great public university.

I know exactly how you feel at this moment.

I'll never forget my own college graduation. In the air, you could feel the same sense of accomplishment, excitement, and the most chilling feeling of all—the absolute fear that the commencement speech would never end.

As a former Governor liked to say, "Commencement speakers should think of themselves as the body at an old-fashioned Irish wake. They need you in order to have the party, but nobody expects you to say very much." Albert Einstein gave one of the shortest graduation speeches ever. He said, "I do not have any particular thoughts to express today, so I wish you all success in the future." Then he sat down.

Well, I do have a few thoughts to share with you.

Because graduation speeches are really about giving advice, in the spirit of David Letterman, as you head out into the world, let me offer you Donna Shalala's top ten pieces of advice for UMBC graduates.

Ten. Face reality. When your alarm goes off at 6:30 a.m., it's not a nightmare—it's a job.

Nine. Be decisive. As Yogi Berra liked to say, "When you come to a fork in the road—take it!"

Eight. Be diplomatic. When your parents ask you how long you'll be living at home after graduation—lie.

Seven. Listen to voices of experience. Lilly Tomlin once said: "The trouble with the rat race is that even if you win, you're still a rat."

Six. Don't procrastinate. Order your World Series tickets now because

Cal and the O's are going all the way.

Five. Be patient. Wait at least twenty-four hours after graduation before asking your parents for money.

Four. Be loyal Americans—vote, pay your taxes, and above all else, always beat the Oxford Debate Team.

Three. Be honest. When relatives ask you what are you going to do the rest of your life, tell them the truth: You have no idea.

Two. Be succinct: When asked what the UMBC chess team has to say to Deep Blue, give just one word: Checkmate.

But in all seriousness—and without the David Letterman drum roll—my number one piece of advice for UMBC grads is: Be more than good at your chosen work—be good citizens as well. In other words, don't confuse having a career with having a life. They are not the same.

Before he died, Paul Tsongas, a former Senator from Massachusetts, and a beloved husband and father, said, "Nobody ever says on their death bed, I wish I had spent more time in the office." I decided to make this point early because, let's face it, if you had a dollar for every time someone asks you, "Now that you've finished school, what are you going to do for the rest of your life?"—you could retire now.

I'll never forget my own college graduation. In the air, you could feel the same sense of accomplishment, excitement, and the most chilling feeling of all—the absolute fear that the commencement speech would never end.

A generation ago, the movie *The Graduate*, made the word "plastics" the favorite answer to that question. But, today, I have come to ask you the only question more important than what are you going to do with your life? It is, how are you going to live your life?

Because the fact is, you are about to enter a world where you will no longer be judged by your grades, but by your character. By the promises you keep and the changes you shape. By the examples you set and the challenges you meet. By your guts and your heart. In short, you will be judged by what kind of citizen you are.

Thirty years ago, when I sat where you're sitting, my parent's generation had just saved our nation from economic collapse and world tyranny. And President Kennedy was challenging my generation to fight for civil rights; join the Peace Corps (which I did); explore space (which I would have liked to do); and carry the American dream to every corner of our country. But, now it's your turn.

The Cold War is over, but as we enter the next century, we face huge new challenges—challenges that are really about you and your future. Will we protect, not neglect, the environment? Will we kick Joe Camel and the Marlboro Man out of young people's lives? Will health care and student loans be there for you, and for your children? And, will we end the racism and division that still plague us and finally emerge as One America? It is up to you.

> **... the fact is, you are about to enter a world where you will no longer be judged by your grades, but by your character.**

Today, too many people think that your generation simply doesn't care about the future. They even call you Generation X. But I don't buy it for a minute. I believe the only "X" that you stand for is excellence. I believe that you and your entire generation will define yourselves not according to someone else's empty labels, but by your words and deeds. Your hopes and dreams. And, I believe that your class—your generation—will redefine what it means to be a citizen in the twenty-first century.

Groucho Marx once posed this interesting question, "Who are you going to believe, me or your own two eyes?" With that warning for the ages, I will not try to define a twenty-first century citizenship for you. But I will offer you some suggestions, with a little help from someone who was the embodiment of early American citizenship—Ben Franklin.

Just a couple of weeks ago, at the volunteer summit in Philadelphia, the President told this story about Franklin. On the last day of the Constitutional Convention, Franklin encountered a woman who asked him, "Well, doctor, what have we got? A monarchy or a republic?" Franklin replied, "A republic if you can keep it."

More than two hundred years later, keeping it is now in your hands.

Keep it by taking the same commitment you brought to the UMBC community and investing it in your local community—and your nation. By never losing the spirit of service that has made your own Shriver Center a national model for mentoring. None of us got to where we are without standing on the shoulders of another. And none of us will get to where we need to go without bending down to lift up someone who comes after us. Keep our republic by taking an active role in your health and your health care. Keep our republic by voting—yes. But also by staying informed, getting involved in public service, and proving that the author William Faulkner was right when he said we are immortal because we are capable of compassion, sacrifice, and endurance.

And, perhaps most important, keep our republic—and your sanity—by always leading a balanced life. Balancing work and family. Work and friendship. Work and spiritual renewal. And perhaps most important, work and having fun. Yes, I said fun.

When I graduated, I did not know exactly where life would take me. But

I promised myself, I would never play it safe. I've kept that promise.

As you prepare to leave UMBC, my deepest hope is that you won't play it safe either. That you'll rise to every challenge, and pick yourself up every time you fall. That you'll stand your ground—and when necessary, stand conventional wisdom on its head.

I wish you the best of everything—and that every dream you carry inside you today comes true. I wish you good health, great friendships, and love. And I wish you uncomfortable but exciting lives—with balance, promise, and many visits back to your wonderful campus. Congratulations and God speed. Thank you.

ESTABLISH THE TRUTH

After July 18, 1965, Jeremiah Denton's life was never the same. Shot down, captured, and held prisoner by North Vietnamese troops, Denton became the first American subjected to four years of solitary confinement. Here he speaks of the assuring love of God, the dependence upon God, and the religious morality graduates must take into the world.

ADMIRAL JEREMIAH A. DENTON
Thomas Aquinas College
June 10, 2000

This is Commencement. What are you supposed to commence? Some of you have your eye on a boy or girl. Some of you have your eye on a job. Some of you don't know what you're going to do. One thing I know you've learned is that if you have Jesus, you have everything, no matter what! So, you can't fail, no matter what you do. Whether you are a spouse, priest, nun, entrepreneur, doctor, musician—your success is assured because it isn't what you do, it's why you do it. Whatever you choose to do, you are going to do it for the honor and glory of God, and He will love you for that. And you will feel that love for you, everyday, in many ways. So, forget about worrying—you're going to succeed.

I believe this class has something in common with my graduating class—the one so touted in recent film and story, which graduated into a war-torn world with our outlooks dominated by a single consciousness. Both your class and mine were called to play a part in the survival of our country—the survival of Western Civilization with its Judeo-Christian foundations and blessings. It's a part that is liable to cause our death, our suffering.

In the prime fifty years of my life, the enemy was, first, the Nazi Pact Nations, and second, the Communist 'Evil Empire.' The first war was won militarily at tremendous cost in blood and treasure. The second—the 'Mostly Cold War'—was decided more by policies, alliances, and defense spending.

But in both cases, we were involved in a war between an atheistic system and a Christian coalition of nations. The atheists wanted to dominate the world, to enslave its peoples, and in one sense, enslave them to sin. The Christians wanted to maintain freedom under the law of God. Winning those wars was not easy. We barely won both of them, to tell you the truth.

Now, like my graduating class, I believe you are graduating in a time of special challenge. You confront a new war. The enemy is not a foreign power.

The enemy is a movement from within this country. Like the cartoon Pogo said, "We have met the enemy, and they is us." The enemy wants to change this from "One Nation Under God," which we affirm as we pledge our allegiance, to "One Nation Without God."

Starting with barring prayer in schools, the Supreme Court has succeeded in implanting the false notion that the First Amendment to our Constitution means this government has nothing to do with God, and God's laws have nothing to do with our laws.

They've removed the laws of God from the halls of justice, the legislative chambers, and the nature and direction of executive policies and programs. We're becoming—we've become—a Godless nation, formally, and we are well on the way to behaving like one. The only thing stopping us is people like you who believe in God.

The Supreme Court ruling, and subsequent court rulings from which this movement stems, are based on a lie. The basic ruling is a lie. The basic ruling that we're not One Nation Under God is a lie. It is just as wrong as the Dred Scott decision of the Supreme Court, which declared slaves to be less than men. It is just as wrong as the Roe v. Wade decision that declared that a baby in the womb is not life and that it is not murder to take a non-life. The war is about lies. Prevailing lies. Steering, domineering lies.

To win means to be able to establish the truth—that this Nation was indeed established as One Nation Under God and cannot survive unless it remains so dedicated. And that's where you fifty-four come in. You know the truth. God is truth. God made man to know Him, to love Him, and to serve Him in this world and to be happy with Him in the next. You know that the beginning of the process of loving with the heart enough to serve Him with your mind and body requires knowing Him. Here you have taken the opportunity to know God in many ways and through different means.

The war is about lies. Prevailing lies. Steering, domineering lies.

Now, yes, Jesus did say we could come to Him as little children—but if we come to Him as educated and enlightened faithful adults, we may lead others to Him. And that's what we need today. We need some action to permit this country to continue to believe in God.

The Lord gave His disciples extraordinary graces for leadership. He shared His physical presence with them and let them see His miracles. He appeared to them after the Resurrection. As He promised, the Holy Spirit came down and gave them the inspirational blessings and bravery of Pentecost Sunday which provided the knowledge and the fire to vault them on their way to their fantastic feats of evangelization. He imparted these blessings that they could teach and testify credibly enough to do their part

William Penn said,

"Men must choose

to be governed by

God or condemn

themselves to be

ruled by tyrants."

in establishing His Church and get footing in the world with that Church. He gave the Twelve what they needed.

. . . You are eminently qualified to take a part in what I am challenging you to take part in—a part in restoring His law, as the basis of the laws of this country, the leader of the Free World, in this year of our Lord, 2000.

I ask you to make some effort to involve yourselves in a specific way in establishing the truth on this issue—in politics, in the courts, in the media, in education, or even by giving a good example as a husband and father or wife and mother. You must pray desperately, because this situation is slipping by. It is becoming possibly irretrievable.

Let's be clear about one thing. The task is simple. The mission is to establish the truth. We sit by while they hammer us with lies—one television program after another, one story, one novel after another. How can we just sit there and let them call us this or that kind of kook while they proceed to demoralize and atheize the United States? They hammer us with lies; let's hammer them with truth!

The First Amendment protects religion from government, not government from religion. It says so in common words. There's no way you can twist it up to mean what they want to say it means, unless you don't read it. The context of the discussions on this subject during the founding days of this nation explicitly recognizes the importance of religion as being the only sufficiently strong source of morality to permit us to enjoy the luxury of democracy. Morality is truly the only alternative to barbarism, and is required not only for nations, especially those with democratic forms of government to exist, but for civilization itself to exist.

In summing up, perhaps better than anybody, William Penn said, "Men must choose to be governed by God or condemn themselves to be ruled by tyrants." George Washington, in three sentences of his farewell address, said: "Of all the dispositions and habits which lead to political prosperity, religion and morals are indispensable supports.

"Let us with caution indulge the supposition that morality can be maintained without religion. Whatever may be conceded to the influence of refined education on minds of peculiar stature, both reason and experience forbid us to expect that national morality can prevail in the absence of religious principle." That's what he said. That's what we had. That's what we're throwing away.

Not enough people have had the guts to try to tell the truth against the loud babble of those liars who want to adopt sin as their way of life and don't want to be bothered. Too many good guys know the truth, (and I include myself here) but they lack the guts to join the battle, to be embarrassed, to be criticized, and maybe someday to be beat up in the streets or even martyred. Father Rutler, in his book *A Crisis of Saints* makes that point clear. He said there are a lot of good people around; and we all talk about these things over the bridge table or golf, we gripe about what's going to happen, but we don't do anything about it. We're not willing to stand up and take the guff.

I believe you have the knowledge and the guts. Now go out and do it. No graduating class in the world today is better qualified to do it. . . . Don't you see yourselves as having a special place in this somehow?

Because truth is truth. Truth sells. The American people are not what they're being portrayed as by these idiots in Hollywood and New York that are selling us sin. They're good people. Appeal to them. This is an issue that can be won. I believe it's an issue that must be won, or we're going to see a Dark Age here in this Millennium now, worse than the one in the previous two that bracketed them.

The United States has been leading the world for fifty years. We started out well. But we became rich and powerful and fell prey to the words of Jesus' own statement, "It is more difficult for the rich man to reach heaven than for the camel to pass through the eye of the needle." Absolute power corrupts absolutely. It takes hardship to naturally induce a nation to pray to God.

It takes what the Founding Fathers had, the Colonialists. They came over that ocean fleeing from all kinds of horrors of government, from tyranny. And they had to survive along the coast

Truth sells.

against the Indians and endure all sorts of hardships. They knew who God was, and they knew they depended upon Him. It was in that religiosity that our Founding Fathers found that they would have to pray if they were to survive, and that their experiment in government would survive only if they were to keep praying. But are we going to stay that way?

You're not having to go through the hell that I went through to get to the point that you believe that Jesus is everything. To me, it's almost a miracle to see how far you have come in your minds. And I'm being honored. I feel I'm old, and I'm just starting to get to know more people—the longer you live, you know more people—and I'm just lucky to be allowed to associate with you. No one, no groups in the Mystical Body of Christ appeal to me more. There's more joy in looking into your faces and seeing that joy and knowing why it's joy, than there is with any other group. Because you are the best.

This College and its graduates typify our best weapons. I hope some of this class will remember and try. I shall pray for you. Our dead from other wars, fighting for our One Nation Under God, will be praying for you. God help you to win back the soul of America.

DUTY, HONOR, COUNTRY

As the last great general of World War II to come home, MacArthur received a hero's welcome when he returned to the United States. Later, retiring from the Korean Conflict, MacArthur is known for his closing lines in an address to Congress in 1951:

The world has turned over many times since I took the oath on the plain at West Point, and the hopes and dreams have long since vanished, but I still remember the refrain of one of the most popular barracks ballads of that day which proclaimed most proudly that old soldiers never die; they just fade away.

And like the old soldier of that ballad, I now close my military career and just fade away, an old soldier who tried to do his duty as God gave him the light to see that duty. Goodbye.

Later, truly a man of the military and a figure of patriotism, a well known hero, General MacArthur speaks to the graduates of West Point.

GENERAL DOUGLAS MACARTHUR
West Point
May 12, 1962

No human being could fail to be deeply moved by such a tribute as this, coming from a profession I have served so long and a people I have loved so well. It fills me with an emotion I cannot express. But this award is not intended primarily for a personality, but to symbolize a great moral code—the code of conduct and chivalry of those who guard this beloved land of culture and ancient descent.

"Duty," "honor," "country"—those three hallowed words reverently dictate what you want to be, what you can be, what you will be. They are your rallying point to build courage when courage seems to fail, to regain faith when there seems to be little cause for faith, to create hope when hope becomes forlorn.

Unhappily, I possess neither that eloquence of diction, that poetry of imagination, nor that brilliance of metaphor to tell you all that they mean.

The unbelievers will say they are but words, but a slogan, but a flamboyant phrase. Every pedant, every demagogue, every cynic, every hypocrite, every troublemaker, and, I am sorry to say, some others of an entirely different character, will try to downgrade them even to the extent of mockery and ridicule.

But these are some of the things they build. They build your basic character. They mold you for your future roles as the custodians of the nation's defense. They make you strong enough to know when you are weak, and brave enough to face yourself when you are afraid.

They teach you to be proud and unbending in honest failure, but humble and gentle in success; not to substitute words for action; not to seek the path of comfort, but to face the stress and spur of difficulty and challenge; to learn to stand up in the storm, but to have compassion on those who fall; to master yourself before you seek to master others; to have a heart that is clean, a goal that is high; to learn to laugh, yet never forget how to weep; to reach into the future, yet never neglect the past; to be serious, yet never take yourself too seriously; to be modest so that you will remember the simplicity of true greatness; the open mind of true wisdom, the meekness of true strength.

They give you a temperate will, a quality of imagination, a vigor of the emotions, a freshness of the deep springs of life, a temperamental predominance of courage over timidity, an appetite for adventure over love of ease.

They create in your heart the sense of wonder, the unfailing hope of what next, and the joy and inspiration of life. They teach you in this way to be an officer and a gentleman.

And what sort of soldiers are those you are to lead? Are they reliable? Are they brave? Are they capable of victory?

Their story is known to all of you. It is the story of the American man at arms. My estimate of him was formed on the battlefields many, many years ago, and has never changed. I regarded him then, as I regard him now, as one of the world's noblest figures; not only as one of the finest military characters, but also as one of the most stainless.

His name and fame are the birthright of every American citizen. In his youth and strength, his love and loyalty, he gave all that mortality can give. He needs no eulogy from me, or from any other man. He has written his own history and written it in red on his enemy's breast.

In twenty campaigns, on a hundred battlefields, around a thousand campfires, I have witnessed that enduring fortitude, that patriotic self-abnegation, and that invincible determination which have carved his statue in the hearts of his people. From one end of the world to the other, he has drained deep the chalice of courage.

> **In twenty campaigns, on a hundred battlefields, around a thousand campfires, I have witnessed that enduring fortitude, that patriotic self-abnegation, and that invincible determination**

As I listened to those songs in memory's eye I could see those staggering columns of the First World War, bending under soggy packs on many a weary march, from dripping dusk to drizzling dawn, slogging ankle deep through mire of shell-pocked roads; to form grimly for the attack, blue-lipped, covered with sludge and mud, chilled by the wind and rain, driving home to their objective, and for many, to the judgment seat of God.

I do not know the dignity of their birth, but I do know the glory of their death. They died unquestioning, uncomplaining, with faith in their hearts, and on their lips the hope that we would go on to victory.

Always for them: duty, honor, country. Always their blood, and sweat, and tears, as they saw the way and the light. And twenty years after, on the other side of the globe, against the filth of dirty foxholes, the strong stench of ghostly trenches, the slime of dripping dugouts, those boiling suns of the relentless heat, those torrential rains of devastating storms, the loneliness and utter desolation of jungle trails, the bitterness of long separation from those they loved and cherished, the deadly pestilence of tropic disease, the horror of stricken areas of war.

Their resolute and determined defense, their swift and sure attack, their indomitable purpose, their complete and decisive victory—always victory, always through the bloody haze of their last reverberating shot, the vision of gaunt, ghastly men, reverently following your password of duty, honor, country.

You now face a new world, a world of change. The thrust into outer space of the satellite spheres and missiles marks a beginning of another epoch in the long story of mankind. In the five or more billions of years the scientists tell us it has taken to form the earth, in the three or more billion years of development of the human race, there has never been a more abrupt or staggering evolution.

> ... in war there is no substitute for victory, that if you lose, the Nation will be destroyed, that the very obsession of your public service must be duty, honor, country.

We deal now, not with things of this world alone, but with the illimitable distances and yet unfathomed mysteries of the universe.

We are reaching out for a new and boundless frontier. We speak in strange terms of harnessing the cosmic energy, of making winds and tides work for us ... of the primary target in war, no longer limited to the armed forces of an enemy, but instead to include his civil population; of ultimate conflict between a united human race and the sinister forces of some other planetary galaxy; such dreams and fantasies as to make life the most exciting of all times.

And through all this welter of change and development your mission remains fixed, determined, inviolable. It is to win our wars. Everything else in your professional career is but corollary to this vital dedication. All other public purpose, all other public projects, all other public needs, great or small, will find others for their accomplishments; but you are the ones who are trained to fight.

Yours is the profession of arms, the will to win, the sure knowledge that in war there is no substitute for victory, that if you lose, the Nation will be destroyed, that the very obsession of your public service must be duty, honor, country.

Others will debate the controversial issues, national and international, which divide men's minds. But serene, calm, aloof, you stand as the Nation's war guardians, as its lifeguards from the raging tides of international conflict, as its gladiators in the arena of battle. For a century and a half you have defended, guarded and protected its hallowed traditions of liberty and freedom of right and justice.

Let civilian voices argue the merits on demerits of our processes of government; whether strength is being sapped by deficit financing indulged in too long, by federal paternalism grown too mighty, by power groups grown too arrogant, by politics grown too corrupt, by crime grown too rampant, by morals grown too low, by taxes grown too high, by extremists grown too violent; whether our personal liberties are as firm and complete as they should be.

> **The twilight is here. My days of old have vanished—tone and tints. They have gone glimmering through the dreams of things that were. Their memory is one of wondrous beauty, watered by tears and coaxed and caressed by the smiles of yesterday.**

These great national problems are not for your professional participation or military solution. Your guidepost stands out like a tenfold beacon in the night: duty, honor, country.

You are the leaven which binds together the entire fabric of our national system of defense. From your ranks come the great captains who hold the Nation's destiny in their hands the moment the war tocsin sounds.

The long gray line has never failed us. Were you to do so, a million ghosts in olive drab, in brown khaki, in blue and gray, would rise from their white crosses, thundering those magic words: duty, honor, country.

This does not mean that you are warmongers. On the contrary, the soldier above all other people prays for peace, for he must suffer and bear the deepest wounds and scars of war. But always in our ears ring the ominous words of Plato, that wisest of all philosophers: "Only the dead have seen the end of war.

The shadows are lengthening for me. The twilight is here. My days of old have vanished—tone and tints. They have gone glimmering through the dreams of things that were. Their memory is one of wondrous beauty, watered by tears and coaxed and caressed by the smiles of yesterday. I listen then, but with thirsty ear, for the witching melody of faint bugles blowing reveille, of far drums beating the long roll.

In my dreams I hear again the crash of guns, the rattle of musketry, the strange, mournful mutter of the battlefield. But in the evening of my memory I come back to West Point. Always there echoes and reechoes: duty, honor, country.

Today marks my final roll call with you. But I want you to know that when I cross the river, my last conscious thoughts will be of the corps, and the corps, and the corps.

I BID YOU FAREWELL.

YES, WE CAN

After serving for six years as Stanford University's Provost, Dr. Condoleezza Rice became the National Security Advisor to President George W. Bush on January 22, 2001. She tells the graduates of Mississippi College School of Law that no matter their background, rich or poor, urban or rural, they will leave today as graduates-and they will be forever changed. "In America, we say 'yes we can,'" she reminds the graduates, and you are obligated to dream higher than you think possible.

CONDOLEEZZA RICE
Mississippi College School of Law
May 16, 2003

To all of you: a sincere congratulations for a job well done! I will always remember my own commencement. I remember the pride written across the faces of my family members. I remember looking at my classmates and wondering if I would ever again find such close friends. I also remember wanting the whole thing to be over with. I do not remember a single word the speaker said. You won't either.

So my duty today is not to say something you will find profound twenty years from now. It is to say something you find interesting for the next twenty minutes. Anything beyond that is a bonus.

I am neither a lawyer nor a Baptist. But I feel very at home before you because I am a strong believer in the transforming power of both education and faith. And I believe that as this school has minted you into lawyers, it has endowed you with enormous opportunities . . . and enormous responsibilities.

First, as educated people—and people who may be called upon in the administration of justice—you have an obligation to be open minded. You have learned how to ask questions, assess evidence, and draw conclusions. You have learned the value of reasoned debate . . . the role of doubt in reaching a conclusion . . . and that it often helps to seek out those who do not think like you do. An "Amen" chorus is satisfying in the short term, but it is not edifying in the long term. By being open to rethinking ideas you once held sacrosanct, you will be better attorneys and better citizens.

Second, you have the responsibility to be optimistic. You have a degree that will create opportunities for you and the learning to help you seize them. Many people just as talented and smart as you did not get to where you are today—often through no fault of their own. So never ask why

> **If you play in C, the foundational key in music, people will come back. Perhaps God plays in C, and that's why we always seem to find our way back to Him, sometimes in spite of ourselves.**

someone else has been given more; ask why you have been given so much.

I first learned this lesson from hearing stories about my paternal grandfather. Grandfather Rice was a poor farmer's son in Ewtah, Alabama. One day, he decided to get book-learning. And so he asked, in the language of the day, where a colored man could go to school. They said that a little Presbyterian school, Stillman College, was only about fifty miles away.

So he saved up his cotton to pay for the first year's tuition. After the first year, he ran out of cotton, and he needed a way to pay. My grandfather asked the school administrators how those other boys were staying in school, and he was told that they had what was called a scholarship. And, they said, "If you want to be a Presbyterian minister, you could have a scholarship too." My grandfather said, "That's just what I had in mind."

What my grandfather found, and what I experienced years later, is that it matters not whether you enter college or graduate school poor or rich, minority or majority, urban or rural, foreign, or American. You emerge as a graduate—and a different person. Some of you may come from a long line of attorneys. Yet there is also the first female member of the Mississippi Band of Choctaw Indians to be admitted to the state bar. Another member of your class was born in a slum in Jamaica. Today, you all leave with the same degree and the same opportunities. You embody the truth that education is a great equalizer, and that here in America it is not about where you are coming from but where you are going.

Your third obligation as educated people is to affirm that values matter and that the law can be, and should be, an instrument for protecting the universal values of freedom that unite people across all cultures.

Here, you have a leg up on many of your colleagues graduating from other schools—because your education has been grounded in faith. Faith provides comfort and hope in times of difficulty . . . and can open the door to understanding of what is important in life.

Throughout my life I have never doubted the existence of God, but, like most people, I have had some ups and downs in practicing my faith. After I moved to California in 1981 to join the faculty at Stanford, there were a lot of years when I was not attending church regularly. I was traveling a great deal, always in a different time zone, and church too often fell by the wayside.

Then one Sunday morning I was approached at the supermarket by a man buying some things for his church picnic. He asked me, "Do you play the piano by any chance?" I said, "Yes." And he said his congregation was looking for someone to play the piano at their church. It was a small African-American church in the center of Palo Alto, and I started playing there every Sunday.

And I thought to myself, "My goodness, God has a long reach—all the way to the spice section of a supermarket on a Sunday morning."

The only problem was, it was a Baptist church, and I don't play gospel very well. I play Brahms. At this church the minister would start with a song and the musicians had to pick it up. I had no idea what I was doing. So I called my mother, who had played for Baptist churches, to ask for advice. She said, "Honey, just play in C, and they'll come back to you." And that's true. If you play in C, the foundational key in music, people will come back. Perhaps God plays in C, and that's why we always seem to find our way back to Him, sometimes in spite of ourselves.

I know there are many outstanding attorneys for whom faith plays little or no role in their lives. But I am confident that by combining your understanding of the law with your understanding of God's ways you will broaden your perspective and multiply your accomplishments and good works.

In Matthew, Jesus warned against the kind of lawyer who knows the law but not its ultimate purposes, saying "Woe to you, teachers of the law and Pharisees . . . [who] give a tenth of your spices—mint, dill and cumin . . . [b]ut neglect the more important matters of the law—[which are] justice, mercy and faithfulness."

This message has particular resonance in Jackson, Mississippi—a place that has been the site of so many key events in America's long-running struggle to define the meaning of justice. This is the city where the Tougaloo Nine and the Freedom Riders were arrested . . . and where Medgar Evers was cut down by an assassin's bullet. It was a focal point of the Freedom Summer of 1964 . . . and it was James Meredith's destination in his 1966 March Against Fear.

The civil rights struggle was America's chance to resolve the contradictions inherent in its birth. And at its roots, it was a legal struggle, pitting the natural law that underpins our Constitution and Declaration of Independence against unjust laws on the books that fell far short of that ideal. The Founding Fathers didn't mean me when they wrote the Bill of Rights. But by their terms, those rights were universal in theory, and you can trace the history of the civil rights era in the court filings of lawyers arguing that they should be universal in fact. The civil rights struggle was in a very real way America's second founding.

It also made real one of America's greatest gifts to the world: the promise of multi-ethnic democracy. We live in an age where too often difference is still seen as a license to kill. That's what terrorism is grounded in—whether it be terrorism in the Middle East or here in America. Growing up in Birmingham, I lived with the home-grown terrorism of that era. And I remember the bombing forty years ago of the Sixteenth Street Baptist Church that took the lives of four young girls, including my friend, Denise McNair. Acts of terror are calculated to propel old fears into the next generation.

America's diversity is a powerful rejoinder to that state of mind. Can the world forge a common future based not on ethnicity but on a commitment to an ideal, a commitment to democracy? A future where people get ahead based on ability—not on circumstances of birth?

In America, we say, "Yes we can."

Our democracy is still a work in progress, not a finished product. The hard work begins anew each day. Yes, we practice what we preach—but 225 years after the fact we are still practicing; practicing each day to get it right. And by doing so we strengthen America's moral authority and the currency of these values across the world.

We must always remember that while America cherishes the ideals of equality, justice, and the rule of law, we do not own them. As President Bush has said, the values of freedom are not America's gift to the world but God's gift to humanity. People everywhere share the most basic yearnings for liberty . . . to create, speak, and worship in freedom.

When these values are under attack, we must not—and we will not—spare any effort in their defense. When freedom is being sought by brave people living under tyranny, we must stand on their side. And when newly free people are seeking to build the institutions of law and democracy, we have an obligation—if asked—to help.

In America, we say,

"Yes we can."

And we are. This summer in Afghanistan a working draft of a new democratic constitution will be presented at town hall meetings across the country. In Iraq, leaders from every province and ethnic group have declared their commitment to a democratic future for their country. And last week, President Bush announced an important initiative for working in partnership with the people of the Middle East to bring more economic opportunity, better education, and more freedom to the region. The United States will help countries seeking to reform their judiciaries, provide training for the growing number of women seeking elective office, establish media law projects, and support new parliamentarians and civil society organizations.

This enterprise will be long, not short. Often, progress will come in small, quiet steps, less dramatic than the toppling of statues. Occasional setbacks are inevitable. But these efforts are vitally important and they are an essential element of the war on global terror. President Bush is fully committed to their success—both as an American, and as a person of faith. As he said last week, "[W]e are determined to help build a Middle East that grows in hope instead of resentment."

My own hope is that some of you have the opportunity to contribute to these efforts directly—or that you find other ways to serve. Because I believe that every American has an obligation to help make the world a better place. As an educated person—and as an attorney—you will have obligations that are weightier than most. Remember that you were admitted to this school, less on the basis of your past achievements than on your potential to continually improve yourself and to contribute to the world once you leave. I urge you to give some of your time, or even part of your career, to give back to a world that has given you so much.

Finally, keep close to your hearts the advice of one of Mississippi's most famous sons, William Faulkner, who said, "Always dream and shoot higher than you know you can do. Don't bother just to be better than your contemporaries or predecessors. Try to be better than yourself."

God bless this Class of 2003—today and every day through the rest of your lives.

William Faulkner, who said, "Always dream and shoot higher than you know you can do. Don't bother just to be better than your contemporaries or predecessors. Try to be better than yourself."

"REMAINING AWAKE THROUGH A GREAT REVOLUTION"

The Rev. Dr. Martin Luther King, Jr., a Christian clergyman who advocated social change through non-violent means, helped shape the American civil rights movement of the 1950s and '60s. In 1963, King organized a march on Washington, D.C., that drew 200,000 people demanding equal rights for minorities. In 1964, King won the Nobel Peace Prize, the youngest recipient at that time. Three years before he was assassinated, King delivered this message to the students of Oberlin College challenging them to work passionately for peace and racial justice. Stay awake, he urges them, during this time of revolution and change.

REV. DR. MARTIN LUTHER KING, JR
Oberlin College
June 1965

Now to the members of the graduating class: today you bid farewell to the safe security of the academic environment. You prepare to continue your journey on the clamorous highways of life. And I would like to have you think with me on this significant occasion on the subject, "Remaining Awake Through a Great Revolution.

I'm sure that you have read that arresting little story from the pen of Washington Irving entitled "Rip Van Winkle." The thing that we usually remember about this story is that Rip Van Winkle slept twenty years. But there is another point in that story that is almost always completely overlooked: it was a sign on the inn in the little town on the Hudson from which Rip went up into the mountain for his long sleep. When he went up, the sign had a picture of King George III of England. When he came down, years later, the sign had a picture of George Washington, the first president of the United States. When Rip looked up at the picture of George Washington, he was completely lost; he knew not who he was. This reveals to us that the most striking fact about the story of Rip Van Winkle is not that he slept twenty years, but that he slept through a revolution. While he was peacefully snoring up on the mountain, a great revolution was taking place in the world—indeed, a revolution which would, at points, change the course of history. And Rip Van Winkle knew nothing about it; he was asleep.

There are all too many people who, in some great period of social change, fail to achieve the new mental outlooks that the new situation demands. There is nothing more tragic than to sleep through a revolution. There can be no gainsaying of the fact that a great revolution is taking place in our world today. It is a social revolution, sweeping away the old order of colonialism. And in our own nation it is sweeping away the old order of slavery and racial segregation. The wind of change is blowing, and we see in our day and our age a significant development. Victor Hugo said on one occasion that there is nothing more powerful in all the world than an idea whose time has come. In a real sense, the idea whose time has come today is the idea of freedom and human dignity. Wherever men are assembled today, the cry is always the same, "We want to be free." And so we see in our own world a revolution of rising expectations. The great challenge facing every individual graduating today is to remain awake through this social revolution.

Victor Hugo said on one occasion that there is nothing more powerful in all the world than an idea whose time has come. In a real sense, the idea whose time has come today is the idea of freedom and human dignity. Wherever men are assembled today, the cry is always the same, "We want to be free."

I'd like to suggest some of the things that we must do in order to remain awake and to achieve the proper mental attitudes and responses that the new situation demands. First, I'd like to say that we are challenged to achieve a world perspective. Anyone who feels that we can live in isolation today, anyone who feels that we can live without being concerned about other individuals and other nations is sleeping through a revolution. The world in which we live is geographically one. The great challenge now is to make it one in terms of brotherhood.

Now it is true that the geographic togetherness of our world has been brought into being, to a large extent, through modern man's scientific ingenuity. Modern man, through his scientific genius, has been able to dwarf distance and place time in chains. Yes, we've been able to carve highways through the stratosphere, and our jet planes have compressed into minutes distances that once took weeks and months. And so this is a small world from a geographical point of view. What we are facing today is the fact that through our scientific and technological genius we've made of this world a neighborhood. And now through our moral and ethical commitment we must make of it a brotherhood. We must all learn to live together as brothers—or we will all perish together as fools. This is the great issue facing us today. No individual can live alone; no nation can live alone. We are tied together.

> **We must all learn to live together as brothers or we will all perish together as fools. This is the great issue facing us today. No individual can live alone; no nation can live alone. We are tied together.**

. . . All mankind is tied together; all life is interrelated, and we are all caught in an inescapable network of mutuality, tied in a single garment of destiny. Whatever affects one directly, affects all indirectly. For some strange reason, I can never be what I ought to be until you are what you ought to be. And you can never be what you ought to be until I am what I ought to be—this is the interrelated structure of reality. John Donne caught it years ago and placed it in graphic terms: "No man is an Island, entire of itself; every man is a piece of the continent, a part of the main." And then he goes on toward the end to say: "Any man's death diminishes me, because I am involved in mankind; and therefore never send to know for whom the bell tolls; it tolls for thee." And by believing this, by living out this fact, we will be able to remain awake through a great revolution.

I would like to mention, secondly, that we are challenged to work passionately and unrelentingly to get rid of racial injustice in all its dimensions. Anyone who feels that our nation can survive half segregated and half integrated is sleeping through a revolution. The challenge before us today is to develop a coalition of conscience and get rid of this problem that has been one of the nagging and agonizing ills of our nation over the years. Racial injustice is still the Negro's burden and America's shame. We've made strides, to be sure. We have come a long, long way since the Negro was first brought to this nation as a slave in 1619. In the last decade we have seen significant developments—the Supreme Court's decision outlawing segregation in the public schools, a comprehensive Civil Rights Bill in 1964, and, in a few weeks, a new voting bill to guarantee the right to vote. All of these are significant developments, but I would be dishonest with you this morning if I gave you the impression that we have come to the point where the problem is almost solved.

We must face the honest fact that we still have a long, long way to go before the problem of racial injustice is solved. For while we are quite successful in breaking down the legal barriers to segregation, the Negro is now confronting social and economic barriers which are very real. The Negro is still at the bottom of the economic ladder. He finds himself perishing on a lonely island of poverty in the midst of a vast ocean of material prosperity. Millions of Negroes are still housed in unendurable slums; millions of

Negroes are still forced to attend totally inadequate and substandard schools. And we still see, in certain sections of our country, violence and man's inhumanity to man in the most tragic way. All of these things remind us that we have a long, long way to go. For in Alabama and Mississippi, violence and murder where civil rights workers are concerned, are popular and favorite pastimes.

. . . We must work for peace, for racial justice, for economic justice, and for brotherhood the world over. We have inherited a big house, a great world house in which we have to live together—black and white, Easterners and Westerners, Gentiles and Jews, Protestants and Catholics, Moslem and Hindu. If we all learn to do this we, in a real sense, will remain awake through a great revolution.

I urge you to continue the tradition that you have followed so long, for this institution has probably done more than any other to support the struggle for racial justice. You have given your time, you have given your earnings, you have given your bodies, you have participated in demonstrations, you have participated in the determined struggle to keep this issue in the forefront of the conscience of the nation. I urge you to continue to do so as you go out into your various fields of endeavor. Never allow it to be said that you are silent onlookers, detached spectators, but that you are involved participants in the struggle to make justice a reality.

We sing a little song in our struggle - you've heard it—*We Shall Overcome*. And by that we do not mean that we shall overcome the white man. In the struggle for racial justice the Negro must not seek to rise from a position of disadvantage to one of advantage, to substitute one tyranny for another. A doctrine of black supremacy is as dangerous as a doctrine of white supremacy. God is not interested in the freedom of black men or brown men or yellow men. God is interested in the freedom of the whole human race, the creation of a society where every man will respect the dignity and worth of personality. So when we sing *We Shall Overcome*, we are singing a hymn of faith, a hymn of optimism, a hymn of faith in the future.

. . . Let us stand up. Let us be a concerned generation. Let us remain awake through a great revolution. And we will speed up that great day when the American Dream will be a reality. We, in the final analysis, can gain consolation from the fact that at least we've made strides in our struggle for peace and in our struggle for justice.

> **God is not interested in the freedom of black men or brown men or yellow men. God is interested in the freedom of the whole human race, the creation of a society where every man will respect the dignity and worth of personality.**

We still have a long, long way to go, but at least we've made a creative beginning.

And so I close by quoting the words of an old Negro slave preacher who didn't quite have his grammar right, but uttered words of great and profound significance:

Lord, we ain't what we oughta be;

We ain't what we wanna be;

We ain't what we're gonna be;

But thank God we ain't what we was!

THE ROOT OF CIVIC DUTY

Charles W. Colson, a widely recognized Christian leader, speaker, advocate of prison reform, and writer today, once referred to himself as "incapable of humanitarian thought." Known as the White House "hatchet man" for President Nixon, Colson turned to the forgiveness of Jesus Christ before serving seven months in prison. Here he speaks of the motivation of gratitude for the duty of a Christian to serve their world.

CHARLES COLSON
Biola University
May 1996

What a joy it is to be here with you this morning; and I must tell you I've only been on the campus for a few hours, but I've been made to feel so very much at home. That's probably not unusual because I've spent much of my life in institutions. Not quite like this, although these students may think there are some similarities.

I congratulate all of you, you students particularly, in having completed the rigorous course of education which you receive here at this great institution. Congratulations to the family as well because this is a day of re-celebration when the financial hemorrhage is over. I know about such things having had three children who went through school, one of whom was able to cram four years of education into five. I'm sympathetic with your celebration today....

You know this is a heady business when you come to these commencements.... It's always a heady time when you put on these robes which haven't been redesigned since the Middle Ages—they're like this because the professors used to put bologna and bread in their sleeves so that they could eat during their six-hour lectures. I have a little bread stuck up in here today....

This is a big occasion, all of these impressive robes and all of this regalia going on. What keeps me humble and what keeps me in perspective is the realization that.... I cannot remember what a single speaker said nor can I even remember who the speaker was [at my own commencements]....

I want to leave you with a four-letter word which I would like to plant in your mind today and have you think about maybe twenty, thirty, forty years down. That four-letter word is duty. Duty is the root of the virtuous and the holy life. Our fathers understood in this country that civic duty was the first of the republican virtues upon which this country was based ... Tocqueville ... when he came to America wrote many things about churches ... and

American democracy, but the thing that struck him most he said was that there weren't ten men in all of France who did what Americans did every day as a matter of course—they helped their neighbors. They had a sense of duty and responsibility to their communities. I believe it is the missing ingredient today in what seems to be the separation between what we know to be right as Christians and what we do as we live our Christian life.

> **. . . there weren't ten men in all of France who did what Americans did every day as a matter of course—they helped their neighbors. They had a sense of duty and responsibility to their communities. I believe it is the missing ingredient today.**

Every summer in August, I set aside a day to often reflect on what God has done in my life. I do it around August 12th because that was the day in 1973 [amidst] a flood of tears in a friend's driveway on a hot summer night outside of Austin that I surrendered my life to Jesus Christ, and my life was transformed. And so I do what Joshua did when he crossed the Jordan and that is he built stones of remembrance so that people coming along after would say, "What are those stones for?" and he would say, "It's to remember what God has done in my life."

And so every year I set aside a little bit of time to remember what God has done in my life. It's a wonderful experience—I recommend it. I build my own stones of remembrance. I look at them and think of the amazing things, now twenty-three years [later], God has done in my life, absolutely extraordinary things. Prison Fellowship in seventy-five countries around the world and 50,000 volunteers and 465,000 kids who got Angel Tree gifts last year . . . [and the] extraordinary movement of God's grace moving into the prisons. . . .

But I have to tell you that the most significant thing that I think about when I look back on what God has done and look at those stones of remembrance . . . is the realization, the historical thought, that Jesus Christ, the son of God, died on a cross, the most hideous death a person could die, to take upon Himself my sins that I could be forgiven. The atonement, his substitutionary death upon the cross in my place, his blood availed for me, forgiving me for what's inside.

Not Watergate . . . not the sins of Watergate. That's child's play compared to what I know was in here, the anger, the covetousness, the bitterness, the pride, far worse than those things I was charged with in Watergate. I reached a point in my life where I realized I could not *live* with myself if I did not know for a fact historically that Jesus went on that cross that I might be forgiven. Camus, the great existentialist philosopher, once said that the only philosophical question in life, there being no God, is suicide. That's true. If it weren't for the Gospel, we would have no way to live with the stench of sin that is inside of every single one of us.

Man only has three choices which I read about, writing my new novel. . . . You can come face to face with the truth and you can accept it, or you can come face to face with the truth and you can reject it, or you can try to juggle the ambiguities of life and you can go mad or end up as one of my characters in my book does, simply killing your conscience or if you can't do that, killing yourself.

What is the response to God's grace? Karl Barth said there is only one possible response to God's grace and it is gratitude—what G.K. Chesterton called "the mother of all virtues." I am overwhelmed with gratitude to God for what He has done in my life and that inspires I me a sense of duty to serve my Lord.

Last night when I met two people dying of AIDS whom I had known in years past in prison. . . . I embraced them in my arms and told them how much I loved them. . . . In prisons with rotten holes, like Ecuador where I was last fall . . . men with arms chopped off, with their eyes gouged out and sores all over their faces, and I found myself bringing them in and embracing them. Why? Not because I like to do that, not because in my flesh I can do that but out of gratitude to God for what He has done in my life, sending His Son to die on the cross that I might be forgiven. That grace invokes in me a sense of gratitude which translates into a sense of duty. . . .

Gratitude is the root of civic duty. I served in the Marines as an infantry captain at the tail end of the Korean War, and I did it out of great loyalty because it was my duty to serve my country. When Richard Nixon asked me to come to the White House, I was in a six-figure income in a law practice and very successful, and I didn't really want to go but I knew it was my duty to go. I know it's my duty as a citizen because Augustine said the Christian is the best citizen of all because he does out of the love of God what others do only because they are required to do it. But if that's a sense of duty, just think how much greater is the sense of duty to Him who paid it all and "all to Him I owe," as the hymn writer put it.

I reached a point in my life where I realized I could not live with myself if I did not know for a fact historically that Jesus went on that cross that I might be forgiven.

Now we serve God and we love God and we obey Him and we defend the truth and we defend His truth in this world and we do acceptable works of service because it is the *only* possible way we can demonstrate our gratitude to God. It's not particularly noble, it's simple duty.

Just as Paul stood before the Sanhedrin near the end of his life and could simply say, "I've done my duty." . . .

My whole attitude about Christian service has changed. It's not noble, it's not heroic. I hear people say, "Oh, what a wonderful man of God, oh, the great things Chuck Colson has done," and I absolutely shrink away because I'm simply a person *doing my duty.*

And each one of you when you graduate from here and you go to live your Christian life, do your duty. First, as citizens because Romans 13 commands it. And then as Christians in obedience to Christ, defending His truth in the world. Out of gratitude for what He has done in your life. Not puffed up, not heavy and arrogant and haughty because you have a great education and a good mind. Always remember those words, the words that are seared in my consciousness that I love so much that we should all remember as Christians because they go to the sense of who we are and how we behave in the world. "Have this mind among yourselves, which is yours in Christ Jesus, who, though he was in the form of God, did not count equality with God a thing to be grasped, but made himself nothing, taking the form of a servant, being born in the likeness of men. And being found in human form, he humbled himself by becoming obedient to the point of death, even death on a cross" (Phil. 2:5-8).

> **Now we serve God and we love God and we obey Him and we defend the truth and we defend His truth in this world and we do acceptable works of service because it is the only possible way we can demonstrate our gratitude to God.**

We are to have that mind in us. Now do your duty. D-U-T-Y, that four-letter word. Strange to many students on the Princeton campus at the time when President Jimmy Carter wanted to reinstate registration for the draft. . . . There was a great protest and a student had a sign up . . . which said, "Nothing is worth dying for." Can you imagine hanging that sign under the cross at Calvary? Nothing is worth dying for? Nothing is worth living for. . . .

Liberty is not what our modern society says—it isn't the right to do what you want to do. Liberty is the right to do what you ought to do. And what you ought to do is to do your duty as citizens and as Christians. It's not understood by this generation. . . . You do it even "unto your own hurt" as Psalm 15 says. A man of honor and a woman of honor is someone who does what he says he is going to do even to his own hurt. Duty is doing what you're called to do, what is right to do, what is out of gratitude to your country, and to your society and to your God. Duty is doing it even when it hurts. . . .

If there's a prayer you pray, pray that God will give you the courage to do your duty. It's central to the Christian life. "All to Him I owe" is the consecrated life. It is the reason I do what I do, it is the reason that you will do what you. Gratitude inspires in you that sense of duty. It's the only way you can do good with your life. . . . It's the only reason to live a virtuous life. . . .

Sure, I knew what was right in the White House. [But] I didn't have within me a sense of duty to God to do what is right. Nothing can overpower that rebellious human will other than a sense of gratitude to God for what He has done in our life. . . .

Liberty is the right to do what you ought to do.

You have a tremendous obligation as educated, thinking Christians to develop a Christian worldview, to be able to defend truth out of gratitude to God for what He has done for you in your life. . . . That's your challenge. A simple four-letter word. Duty. Do your duty. Fear God and keep His commandments. Think Christianly. Use the good mind that God has given you . . . to defend Christian truths in the world. . . . Care for the poor and the sick and the needy and the suffering and the hungry and the imprisoned. . . . Cultivate virtue. . . . Love one another, honor the righteous, spread the good news.

If you do your duty out of gratitude to God for what He has done in your life, you'll be a better person for it, liberty in our land will be strengthened, and the kingdom of God will be glorified.

GOD BLESS YOU AND CONGRATULATIONS.

A LIFE OF SERVICE

President George W. Bush challenges graduates at Ohio State University to consider their path: will they become a selfish generation or a generation of service? In the fresh remembrance of September 11ᵗʰ, 2001, President Bush urges them not to forget the courageous heroes of 9-11 and the patriotism we all must demonstrate through service and love for our country.

GEORGE W. BUSH
Ohio State University
June 14, 2002

Members of the mighty class of 2002. Congratulations. You have earned a degree at a great American institution, and you have every right to be proud. I want to congratulate your parents. Many of you have written your last tuition check. That must be nice—I'm still writing them. You've given so much encouragement and support to your children, and their gratitude will only increase over the years . . .

I am now the only person standing between you and your diploma. The tradition of commencement addresses is to be brief—and forgotten. I assure you that this speech will be shorter than it seems.

Your senior year was special in your life—and the months since last September have been extraordinary in our country's history. On a Tuesday morning, America went from a feeling of security to one of vulnerability, from peace to war, from a time of calm to a great and noble cause. We are called to defend liberty against tyranny and terror. We've answered that call. We will bring security to our people and justice to our enemies.

In the last nine months, we've seen the true character of our country. We learned of firefighters who wrote their Social Security numbers on their arms with felt tip pens—to mark and identify their bodies—and then rushed into burning buildings. We learned of the desperate courage of passengers on Flight 93—average citizens who led the first counter-attack in the war on terror. We watched the searchers, month after month, fulfill their grim duty—and New Yorkers line the streets to cheer them on their way to work each morning. And in these events we relearned something large and important: the achievements that last and count in life come through sacrifice and compassion and service.

Some believe this lesson in service is fading as distance grows from the shock of September the 11th, that the good we have witnessed is shallow and temporary.

Your generation will respond to these skeptics—one way or another. You will determine whether our new ethic of responsibility is the break of a wave or the rise of a tide. You will determine whether we become a culture of selfishness and look inward—or whether we will embrace a culture of service and look outward. Because this decision is in your hands, I'm confident of the outcome. Your class and your generation understand the need for personal responsibility—so you will make a culture of service a permanent part of American life.

After all, nearly 70 percent of your class volunteers in some form—from Habitat for Humanity to Big Brothers and Big Sisters, to OhioReads. Ohio State has been a leading source of Peace Corps volunteers since 1961. I honor the twenty-nine ROTC members in today's graduating class for their spirit of service and idealism.

> **. . . service is important to your neighbors; service is important to your character; and service is important to your country.**

I hope each of you—I hope each of you will help build this culture of service, for three important reasons: service is important to your neighbors; service is important to your character; and service is important to your country.

First, your idealism is needed in America. In the shadow of our nation's prosperity, too many children grow up without love and guidance, too many women are abandoned and abused, too many men are addicted and illiterate, and too many elderly Americans live in loneliness.

These Americans are not strangers, they are fellow citizens; not problems, but priorities. They are as much a part of the American community as you and I, and they deserve better from this country.

Government has essential responsibilities: fighting wars and fighting crime; protecting the homeland and enforcing civil rights laws; educating the young and providing for the old; giving people tools to improve their own lives; helping the disabled and those in need.

But you have responsibilities, as well. Some government needs—some needs, government cannot fulfill: the need for kindness, and for understanding, and for love. A person in crisis often needs more than a program or a check; he needs a friend—and that friend can be you. We are commanded by God and called by our conscience to love others as we want to be loved ourselves. Let us answer that call with every day we are given.

Second, service is important in your own life, in your own character. No one can tell you how to live or what cause to serve. But everyone needs some cause larger than his or her own profit. Apathy has no adventures. Cynicism leaves no monuments. And a person who is not responsible for others is a person who is truly alone.

Apathy has no adventures. Cynicism leaves no monuments.

By sharing the pain of a friend, or bearing the hopes of a child, or defending the liberty of your fellow citizens, you will gain satisfaction that cannot be gained in any other way. Service is not a chain or a chore—it gives direction to your gifts, and purpose to your freedom.

Lyndsey Holben is an OSU sophomore majoring in business. When she was in high school, Lyndsey had a friend and a classmate who died from an illness—and Lyndsey decided she wanted to work with children who suffer from life-threatening diseases. Today, Lyndsey is a leader among volunteers for the Make-A-Wish Foundation. Here's what she had to say: "It's hard enough to put a smile on someone's face, but especially someone who is hurting. Even if that's all you can do, that is something—and there is no better feeling in the world." Lyndsey and others here today have learned that every life of service is a life of significance.

Third, we serve others because we're Americans, and we want to do something for the country we love. Our nation is the greatest force for good in history—and we show our gratitude by doing our duty.

Patriotism is expressed by flying the flag, but it is more. Patriotism means we share a single country. In all our diversity, each of us has a bond with every other American. Patriotism is proven in our concern for others—a willingness to sacrifice for people we may never have met or seen. Patriotism is our obligation to those who have gone before us, to those who will follow us, and to those who have died for us.

In March of this year, Army Ranger Marc Anderson died in Afghanistan, trying to rescue a Navy SEAL. Marc and five others gave their lives in fulfilling the Ranger creed: "I will never leave a fallen comrade to fall into the hands of the enemy."

Marc, from Westerville, Ohio, was a remarkable man. Instead of pursuing a career that might have made him wealthy, Marc decided to be a math teacher in a high school in a tough neighborhood. He was a mentor, a tutor, and the best teacher many students ever had.

After September the 11th, Marc joined the fight against terrorism. "I'm trained and I'm ready," he wrote to his friends. Before Marc left for Afghanistan, he arranged for part of his life insurance to pay for one of his former students to attend college. Today, that student—Jennifer Massing—plans to go to the University of Florida to study architecture.

Marc Anderson considered this country great enough to die for. Surely it is great enough to live for. And we live for America by serving others. And as we serve others, this challenge can only be answered in individual hearts. Service in America is not a matter of coercion; it is a matter of conscience. So today I'm making an appeal to your conscience, for the sake of our country.

America needs more than taxpayers, spectators, and occasional voters. America needs full-time citizens. America needs men and women who respond to the call of duty, who stand up for the weak, who speak up for their beliefs, who sacrifice for a greater good. America needs your energy, and your leadership, and your ambition. And through the gathering momentum of millions of acts of kindness and decency, we will change America one soul at a time—and we will build a culture of service.

A life of service isn't always easy. It involves sacrifices, and I understand many other things will lay claim to your time and to your attention. In serving, however, you will give help and hope to others. You will—your own life will gain greater purpose and deeper meaning. You will show your love and allegiance to the United States, which remains what it has always been: the citadel of freedom, a land of mercy, the last, best hope of man on Earth.

And so to the graduates of Ohio State University: Congratulations on your achievement. I want to thank you for this honorary degree. I leave here a proud member of the class of 2002. I leave here confident that you will serve our country, and a cause greater than self. May God bless you your families, and may God bless America.

> **America needs men and women who respond to the call of duty, who stand up for the weak, who speak up for their beliefs, who sacrifice for a greater good.**

FIND YOUR PASSION,

Follow Your Dreams

*"Call to Me, and I will answer you, and show you great
and mighty things, which you do not know."*

JEREMIAH 33:3 NKJV

INSIGHTS *for* LIVING

I HAVE SEEN THE GOD-GIVEN TASKS WITH WHICH
THE SONS OF MEN ARE TO BE OCCUPIED.
HE HAS MADE EVERYTHING BEAUTIFUL IN ITS TIME.
ALSO HE HAS PUT ETERNITY IN THEIR HEARTS . . .
ENJOY THE GOOD OF ALL [YOUR] LABOR—IT IS THE GIFT OF GOD.

—ECCLESIASTES 3:10-13 NKJV

We are face to face with our destiny, and we must meet it with a high and resolute courage. For ours is the life of action, of strenuous performance of duty. Let us live in the harness, striving mightily. Let us run the risk of wearing out, rather than rusting out.

—THEODORE ROOSEVELT

TO ACCOMPLISH GREAT THINGS, WE MUST DREAM AS WELL AS ACT.

—ANATOLE FRANCE

I remember my son when he was five, explaining to his kindergarten class what his father did for a living. "My Daddy," he said, "pretends to be people." There have been quite a few of them. Prophets from the Old and New Testaments, a couple of Christian saints, generals of various nationalities and different centuries, several kings, three American presidents, a French cardinal and two geniuses, including Michelangelo. If you want the ceiling re-painted I'll do my best.

—CHARLETON HESTON

All people dream, but not equally. Those who dream by night in the dusty recesses of their mind, wake in the morning to find that it was vanity. But the dreamers of the day are dangerous people, for they dream their dreams with open eyes and make them come true.

—T.E. LAWRENCE

TRUST YOUR INSTINCTS

George Herbert Walker Bush was himself a man of dreams. On his eighteenth birthday, he enlisted in the Navy, later proving to be the youngest pilot in the Navy when he received his wings. A Yale University graduate, he quickly excelled in the oil industry, public service, and politics. When he became President in 1988, he pledged in "a moment rich with promise" to use American strength as "a force for good." In his address to the graduates of Alcorn State University, he assures them that they must trust their instincts by following their dreams.

GEORGE BUSH, SR.
Alcorn State University
May 13, 1989

Today every senior here is an educated man or woman, proud, self-assured. With all the cockiness of youth, some of you—I hope most of you—must be feeling like anything is possible today. Well, trust those instincts. Everyone has a dream. Everyone has something to give. . . .

And, yes, there is enough magic out there, enough for all Americans. And, yes, you can seize the magic with the power of your own hands and with the skills bequeathed to you by this special university. And, yes, just as Alcorn's 1988 yearbook was dedicated to Dr. King, you can honor his memory by doing what he taught this nation to do: to have a dream and to work every day to make that dream come true.

America is proud of you and of your families that you represent. God bless you in the challenge to come, and God bless the United States of America. I am honored to be your guest today. Thank you.

INSIGHTS *for* LIVING

THE VICTORY OF SUCCESS IS HALF WON WHEN ONE GAINS
THE HABIT OF SETTING GOALS AND ACHIEVING THEM.
EVEN THE MOST TEDIOUS CHORE WILL BECOME ENDURABLE
AS YOU PARADE THROUGH EACH DAY CONVINCED THAT EVERY
TASK, NO MATTER HOW MENIAL OR BORING,
BRINGS YOU CLOSER TO FULFILLING YOUR DREAMS.

—OG MANDINO

*I used to tell my children . . . if you don't take a risk, you're probably not
doing anything of value. If you don't feel a little fear, or at least some
nervousness, if you're constantly comfortable, then how creative are you
being? How are you challenging yourself? What good are you doing? Don't
stay in your comfort zone. Step out to the edge or beyond and push yourself
further than you think you can go. . . . You will give more richly if you give of
all your talents to the larger world.*

—DAVID SHIPLER

UNTIL PEOPLE SEE THE BIBLE AS A PRACTICAL GUIDEBOOK
FOR THEIR EVERYDAY EXISTENCE, IT WILL PROBABLY CONTINUE
TO REMAIN ON THE SHELF.

—GEORGE BARNA

DESTINY WAITS IN THE HAND OF GOD,
NOT IN THE HANDS OF STATESMEN.

—T. S. ELIOT

"FLY, EAGLE, FLY!"

Desmond Tutu, a South African1985 Nobel Peace Prize Laureate, delivers his uplifting message, "Fly, Eagle, Fly!" to American students. In the midst of evil, Tutu says, we must acknowledge our "infinite worth" to God as His created beings and therefore "rise toward the compassionate and the gentle and the caring." We must not be mere chickens but soaring eagles of confidence and beauty. Tutu's latest book is God Has A Dream: A Vision Of Hope For Our Time *(Doubleday, March 2004).*

ARCHBISHOP DESMOND TUTU
Brandeis University
May 21, 2000
Copyright Desmond Tutu, used with permission.

Mr. President, chairperson of the Board of Trustees, graduates, friends, ladies and gentlemen: What a glorious, glorious occasion today is turning out to be. What a great joy to be here with all of you celebrating the outstanding achievements of those who are graduating on this occasion. . . .

Sometimes when one is introduced to gatherings such as these they will sometimes say, "Oh he doesn't need to be introduced. Everybody knows him." Well, I'm not quite sure after what happened to me when I was with my wife in Atlanta a few years ago at the Olympic Games. We were traveling on the subway and somebody, I think, thought they recognized me and came up and said, "Can I have your autograph? "And so, one or two people came along, and I was signing autographs. And then a woman came up, and she pushed a piece of paper, and as I was signing she turned to people and said, "Who is it? Who is it? Who is it?" which I thought was very good for her soul.

But I want, first of all, to say what is quite right and fitting at this moment. Heartiest congratulations to all of you who are graduating. It is a splendid, splendid achievement, and I know that you are going to keep getting applause. But I'd like to suggest to this great gathering that we ought to give them at this point a very, very special—a real humdinger—of an applause. Let's just give them a wonderful [applause]. . . . Thank you. It is very, very richly deserved, and I have no doubt at all that all of you are going to make a very significant contribution to the world out there.

Who are the people we look up to most? Who are the people we most admire? It is not aggressive, the macho, the belligerent, the intransigent ones as you might have expected. No, no, no, no, no, no, it isn't. It is that we revere a Mother Theresa. She's anything but macho. And why? Because she's good. She's someone who's spent herself prodigally on behalf of others. And we, each one of us, have inside us a [potential] that hems in on goodness. We hold in the highest possible regard, not the ones who are the powerful militarily, no, no, no.

Who is the most admired statesperson in the world today? And I would venture to say and know that there are very few who would dare say me. That it is a Nelson Mendela who was president, not of one of the most powerful militarily or the most successful economically. No. It is this man who amazed the world when he emerged from prison after twenty-seven years of incarceration. When people had thought he would be spewing bitterness and anger and seeking retribution and revenge, he amazes the world by his readiness to forgive, to speak about reconciliation. And today he stands as a colossus in the world; he is an icon of reconciliation of goodness. And you and I testify to the fact that we recognize goodness when we see it. For, you see, we are in fact made for goodness.

We are created by God. You and I are created by God, not by some junior, subordinate God. We are created by the Transcendent One, the One who is able to speak and things happen. Let there be light, and light happens. That is the God who creates us. And we are created like God. That each one of us, however we may be in our circumstances material and otherwise, whether we are tall or short, whether we are substantial or we have, whether we are beautiful or not so beautiful, whether we are rich or poor.

How incredible that each one of us because we are created in the image of God are creatures of incredible worth, infinite worth. Each one of us is a stand-in for God. And so, to treat one such as if they were less than this is not just easy. It's a blasphemy. It is as if we were speaking in the face of God. If we are created by God, we are created like God, and then we are created for God. We are this extraordinary paradox really. The finite created for the infinite, but we are created for the transcendent.

> . . . we are family and all belong, all belong—rich, poor, black, white, red, green, . . . all, all belong. All belong, and God says this is my dream. . . .

We are created for the beautiful, for the truth, for the good. And we know it. For there are those moments when we try to find satisfaction in anything less than God, and it ends up being like ashes in our mouth. It ends up and fills us with a terrible, terrible dissatisfaction of people [who] could say, "God, thou hast created us for thyself, and our hearts are restless until they find their rest in Thee. We are created for God, and anything less than God would never, never satisfy us." And so, we are aware that this is a moral universe, that good and evil matter, that right and wrong matter, that life and truth matter. And, that, yes, there are frequently many, many times when we think that evil is on the rampage, that evil seems to be going to have the last word. It doesn't; it doesn't. Isn't that exhilarating? It isn't Hitler who has won; it is those he tried to destroy. They have survived; they have survived and have left the world an incredible, incredible legacy.

It isn't Stalin who has won. Communism, fascism, Nazism have bitten the dust, have bitten the dust ignominiously. It isn't slavery that has won; slavery has been done away with, and people are entering into what has been called the glorious liberty of the children of God. It isn't Apartheid that's won. No, no, no. It may be, it takes a long time for goodness to be vindicated, but goodness in the end is vindicated. For God has created this world for laughter and joy and caring and compassion. . . .

God wants us to shake ourselves, spread our pinions, and then lift off and soar and rise, and rise toward the confident and the good and the beautiful. Rise towards the compassionate and the gentle and the caring.

But friends, courses like Martin Luther King, Jr., I, God, have a dream too. I have a dream that my children one day will recognize that they are members of a family. Really, truly, that they are sisters and brothers one of another, that they belong together in a family where there are no outsiders. All are insiders, that they are family. They are family in which the ethical family obtains, and where the ethical family obtains you don't say, "Hey, granny, granny, your contribution to the family budget is, you know. And baby, yours is nil; and you're going to get from the family in proportion to what you put in." No family, no good family, no healthy family says that.

The true family says from each according to their ability, to each according to their need. . . . If we are family, how can we, how can we have problems about a budget surplus? Ha, ha. A budget surplus—God gives us a budget surplus and says, "You've got sisters and brothers over there who are hungry."

I have given you these resources so that you can be my hands and my feet, so that you can feed your sisters and brothers over there. You can't be arguing about this; this is not for your sake. It is for your sisters and brothers over there. It is that we are family and all belong, all belong—rich, poor, black, white, red, green, . . . all, all belong. All belong, and God says this is my dream, this is my dream.

You know the story of the farmer who in his back yard had [a] chicken, and then he had a chicken that was a little odd looking, but he was a chicken. It behaved like a chicken. It was pecking away like other chickens. It didn't know that there was a blue sky overhead and a glorious sunshine until someone who was knowledgeable in these things came along and said to the farmer, "Hey, that's no chicken. That's an eagle."

God says to all of us, "You are no chicken; you are an eagle.

Then the farmer said, "Um, um, no, no, no, no man. That's a chicken; it behaves like a chicken."

"And the man said, "No; give it to me please." And he gave it to this knowledgeable man. And this man took this strange looking chicken and climbed the mountain and waited until sunrise. And then he turned this strange looking chicken towards the sun and said, "Eagle, fly, eagle." And the strange looking chicken shook itself, spread out its pinions, and lifted off and soared and soared and soared and flew away, away into the distance.

And God says to all of us, "You are no chicken; you are an eagle. Fly, eagle, fly." And God wants us to shake ourselves, spread our pinions, and then lift off and soar and rise, and rise toward the confident and the good and the beautiful. Rise towards the compassionate and the gentle and the caring. Rise to become what God intends us to be —eagles, not chickens.

INSIGHTS *for* LIVING

[GRADUATES] ARE LIVING IN ANY TENSE BUT THE PRESENT
TENSE; THEY'RE REALLY NOT THERE. IT'S LIKE THEY'RE IN AN
AIRPORT, BETWEEN FLIGHTS. THEY HAVE A FLIGHT TO CATCH
AND THE FLIGHT IS THEIR LIFE.

—PETER SMITH

The Bible has shown me that with all my effort, all my
discipline, I will never be able to make myself perfect.
If I want to know God and be a part of his kingdom, then
God himself is going to have to remake me. . . . I'm always
trying to give 100 percent to God—anything less would be
unacceptable as far as [I am] . . . concerned. He went in
and gave 100 percent of himself for us—he died for us!

—DAVE JOHNSON, U.S. DECATHLON BRONZE MEDAL WINNER

THE DESTINY OF EVERY HUMAN BEING DEPENDS
ON HIS RELATIONSHIP TO JESUS CHRIST. IT IS NOT
ON HIS RELATIONSHIP TO LIFE, OR ON HIS SERVICE OR HIS
USEFULNESS, BUT SIMPLY AND SOLELY ON HIS RELATIONSHIP
TO JESUS CHRIST.

—OSWALD CHAMBERS

There are no disappointments to those whose wills
are buried in the will of God.

—FREDERICK WILLIAM FABER

INVEST YOUR LIFE IN PEOPLE

One of the most admired men in America, William Franklin Graham, Jr., decided to devote his life to Christ in 1934 when he was sixteen. International fame came in 1949 when Rev. Graham's crusades in Los Angeles attracted overflow crowds. Through television, videos, best-selling books, and an intensive travel schedule, Rev. Billy Graham and his organization have touched every corner of the world for the gospel of Jesus Christ. Here he encourages graduates to make use of the investment God has given them—time. "You can't count your days," he tells them, "but with Jesus Christ as your Savior and Lord, you can make your days count."

Billy Graham
Wheaton College
May 9, 1993
"Address to Graduating Class at Wheaton College" by Billy Graham, May 9, 1993,
© *1993 Billy Graham, used by permission, all rights reserved*

Unless things have changed since I was here as a student, you haven't managed to save a great deal of money while you were here. There aren't many wealthy graduating seniors. But you do possess something of great value, a non-renewable resource that is moving inevitably toward total depletion—and there is nothing you can do to stop it. That resource is *time*.

In a few minutes, you'll walk out the door of Edman Chapel with a diploma in your hand and a life of uncertain length ahead of you. For some, it will be a long life; for others, it will be a surprisingly short life— and if you reach my age, you'll wonder where the time has gone, because it's so quick, it's just like that. And you're ready now for whatever God planned for you in eternity.

A student at a university asked me some time ago what was the greatest surprise of my life, and I said the greatest surprise of my life was the brevity of life. So let me urge you to consider some things as you decide how you will invest your life.

Time is our investment capital. A recent issue of *Time* magazine focused on the year 2000 and life beyond it. In that issue Lance Morrow wrote, "Time is all we have. It's the medium in which we swim." Your only choice is to use it or lose it. Either invest it or let it dribble away, like sand through your fingers.

Jesus told the story in Luke 19 of a nobleman, who before going on a journey, commanded his stewards to invest his money very carefully. The Lord expects us to use whatever He has given us—whether it's in money, time, or talents—in profitable ways. And He promises us His personal audit of our lives when He returns.

Time is an equal opportunity employer. Each human being has exactly the same number of minutes in every day—1400 minutes. It adds up to 168 hours per week. In Psalm 90:10, the Bible indicates our allotted time on earth may be seventy years. I passed that nearly five years ago.

The Psalmist therefore goes on to say, "Teach us to number our days aright that we may gain a heart of wisdom."

Let's think about the numbers in our lifetime. Our first fifteen years are in childhood and adolescence. We spend a total of twenty years sleeping. Maybe some of you don't—some of you sleep more than that. In our final years, physical limitations curtail our activities usually. So we may have only thirty years left, and part of that time must be spent eating meals, building family and social relationships, working at our jobs and figuring out our income tax!

Rich people cannot buy more hours than the rest of us. Scientists cannot invent new minutes. Each day you have 86,400 seconds to invest. Time allows no balances, no overdrafts. If you fail to use each day's deposit, your loss cannot be recovered. It's not like putting savings in a bank and getting interest. You cannot hoard time to spend on another day.

Paul tells the Ephesians to redeem the time because the days are evil. "Redeem" is a word from the business world, and it means to "buy" the time. Redeeming the time means making the most of every opportunity you have—every minute, every second. And when you leave here, don't finish studying. This is only the beginning of a life of study. And I would advise you to keep up in the discipline you've been working in. That's something I didn't do, and I remember one of my professors wrote me a letter and he said, "In your sermons that I watch, I don't see you use enough illustrations from anthropology!" Your professor may be watching you.

God calls us to invest our time capital in the very lives of people—not in projects, not in possessions.

Former President Nixon wrote a best selling book entitled *Seize the Moment.* But for the Christians, we must be sure it's God's moment—an opportunity He has provided. That's what Bishop Fulton Sheen called "the sanctification of the now moment." Our natural tendency is to count the days, but God tells us to make every day count.

Time is the capital we've been given by God to invest wisely, so the question is, where do we invest it? God calls us to invest our time capital in the very lives of people—not in projects, not in possessions. God invested His only begotten Son in us as sinners, not because we were prime prospects to give Him a good payout, but because His heart is overflowing with love for us.

People in our world are suffering greatly from the consequences of ignoring God. I've seen it all over the world. Sometimes it's open and glaring, like the hatred and civil war in former Yugoslavia today. I've preached in various places in Yugoslavia, and when I see the pictures on television of the slaughter that's going on there my heart is broken, because it seems to me that we may be on the verge of a Third World War. And I remember when the Japanese attacked Pearl Harbor, and Dr. Edman stood before us the next morning and tears were coming down his cheeks; and he said, "I had hoped we would not have this," because he had served in World War I, and he knew something about how terrible war was.

But sometimes our errors and terrors are more subtle—equally frightening, but in a different way. Physical beauty or brawn may conceal a bewildered mind or a battered spirit, even on a college campus like this. As you graduate today, I can hear some of you saying, "I wish I knew the Lord's will. I've prayed about it, struggled with it, but I do not know what God's will for me is in the future."

All of us occasionally grapple with discovering the will of God in specific matters that concern us. I do at my age and time of life in my ministry: shall we go to this city or that city, or shall we go in this direction with all the new technology that's coming?

At your age, I knew one thing: I had said to people, "There's one thing I don't ever want to be. I don't ever want to be an undertaker or a preacher." And I put them in the same category. But one night fifty-five years ago, I said with tears, "Oh God, I'll go where you want me to go and be what you want me to be." I never dreamed what He had planned out in the future.

> **But one night fifty-five years ago, I said with tears, "Oh God, I'll go where you want me to go and be what you want me to be." I never dreamed what He had planned out in the future.**

God's will first and foremost for all of us is that you love Him with all your heart, soul, mind, and strength. Then God's will for you is that you live a holy life, to become like His Son—in your attitudes and actions, in your thoughts and words, to be and behave like Jesus did—which means delighting in doing His will and serving our neighbors.

Jesus said, "I must work the works of Him

that sent Me while it is day. The night is coming when no man can work." What was the work of Jesus? Simply to do the will of His Father and finish the work that had been assigned to Him. He lived and died for others—for His friends and enemies alike.

Jesus told His disciples, "Lay up for yourselves treasures in heaven."

What are those treasures, those investments? They are people who need to know God, and I've seen them all over the world. I've seen them in every kind of situation, every kind of culture, and I know that the great thing they're searching for can only be met in a relationship with God. And they need us to demonstrate His love to them.

We need to be reminded of people everywhere who are unemployed, demoralized, despairing, and addicted to one habit or another. All these kinds of people are the stocks in which we are to invest our time. Time is the capital that God has given us to invest. People are our investment, whether they're blue chips, or penny stocks, or even junk bonds. Jesus was willing to take risks with twelve diverse disciples, and He took a great risk with us.

But when we talk of investments, everyone asks, "What return will we get?" A meaningful life that will count for God and fulfillment in our lives.

You look on the television today and see all those people. Most of them are searching for fulfillment in their lives. Last week I spoke at a dinner honoring Roy Rogers. There were about eight hundred there, including some of the old-time film stars. And some of them were still searching for something that Roy and Dale had already found in their relationship with God. Jesus said, "Give and it will be given to you." He was talking here not just about money, but about lives.

The other night I saw a film produced by the Salvation Army that showed young people walking down Hollywood Boulevard. These young people were asked questions about their lives. Each one seemed to be searching for purpose and satisfaction. People are so constituted that they need something to believe in that will be fulfilling.

I was at Harvard to speak at the John F. Kennedy School of Government,

God's will first and foremost for all of us is that you love Him with all your heart, soul, mind, and strength. Then God's will for you is that you live a holy life, to become like His Son—in your attitudes and actions, in your thoughts and words, to be and behave like Jesus did—which means delighting in doing His will and serving our neighbors.

and I was entertained by the president of the University. And as I was sitting in his office and we were talking, I said, "Sir, what is the greatest need that students on Harvard University campus have?" And he thought for a moment, and he said, "Fulfillment." He said, "They're searching for something, but they don't know what it is—to satisfy them, to bring fulfillment in their lives."

From my more than fifty years of experience, may I say to you young people today facing your careers and the uncertainties of life, the best of all investments you can make is to help people come to the Giver of Eternal Life and Peace, who is the Lord Jesus Christ.

> **At this commencement, this beginning of a new phase in your life, you can make that commitment to love God and your neighbors right here, right now. Don't wait until tomorrow.**

One of our daughters wanted to witness in her community and she started by taking pies to her neighbors. When she asked one neighbor, "Would you like to come to my home and start a prayer time, a Bible study together?" the neighbor began to cry and said, "I long to; I would love to." And so our shy little daughter invited that neighbor over and they started a small Bible study. That grew to 500 every week and went on for thirteen years, until today it has reached 2,500 every week in that city. It started because of taking those pies as a witness to her neighbor. A life of rich fulfillment is the dividend we receive for putting our trust in Christ, and putting our time into people.

At this commencement, this beginning of a new phase in your life, you can make that commitment to love God and your neighbors right here, right now. Don't wait until tomorrow. Half a century ago, Ruth and I graduated from Wheaton and we were married two months later. World War II was raging when we were students here, and we had almost daily reminders of the brevity of life. Many times in Pierce Chapel we prayed for the families of our classmates who were being called to military service.

At this very hour, we're wondering how many young American and Allied troops will be caught up in the Balkans, where the First World War began. And there are also many other dangerous frontiers in the world. One of our great leaders said the other day that the most dangerous frontier in the world today is the Korean border. It could be. But we also know that this war has moved to the sidewalks of our own cities and suburbs. Read the newspapers and watch the television news at night—it's filled with crime and fraud. It's even now in our schools and homes.

Your generation will bear the brunt of the future's uncertainties. Not one of us at any age has a clue as to how long we're going to live. That's why the Bible says, "Now is the accepted time. Today is the day of salvation." You can't count your days, but with Jesus Christ as your Savior and Lord, you can make your days count. You can invest whatever time is yours for a high yield return in the lives of people whom you introduce to Christ.

Right now you can decide to invest your life in such a way that some day you will hear God say, "Well done, good and faithful servant. Come and share in your Master's happiness."

PREPARE FOR OPPORTUNITY

Graduating from Stanford Law School and later serving as an Arizona assistant attorney general and on the Arizona Court of Appeals, Sandra Day O'Connor was nominated by President Ronald Reagan in 1981 to the Supreme Court. She was the Court's 102nd justice and its first female member. Here she speaks to law graduates about the importance of striving for excellence and the meaning of the individual.

Sandra Day O'Connor
Georgetown University
May 26, 1986

Today we note and celebrate the Class of 86's liberation from the rigors of academic life. Tomorrow the public will experience the impact of your presence as a member of the legal profession. . . .

I want to mention two things that I think are very important . . . to keep in mind. One relates to how you should go about performing the tasks you will soon undertake, and the other deals with the quality of your relationship with your community.

The first suggestion is to aim high but to be aware that even before you have reached your ultimate professional destination, if you strive for excellence, you can and should have a substantial impact on the world in which you live. . . . But if your career path is at all like mine, . . . you won't be starting at the top of the ladder.

As some of you may have read, the only job offer I received in the private sector on my graduation from law school was a job as a legal secretary. So I started my own private practice, sharing a small office with another lawyer in a shopping center in a small community in Arizona. Other people who had offices in the same shopping mall repaired TVs, cleaned clothes, or loaned money. It was not a high rent district. I got walk-in business. People came to see me about grocery bills they could not collect, landlord-tenant problems, and other everyday matters not usually considered by the United States Supreme Court. But I did the best I could with what I had

When I applied to the Arizona attorney general's office for work, they did not have a place for me. I persisted, however, and got a temporary job and quickly rose all the way to the bottom of the totem pole at the attorney general's office. As was normal for a beginner, I got the least desirable assignments. But that was all right because I managed to take away from these rather humble professional beginnings a valuable lesson. I learned, for example, the habit of always trying to do the best I could with every task, no matter how unimportant it might seem at the time. Such habits can breed future success.

As Abraham Lincoln once observed, "I always prepared myself for the opportunity I knew would come my way." As his career attests, devotion to excellence in all things, even when it seems that "the world will little note nor long remember" the small tasks in which you find yourself engaged can have its rewards.

Starting at the bottom and working hard while you are there can have its present consolations and benefits as well. The pay is lower, the prerequisites are nonexistent, and usually the title is not that impressive. But you will quickly learn, as I did, that the person at the bottom, despite a low rank on the totem pole, can have great power. This is true because that person develops the factual predicate on which everyone else acts. No one learns more about a problem than the person at the bottom whose job it is to develop the facts and make the first analysis. . . .

Remember, although you may begin as a lowly foot soldier, your power rests in your ability to see, interpret, and communicate the facts, and even make those facts happen. . . .

Now the second suggestion I have to help make your life in the legal profession meaningful and fulfilling is to become involved in the community in which you find yourself. Be a part of it. . . . You will find that the individual can and does make a real difference even in this increasingly populous, complex world of ours. The individual can make things happen. It is the individual who can bring a tear to my eye and cause me to take a pen in my hand. It is the individual who has acted or tried to act, who will not only force a decision but have a hand in shaping it. . . .

> **The individual can make things happen. It is the individual who can bring a tear to my eye and cause me to take a pen in my hand. It is the individual who has acted or tried to act, who will not only force a decision but have a hand in shaping it. . . .**

When I was first admitted to the Arizona Bar, it was still customary for federal district court judges to appoint young lawyers to provide free legal services for certain criminal defendants in federal courts. And I can remember to this day the excitement of handling several such matters and the feeling of service to one's fellows that it gave me to render that needed legal assistance. I do not think that any legal service for which I was paid gave me more satisfaction than simply helping someone who needed it without any expectation of financial compensation. . . .

I hope every single graduate here today of this law school will take some of the opportunities that will surely come your way to perform some *pro bono* legal services for others in need. Without a doubt, you will look back on that with a great deal of pride. My wish is that you will be full participants in life's opportunities, that you will join in trying to leave the world a little better than you found it on your arrival. . . . Justice Holmes once said that every calling is great when greatly pursued. On this, your graduation day, I urge you to greatly pursue high standards in your new calling. In doing so, you will bring credit to our profession, to this law school, and to the families who helped you achieve your status. . . .

"THE HARVARD SPIRIT"

Known for his "Rough Riders," his endless ambition, and his words of policy
"speak softly and carry a big stick," Theodore Roosevelt, the twenty-sixth
President of the United States, proved to be the epitome of the work ethic. As a
weak, asthmatic child, Roosevelt grew to become a U.S. colonel, the governor
of New York, and United States President for two terms (1901-1909). Here he
speaks to the Harvard graduates of the importance of hard-earned work,
moral fiber, and the practical achievement of those ideals.

PRESIDENT THEODORE ROOSEVELT
Harvard University
June 28, 1905
Copy taken from the Harvard Graduates' Magazine *(September 1905),*
supplied courtesy of the Theodore Roosevelt Collection, Harvard College Library.

A great university like this has two especial functions. The first is to produce a small number of scholars of the highest rank, a small number of
men, who, in science and literature, or in art, will do productive work of the
first class. The second is to send out into the world a very large number of
men who never could achieve, and who ought not to try to achieve, such a
position in the field of scholarship, but whose energies are to be felt in every
other form of activity; and who should go out from our doors with the balanced development of body, of mind, and above all, of character, which shall
fit them to do work both honorable and efficient. . . .

What counts infinitely more than any possible outside reward is the
spirit of the worker himself. The prime need is to instill into the minds of
the scholars themselves a true appreciation of real as distinguished from
sham success. In productive scholarship, in the scholarship which adds by its
work to the sum of substantial achievement with which the country is to be
credited, it is only first-class work that counts. . . . The smallest amount of
really first-class work is worth all the second-class work that can possibly be
produced; and to have done such work is in itself the fullest and amplest
reward to the man producing it. We outsiders should according to our
ability aid him in every way to produce it. Yet all that we can do is but little
compared to what he himself can and must do. The spirit of the scholar is
the vital factor in the productive scholarship of the country. . . .

Of course, if in any individual university, training produces a taste for
refined idleness, a distaste for sustained effort, a barren intellectual arro-

gance, or a sense of supercilious aloofness from the world of real men who do the world's real work, then it has harmed that individual; but in such case there remains the abiding comfort that he would not have amounted to much anyway. Neither a college training nor anything else can do much good to the man of weak fibre or to the man with a twist in his moral or intellectual make-up. But the average undergraduate has enough robustness of nature, enough capacity for enthusiasm and aspiration, to make it worthwhile to turn to account the stuff that is in him. . . .

But in addition to having high ideals, it cannot too often be said to a body such as is gathered here today, that together with devotion to what is right must go practical efficiency in striving for what is right. This is a rough, workaday, practical world, and if in it we are to do the work best worth doing, we must approach that work in a spirit remote from that of the mere visionary, and above all remote from that of the visionary whose aspirations after good find expression only in the shape of scolding and complaining. . . . There can be nothing worse for the community than to have the men who profess lofty ideals show themselves so foolish, so narrow, so impracticable, as to cut themselves off from communion with the men who are actually able to do the work of governing, the work of business, the work of the professions. It is a sad and evil thing if the men with a moral sense group themselves as impractical zealots, while the men of action gradually grow to discard and laugh at all moral sense as an evidence of impractical weakness. . . .

> **. . . together with devotion to what is right must go practical efficiency in striving for what is right.**

The men who go out from Harvard into the great world of American life bear a heavy burden of responsibility. The only way they can show their gratitude to their *Alma Mater* is by doing their full duty to the nation as a whole; and they can do this full duty only if they combine the high resolve to work for what is best and most ennobling with the no less resolute purpose to do their work in such fashion that when the end of their days comes, they shall feel that they have actually achieved results and not merely talked of achieving them.

INSIGHTS *for* LIVING

REST IS NOT IDLENESS, AND TO LIE SOMETIMES ON THE GRASS
UNDER THE TREES ON A SUMMER'S DAY, LISTENING TO THE
MURMUR OF WATER, OR WATCHING THE CLOUDS FLOAT ACROSS
THE SKY, IS BY NO MEANS A WASTE OF TIME.

—SIR J. LUBBOCK

*I learned years ago . . . that the richest and fullest lives attain
an inner balance of work, love and play, in equal order, that
to pursue one to the disregard of others is to open oneself to
ultimate sadness in older age, whereas to pursue all three
with equal dedication is to make possible an old age filled
with serenity, peace and fulfillment.*

—DORIS KEARNS GOODWIN

*Our society's problems of productivity come, in part,
because our young . . . are so burdened by debt that they
rush unthinkingly to the highest-paying entry-level job. But
a true vocation brings our best talents to bear on tasks
society needs, and through working on them, we focus our
most creative energies. So, look for that vocation.
Forget the starting salary and remember that your
biggest debt is to your talents—and to the people who
have helped you foster them so far.*

—JILL KER CONWAY

*Here comes my piece of advice: watch out, watch out, as you
go along that what you're doing is not merely a job, not
merely a career, but your work, the thing that you really
want to do.*

—FRANCES FITZGERALD

AIM HIGH AND TRUST GOD

Mr. Luis Bush, International Director for the AD2000 & Beyond Movement, urges graduates at Biola University to "aim high and trust God." Through his ministries and evangelism in more than 50 countries, many of them in the "10/40 Window," Mr. Bush has himself aimed high and has seen the ways that God has been "able to do exceeding abundantly beyond all that you can ask or imagine."

> LUIS BUSH
> *Biola University*
> *December 1997*

It's been said it's better to aim high at an eagle and miss it than to aim low at a skunk and hit it. For some two hundred of you, the honor has come. You're commencing a new chapter in your journey of life. It's a time for a great point, a gearshift. And you're going to go places and do things perhaps that nobody felt you would be going to and doing. My encouragement to you is to aim high and trust God.

Someone entered into the international headquarters of the Coca Cola company and said, "Immediately I knew what the goal of that company was because it said in very large letters on the wall 'A can of Coke in the hand of every person by the year 2000.'" And being a committed Christian, [this person] coming up from that headquarters wrestled with the concept of how could a commercial company without the power of God and the people of God expect such great things when sometimes we as the people of God, with the power of God, don't expect such great things?

This applies to you as you graduate from this place. You can trust God because God, the Scriptures say in Ephesians 3, is "able to do exceeding abundantly beyond all that you can ask or imagine." And as you move from this place, I believe that the greatest challenge that you will face as you leave these beautiful Biola grounds is to recognize your potential in Christ Jesus, to step forth boldly, to go out by faith to make a difference for all eternity. To recognize that God is able not only to do exceeding abundantly beyond all you ask or think *but* that you can do something about it that no one else can do as He calls you very specifically to a task, a ministry, or work opportunity.

The Scriptures in Ephesians 3:20 indicate "Him who is able to do exceeding abundantly according to the power that works in us;" and this is the hour, the moment, the time when you are stepping out, and it's a brand new step in your journey of life. In that text of Scripture contains the clue I believe to a glorious transition from your coming to Biola to your going from Biola, from your preparation to your presentation, from here to there as Ephesians would have it, from your call, as you are being called to Christ, to your conduct. . . . The conduct to walk in love, in light, in unity, in holiness . . . in warfare into battle . . . These verses are the hinge from the call to the conduct which has the key to making that conduct a conduct that will count for all eternity. And that key is the effectiveness of your stewardship of life as you aim high and trust God in you to do *beyond* . . . what you're asking or even imagining.

In that text of Scripture, there are two phrases that wrap up the very core of the truth that Paul, if he were here tonight, would probably be articulating and addressing. The first terms . . . "God is able . . . "; the second "in you with His power.". . . The explosion of His power is like the power of dynamite produced by the Holy Spirit. . . . That which energizes the Christian . . . a habitual, ongoing, continuous pattern of life as you trust in Him. He gives us the key, faith, to unlock the doors, spiritual power that turns dynamite into explosive power. And you commencers, go with this word in your heart and in your mind: . . . God's power. Go with the expectation that He will inspire and energize you beyond all imagination as you trust in Him. Believe Him for the impossible because our God is the God of the impossible. Paul said, "I am able to do all things through Christ who strengthens me." . . .

Why aim high and trust God *first*? Because God is able to do above all. There are many along the road that would be surprised for me to be here tonight, for you see, in my home the most important thing to my father was the education of the four boys [in our family]. All four aspired to a good education. But in my particular case, I competed in high school not to come in first but to avoid coming in last. My mother was the kind that kept the report cards and the teachers were all consistent in their reporting along those years when they wrote in and said, "He tries hard, but he just doesn't have it together."

Then it came time to go to university. The oldest of the four brothers graduated from Cambridge University in England and things got a little hotter in the home front. The second one graduated from Yale University. . . . The other brother graduated from Stanford Business School—and then it was my turn. And seeing the trend in high school, my father thought the best

Some of you here will be told along the journey of life that you lack what it takes, that you just don't have it together, that you're missing a necessary ingredient. Don't believe it. Believe God.

> **. . . you who are graduating, expect great things from God, great things— whatever your profession or ministry might be. Aim high and trust God . . .**

thing for me was a finishing school so they sent me to Great Britain for several years. . . . Then it came time to apply to university and there was some real suspense in the home front at that point. I ended up applying to twenty universities—in four continents. . . .

Some of you here will be told along the journey of life that you lack what it takes, that you just don't have it together, that you're missing a necessary ingredient. Don't believe it. Believe God.

Why aim high and trust God? Second, because not only is God able to do beyond all you ask or imagine, but the Scripture tells us that God is able to do exceedingly beyond all you can think or imagine. William Carey was an impoverished English shoemaker born in the late eighteen century. He had to overcome great odds to pursue the call of God to become a missionary to India . . . He was accused of being a dreamer who dreamed. He was dreaming but his passion, his God-given passion for the heathen that could not be extinguished, brought the whole world especially India into the hearts of western Christians. It was Carey who said, perhaps he would do so tonight to you commencers, you who are graduating, expect great things from God, *great things*—whatever your profession or ministry might be. Aim high and trust God. . . .

Why aim high and trust God? Thirdly because He is able not only to do exceedingly beyond what we ask or think but exceeding abundantly beyond what we can ask or think. This is where you need to start to write your story. It's yet untold. The page is blank. It still must be written. Where do you want to go? Is it to the eagle or the skunk?

Regardless of where you go and what you decide to do, the main question of the moment is what will you do with what you have been given in Jesus Christ? The next step of faith is the step that unlocks the door, which is up to you so that one day when it is all over and you enter that heavenly pearly gate, it might be said of you, "Well done, well done, thou good and faithful servant. You have been faithful with a few things. Come and share your Master's happiness." Aim high and trust God. Step forth in faith and pray as you go, . . .

You've been ministered by Jesus Christ and by other students and by the Holy Spirit—NOW to move into commencement, into a new chapter. It's time to *fly*. Aim *high* and trust God. God bless you.

THE STUDENT

Born in Scotland in 1874, Oswald Chambers became an itinerant Bible teacher following training at London's Royal Academy of Art, the University of Edinburgh, and Dunoon College (theology). Later he and Mrs. Chambers founded the Bible Training College in London where he lectured and she diligently wrote his notes out in shorthand. In 1915, he left Britain with his family to become Y.M.C.A. chaplain to British Commonwealth troops in Egypt, where he died in 1917. The following text is a class lecture Mr. Chambers gave to his students at the BTC, emphasizing the importance of not separating sacred and secular, study and activity, but rather acknowledging God in all one's ways. This lecture is the one exception in this book in that it was not given as a commencement speech; nevertheless, it communicates important values for those launching out into their chosen fields of study.

Oswald Chambers

Bible Training College

London, England
"The Student" Taken from Approved Unto God © *1936, by the Oswald Chambers Publications Assn., Ltd., as published in* The Complete Works of Oswald Chambers © *2000 by the Oswald Chambers Publications Assn., Ltd., published by Discovery House Publishers, 3000 Kraft Ave., SE, Grand Rapids, Michigan 49512. Reprinted by permission. All rights reserved*

The difficulty in Christian work today is that we put it into a sphere that upsets the reasoning of things—this sphere for sacred and that for secular; this time for activity and that for study. God will never allow us to divide our lives into sacred and secular, into study and activity.

We generally think of a student as one who shuts himself up and studies in a reflective way, but that is never revealed in God's book. A Christian's thinking ought to be done in activities, not in reflection, because we only come to right discernment in activities. Some incline to study naturally in the reflective sense, others incline more to steady active work; the Bible combines both in one life.

We are apt to look on workers for God as a special class, but that is foreign to the New Testament. Our Lord was a carpenter; Paul was a weaver. If you try and live in compartments, God will tumble up the time. Acknowledge Him in all your ways, and He will bring you into the circumstances that will develop the particular side of your life that He wants developed, and be careful that you do not upset His plans by bringing in your own ideas.

Another danger in work for God is to make natural temperament the line of service. The gifts of the Spirit are built on God's sovereignty, not on our temperament. We are apt to limit God by saying, "Oh, I'm not built like that;" or, "I have not been well educated." Never limit God by those paralyzing thoughts; it is the outcome of unbelief. What does it matter to the Lord Almighty of heaven and earth what your early training was like! What does matter to Him is that you don't lean to your own understanding, but acknowledge Him in all your ways. So crush on the threshold of your mind any of those lame, limping "I can'ts,"—"you see I am not gifted." The great stumbling block that prevents some people being simple disciples of Jesus is that they *are* gifted—so gifted that they won't trust in the Lord with all their hearts. You have to learn to break by the power of the Holy Spirit the fuss and the lethargy which alternate in your life and remember that it is a crime to be weak in His strength.

> Remember you are accountable to no one but God; keep yourself for His service along the line of His providential leading for you, not on the line of your temperament. The servant of God has to go through the experience of things before he is allowed to go through the study of them.

Our Lord Jesus Christ became poor for our sakes not as an example, but to give us the unerring secret of His religion. Professional Christianity is a religion of possessions that are devoted to God; the religion of Jesus Christ is a religion of personal relationship to God and has nothing whatever to do with possessions. The disciple is rich, not in possessions but in personal identity. Voluntary poverty was the marked condition of Jesus (Luke 9:58), and the poverty of God's children in all ages is a significant thing.

Today we are ashamed and afraid to be poor. The reason we hear so little about the inner spiritual side of external poverty is that few of us are in the place of Jesus or of Paul. The scare of poverty will knock the spiritual backbone out of us unless we have the relationship that holds. The attitude of Our Lord's life was that He was disconnected with everything to do with things that chain people down to this world; consequently, He could go wherever His Father wanted Him to.

Remember you are accountable to no one but God; keep yourself for His service along the line of His providential leading for you, not on the line of your temperament. The servant of God has to go through the experience of things before he is allowed to go through the study of them. When you have had the experience, God will give you the line for study; the experience first, and then the explanation of the experience by the Spirit of God. Each one of us is an isolated person with God, and He will put us through experiences that are not meant for us at all but meant to make us fit stuff to feed others.

How much time have you given to wondering what God is doing with you? It is not your business. Your part is to acknowledge God in all your ways; and He will blend the active and the spiritual until they are inseparable, and you learn to live in activities knowing that your life is hid with Christ in God.

IF YOU HAD IT TO DO OVER...

Dr. Tony Campolo is Professor Emeritus of Sociology at Eastern University in St. Davids, Pennsylvania, and an ordained Baptist minister. As founder of the Evangelical Association for the Promotion of Education (EAPE), Dr. Campolo has helped at-risk children in cities and helped develop schools and universities in developing countries. In his speech, Dr. Campolo challenges the graduates to risk more, to reflect more, and to make a difference on this earth, to the point of altering the course of history.

TONY CAMPOLO
Oakwood College
May 10, 2003

There was a study that was done . . . in which ninety-five people over the age of ninety-five were asked one question, open-ended answers: if you had it to do over again, what would you do differently? That's what I have to ask of [you]. Will you be wise enough to listen to elderly people? . . .

The first thing they said was *we would risk more.* There's a good word—risk. There are a lot of things that we could do and would do for Jesus but we become threatened, we become intimidated, we hang back, and we fail to see the opportunities that are available to us. I call upon you the class of this year to risk great things for God, to attempt great things for God, and to expect great things from God.

Let me just say that you have a lot of risks to take in the years that lie ahead. I don't know how many of you are married, but the truth is that getting married is a risk. Amen? Now people say it's not a risk; they say it's not a risk if you marry the right one. So you ask your mother, "Mother, how will I know if I've met the right one?" Every mother answers the same way, "When you meet the right one, you'll know." That really clarifies everything, doesn't it? It doesn't end there, graduates. I guarantee you that three weeks before the wedding she's going to say to you, "Are you sure?" It's too late, the invitations are out, the gifts are coming in—you are dead meat.

The important thing to recognize is that marriage is what you create after the wedding is over. When romanticism has died down. You say, it will never die down. It *will* die down. You will wake up one morning in the middle of the bed, she won't be awake, her hair will be hanging down over her face, her mouth will be open. Worse than that, *she* will wake up in the middle of the bed, and there will BE no hair hanging down. At that particular point, you have to say that it's time for commitment to take over for romance will not carry it. I have to commit myself to create love.

And that's why we Christians are unique. We do not believe that romance is an emotion that overtakes us but for Christians, love is something that has been deliberately created, it is a decision of the will and it comes as you commit yourself to allowing Jesus to invade you and to empower you, to envelop this person with His love: when you can, in fact, encounter the other person as one in whom Christ dwells. . . .

> **If you are going to be a risk-taker, there will be an excitement and a joy to your life. Don't be afraid to do the daring things for God that need to be done.**

You've got to take risks, you've got to make the commitment but after you've made the commitment, you have to work to create a life that will carry you over the low bridge of life. I must say this, I love my wife MORE today than the day I married her. I'm not as romantic but I do love her more. . . . Love goes much deeper. Love is a gift that God gives to those who are surrendered to Him. . . . If we do the things that love requires, the emotion will tend to follow. Risk taking is crucial. . . . If you are going to be a risk-taker, there will be an excitement and a joy to your life. Don't be afraid to do the daring things for God that need to be done. . . . Take the risks. Attempt to do the great things that God told you to do.

The second thing is this. You must not only risk more, say these old people, *you must reflect more.* They look back on their lives, and they wish they had taken more time to pay attention. They let so much of life slip away without focusing on it.

When Mike was four, he wanted a sandbox but his father said, "If they put a sandbox in that yard, there'll be sand all over the place. The sand will kill the grass." And Mike's mother said, "The grass will grow back." When he was five, he wanted a jungle gym that would climb to the sky with swings that would take his breath away. His father said, "If you put that thing in the backyard, every kid in the neighborhood will be here, they'll run back and forth and back and forth—they'll kill the grass." And Mike's mother smiled and said, "The grass will grow back." . . .

The basketball hoop on the side of the garage grew a bigger crowd than the Summer Olympics and the barren spot underneath the hoop got larger and larger . . . winter came, snow fell, sludge beat the grass into the ground and Mike's father said, "I never asked for much in this life, just a few crummy blades of grass." And Mike's mother smiled and said, "The grass will grow back." Well, the grass this year was beautiful. It rolled out like a green sponge, out of the flowerbeds where little boys once dug with tea-spoons, out along the driveway where bicycles once fell, but Mike's father never saw the grass. Instead, his eyes were lifted beyond the yard, and he said with a catch in his voice, "He *will* come back, he *will* come back, he *will* come back, won't he?"

Listen to me, students, you're so young and you're so full of life, and so much is ahead of you, I want to inform you that it will be gone before you can even catch your breath. You need to stop and pay attention with your eyes wide open to the mercies of God. Look around you, take it in, live life with intensity, live it with passion, don't let life get away from you without you focusing on it, reflecting on it, and understanding how fresh it all is. *Count* your blessings. *Name* them one by one. Pay attention to what God has done, is doing, and will do in your life. Reflect more.

> **The purpose of an education and the life of a Christian is not to equip you to climb the ladder of socio-economic success so that you can buy stuff.**

The last thing [the elderly said] is *do more things that live on after you're dead.* Now that's a funny thing to say to [those of your age]. It seems like I just graduated, and yet I'm an old guy. I don't know where my life has gone. I've reached that age where my idea of a "happy hour" is a nap. I go to weddings, the bride's *mother* looks better to me than the bride. . . . Listen to me, class, . . . Jesus gave to create a church who throws parties for people who don't have parties, for those who are rejected and left behind. Look at us here, well-dressed, we are the elite, the educated, the sophisticated. When it's all said and done, let us all be aware that "to whom much is given, from them much is expected." Do not leave your brothers and sisters behind. Do things that are worthy of followers of Jesus Christ. Pick up those who have fallen by the wayside, strengthen those who are weak, reach out to those who are poor. . . .

The purpose of an education and the life of a Christian is not to equip you to climb the ladder of socio-economic success so that you can buy stuff. The purpose of an education is to equip you to serve others in the name of Jesus Christ.

I ask you quite simply are you ready to take your stand? I belong to an African American church in west Philadelphia. I'm the only white guy left in the place. It's a great church. . . . Our preacher said one time in a sermon one line over and over again. "It's Friday but Sunday's coming." It doesn't sound like much, does it, but you weren't there. It started nice and softly, "It's Friday, and Jesus is dead on the cross. It's FRIDAY but Sunday's coming." And the men yelled "keep going," and that's all he needed and he took off. "It's *Friday* but Sunday's coming. . . . Friday, Satan's dancing a little jig and the Pharisees are yelling" . . . and the preacher's yelling "FRIDAY, Sunday's coming." . . .

Friday, they're saying the class of 2003 cannot shake the foundation, cannot alter the course of history. But I'm here to say it's only *Friday*—Sunday's coming! . . . When we commit ourselves to Christ, when we take the risks, when we live passionately and pay attention to what's going on around us, and what God is doing through us, when we commit ourselves to living out the great visions and dreams that God has placed in our hearts and minds, if we are willing to be used by the Spirit to expect great things from God, then the world will have the good news. My preacher said it best: The good news is it's Friday—but Sunday's coming!

REACH BEYOND
YOUR BEGINNINGS
Profiles of Excellence

*Forgetting what lies behind and reaching forward to
what lies ahead, I press on toward the goal for the prize
of the upward call of God in Christ Jesus.*

PHILIPPIANS 3:13-14 NASB

PHILIP EMEAGWALI:
A STORY OF INCALCULABLE ODDS

His classmates called him Calculus, his teachers called him "young Chike Obi," in honor of a well-known mathematical genius from Nigeria. As an eight-year-old Nigerian, Philip Emeagwali wanted to be playing soccer with his friends, but he was forced by his father to sit in front of an alarm clock and answer three hundred math questions within three hours—before the alarm could sound. Realizing that thirty-six seconds per questions was not enough time, Philip began to learn how to calculate the answers in his head rather than on paper. Philip's father knew that his son's quick answers and mathematical ability would one day remove the young boy from the hopeless world of poverty in which he lived to a future world of success. And he was right.

Philip's potential first revealed itself in the family's living room in front of an annoying alarm clock. It was then his father knew he had no ordinary son. But then his classmates noticed that he was able to solve mathematics problems before they could even write them down. Some classmates raved, others were jealous, and still others suspected him of using magic during math exams. The problems began as simple addition sums, then algebra, then geometry, then trigonometry equations. Before long, Philip Emeagwali could easily outdo his instructors; in fact, if the math teacher were absent, the school's headmaster would allow Philip to teach. But Philip's mathematical genius backfired in 1965 when he was ten; Philip was denied admission into a grammar school in Nigeria because he finished a one-hour examination in five minutes, scoring one hundred percent—unheard of for anyone, much less a ten year old. And then once again, tragedy hit, and it appeared as if Philip Emeagwali would not excel or even live.

In April 1967 during an ethnic cleansing in which fifty thousand Igbos indigenes were killed, Philip was forced to withdraw from school as he and his family hid in refugee camps. "We slept in refugee camps, abandoned school buildings, and bombed houses," he says. "We stood in long lines to receive food from charity organizations." However, Philip didn't leave the camps without having gained from the experience. "The hardship of living in a refugee camp made me psychologically strong. It made me street smart. It equipped me [with] a greater sense of determination and vision."

One year later, Philip was forced to serve the Biafran army as a child-soldier in an ethnic civil war. In six month's time, he was reunited with his family only to have to leave school because his parents could no longer afford it. Though his father continued teaching him, the teenager had to study on his own because his father could no longer keep up with his son's mathematical skills. Philip soon earned a General Certificate of Education from the University of London, and then at the age of seventeen, Philip won a scholarship to Oregon State University. The young math genius began to follow his dreams in America, leaving behind his cherished family and the impoverished country he had always known.

Emeagwali had little idea of the advanced technology and possibilities that lay before him. He recounts his first exposure to a new continent. "When I got to America, I was amazed at the level of technological development there. In one day I saw an airport, used a telephone, used a library, talked with a scientist, and was shown a computer for the first time in my life. Not in my wildest dreams did I expect to be recognized as a contributor to American technology."

With degrees from several American universities including George Washington University and the University of Maryland, Mr. Emeagwali began working in civil and marine engineering as well as information technology. While observing bees building their honeycombs one day, Emeagwali conceived the idea of programming a computer that used thousands of other computers (like bees) to work together. Instead of using a single extraordinarily large computer to do the work, Philip used the Internet to connect to 65,000 smaller computers, discovering that the computer could work at an amazing rate of 3.1 billion calculations a second.

Because of his technological and scientific discoveries, Philip Emeagwali has been given numerous awards including Africa's Best Scientist, the 1989 Gordon Bell Prize (equivalent to the Nobel Prize in computers), America's Best & Brightest Inventor in 1996, and Nigerian Achiever of the Year. But amidst these honors and awards, Emeagwali has not forgotten where he began and how far he has come.

"My son is going to encounter racism in the US which will deny him the opportunity to contribute as much as he can to society," Emeagwali says. "I want him to be inspired by the fact that I was a high school drop-out and ex-refugee who overcame racism and made scientific contributions that benefited mankind."

Philip Emeagwali remembers his personal struggle for an education and has seen the direction one can go when given an opportunity. "We must ensure that our children are properly educated," he tells South African parents. "When we invest in our children, we will find that our standard of living grows, too. We should invest in education and technology not because it is easy, but because our children will be the beneficiaries tomorrow of the decisions we adults make today."

JOSH McDOWELL: A SKEPTIC'S QUEST

One day I was in Newport Beach, California, riding on a motor scooter with a friend. We were zipping along having a great time, laughing, when two women pulled up beside us in a brand new Continental (that's a Newport Beach Chevy). After staring at us for about three blocks, the woman on the passenger side rolled down her window and yelled, "What right do you have to be so happy?"

Well, I couldn't see anything wrong with being happy. I love to laugh. What's wrong with wanting to be one of the happiest individuals in the whole world? Not only did I want to be happy and have meaning and purpose in life, but I also wanted to be free. See, most people know what they ought to do, but they don't have the capacity, the strength, to do it. They're not free. They're in bondage. To me, freedom is having the capacity to do what you know you ought to do.

So I started looking for answers. Now, where I was brought up, a lot of people had religion. So, I took off on religion. I was involved in it morning, afternoon, and night. But I must have gone to the wrong church because I actually felt worse.

Next, I thought, "Well, maybe education is the answer." So, I enrolled in the university. I was probably the most unpopular student with the professors in the first university I went to in Michigan. I wanted answers. My economic theory professor could tell me how to make a better living, but he couldn't tell me how to live better. It didn't take me long to realize that a lot of faculty members, and students too, had more problems, less meaning to life, and more frustration than I did.

Then I thought, "Maybe prestige is the answer." Find a "calling" and give your life to it. So I ran for various student body offices and got elected. It was neat . . . knowing everyone on campus, making decisions, spending other people's money to do what I wanted. I enjoyed it.

But every Monday morning I woke up the same individual, usually with a headache because of the night before, with the same attitude, "Well, here we go again for another five days." Monday through Friday I sort of endured. Happiness revolved around three nights a week: Friday, Saturday, and Sunday. Then I'd start the whole cycle again.

Eventually I became frustrated. I doubt if too many students in the universities of our country have been more sincere in trying to find meaning and truth and power and purpose in life than I was—yet I hadn't found it.

About that time, around the campus I noticed a small group of people—eight students and two faculty. There was something different about their lives. They seemed to have direction. They seemed to know where they were going, and that was very unusual.

Further, they seemed to have a type of love that was manifested in the way they treated people. I had observed that most people talked a lot about love, but these people demonstrated something special in their relationships with others. They had something I didn't have, so I made friends with them.

After a couple of weeks, we were sitting around a table in the student union. I recall that six of the students were there and both of the faculty and one of their wives. The conversation started to get to God.

Let's face it: if you're an insecure student or professor or businessperson, or an insecure anything, and the conversation gets to God, you have to put on a big front. You know what I've found to be true? The bigger the mouth, the greater the vacuum. The bigger the front an individual puts on, the greater the emptiness inside. Well, I was putting on that kind of front.

Their talk irritated me. I wanted what they had, but I didn't want them to know it. I leaned

I noticed a small group of people— eight students and two faculty. There was something different about their lives. They seemed to have direction. They seemed to know where they were going, and that was very unusual.

back on my chair and tried to act nonchalant. I looked over at one young woman and said, "Why are you so different from the other students on campus?" She said two words I never thought I'd hear in the university as part of the "solution." She said, "Jesus Christ."

"Oh, come on," I fired back at her. "Don't give me that garbage about religion." She must have had a lot of courage and convictions.

"Look," she said, "I didn't tell you *religion*; I told you Jesus Christ." Well, I apologized to her because I'd been very rude. . . . "Please forgive my attitude, but to tell you the truth, I'm sick and tired of that kind of thing. I just don't want anything to do with it."

Then you know what happened? These students and faculty challenged me to examine intellectually who Jesus Christ was. At first I thought it was a joke. How ridiculous. It was my opinion that most Christians had two brains. I thought one was lost, and the other was out looking for it!

But these people kept challenging me over and over and over again, until finally I accepted their challenge.

I spent a lot of money to completely discredit Christianity, but it backfired. I concluded that Christ had to be who He claimed to be. . . . So I had a problem. I found out that becoming a Christian (or I prefer the term *a believer*) was rather ego-shattering. My intellect was convinced, but a struggle began in my life. Jesus Christ directly challenged me to trust Him as Savior, as the One who died on the cross for my sins. "To all who received Him, to those who believed in His name, He gave the right to become children of God" (John 1:12). But I didn't want a "party pooper" invading my life. I couldn't think of a faster way to ruin a good time or destroy intellectual pursuits or impede scholarly acceptability with my peers.

My mind told me that Christianity was true: but my will said, "Don't admit it."

> **I spent a lot of money to completely discredit Christianity, but it backfired. I concluded that Christ had to be who He claimed to be. . . . So I had a problem.**

It came to the point where I'd go to bed at ten at night but I couldn't fall asleep until four in the morning. I knew I had to get Jesus off my mind or go out of my mind!

On December 19, 1959, at 8:30 p.m., during my second year at the university, I became a Christian. That night I prayed. I prayed four things in order to establish a relationship with God—a personal relationship with His Son, the personal, resurrected, living Christ. Over a period of time, that relationship has turned my life around.

First, I prayed, "Lord Jesus, thank You for dying on the cross for me." Second, I said, "I confess those things in my life that aren't pleasing to You and ask You to forgive me and cleanse. Me." The Bible says, "Though your sins are like scarlet, they shall be as white as snow" (Isaiah 1:18). Third, I said, "Right now in the best way I know how, I open the door of my heart and life and trust You as my Savior and Lord. Take control of my life. Change me from the inside out. Make me the type of person You created me to be."

The last thing I prayed was "Thank You for coming into my life by faith." It was a faith produced by the Holy Spirit, based on God's Word and supported by evidence and the facts of history.

I'm sure you've heard religious people talk about their "bolt of lightning." Well, after I prayed, nothing happened. In fact, after I made that decision, I felt sick to my stomach.

"Oh no, McDowell, what'd you get sucked into now?" I wondered. I really felt I'd gone off the deep end—and some of my friends agreed. But I can tell you one thing: In six months to a year and a half, I found I hadn't gone off the deep end. My life was changed.

A few years ago, I was in a debate with the head of the history department at a Midwestern university, and I said, "My life has been changed." He interrupted me rather sarcastically. "McDowell, are you trying to tell us that God really changed your life in the twentieth century? What areas?"

After forty-five minutes of my describing changes, he said, "Okay, that's enough."

I told him about my restlessness. I was a person who always had to be occupied. I had to be over at my girlfriend's place or somewhere in a rap session. My mind was a whirlwind of conflicts. I'd sit down and try to study or think, and I couldn't.

But a few months after I made that decision to trust Christ, a kind of mental peace began to develop. Don't misunderstand. I'm not talking about the absence of conflict. What I found in this relationship with Jesus wasn't so much the absence of conflict as it was the ability to cope with it. I have come to experience in a very real way Christ's promise when He said, "Peace I leave with you; My peace I give you. I do not give to you as the world gives" (John 14:27).

Another area that changed was my bad temper. I used to "blow my stack" if somebody just looked at me cross-eyed. I still have the scars from almost killing a man my first year at the university. My temper was such an integral part of me that I didn't consciously seek to change it.

One day after my decision to put my faith in Christ, I arrived at a crisis, only to find that my temper was gone! And only once in the many years since 1959 have I lost it.

There's another area that I'm not proud of. Hatred. It wasn't something outwardly manifested, but a kind of inner grinding. The one person I hated more than anyone else in the world was my father. I despised him. To me he was the town alcoholic. If friends were coming over, I would take my father, tie him up in the barn, and park the car up around the silo. To avoid embarrassment, we would tell our friends he had to go somewhere. I don't think any person could hate someone more than I hated my father.

A relationship with Jesus Christ changes lives. You can ignorantly laugh at Christianity; you can mock and ridicule it. But it works.

Maybe five months after I made that decision for Christ, love for my father—a love from God through Jesus Christ—inundated my life. It turned my hatred upside down. It enabled me to look my father squarely in the eyes and say, "Dad, I love you." After some of the things I'd done, that really shook him up.

When I transferred to a private university, I was in a serious car accident. With my neck in traction, I was taken home. I'll never forget my father coming into my room and asking, "Son, how can you love a father like me?" I said, "Dad, six months ago I despised you." Then I shared with him my conclusions about Jesus Christ.

"Dad, I let Jesus come into my life. I can't explain it completely, but as a result of this relationship, I've found the capacity to love and accept not only you, but other people—just the way they are."

Forty-five minutes later, one of the greatest thrills of my life occurred. Somebody in my own family, someone who knew me so well I couldn't pull the wool over his eyes, my own father, said to me, "Son, if God can do in my life what I've seen Him do in yours, then I want to give Him the opportunity." Right there, my father prayed with me and trusted Christ.

Usually changes take place over several days, weeks, months . . . even years. The life of my father was changed right before my eyes. It was as though somebody reached in and turned on a light bulb. I've never seen such a rapid change before or since. My father touched alcohol only once after that. He got it as far as his lips and that was it. He didn't need it anymore.

I've come to one conclusion: A relationship with Jesus Christ changes lives. You can ignorantly laugh at Christianity; you can mock and ridicule it. But it works. If you trust Christ, watch your attitudes and actions—because Jesus Christ specializes in changing lives, forgiving sins, and removing guilt.

JIM STOVALL: "YES, YOU CAN!"

It was devastating and unexpected news the seventeen year old heard that day. He had never known a visually handicapped person or dreamed that he would become blind in his young adulthood. But on the day of his routine eye exam in the early 1980s, a team of doctors surrounded Jim Stovall with the news: "You have a degenerative eye disease and you will eventually lose your sight."

A young teenager, eager to participate in college, sports, and eventually a successful career, Jim knew it had all come to an end. Slowly his sight began to worsen but in the meantime, he forced himself to attempt college classes; unfortunately, in the early 1980s, no facilities or arrangements for handicapped students existed. "I always seemed to be groping around in a gray haze," Stovall remembers. For something to do, the young man losing his sight decided to investigate a school for blind children that was across the street from the college he attended. There he found a four-year-old boy who would forever change Jim's outlook and success in life.

The boy, a difficult child who had accomplished very little while in the school, was Stovall's first and only responsibility. His task? To teach the boy to tie his own shoes and climb stairs. The teaching staff of the school had long ago given up on the boy and because of his multiple handicaps, they had concluded he would never learn to do either.

"You can tie your shoes," Stovall told him when they were first introduced. "You can climb stairs."

"No, I can't," he replied.

"Yes, you can," Stovall insisted.

Jim Stovall wanted to believe the young boy could accomplish two simple tasks. But the truth was, Stovall admits, he was struggling to say "Yes, I can" in his own life. Classes had become too difficult, and he had finally come to the point of quitting. He could no longer put in the time, energy, and frustration required to study with failing sight. As he began to walk to the college administration building to withdraw, he decided to tell them at the blind school that he was also calling it quits there. "It's too tough," he told the school staff. "I can't do it."

"Yes, you can," a small voice spoke up from beside Stovall. The little four-year-old boy had been listening all along.

It was then that Stovall realized what had to be done. "I had to keep on trying or admit I had been lying to this kid that the extra effort was

> "I had to keep on trying or admit I had been lying to this kid that the extra effort was worth it. And in that second, I knew: it was worth it—for him and for me."

worth it. And in that second, I knew: it was worth it—for him and for me."

Stovall graduated three and a half years later with the help of a nice young woman, Crystal, who had patiently read his books for him during the semesters. Later, that kind college friend would become his wife.

With dreams of becoming a small business owner, Stovall was encouraged by a seventy-year-old man his father knew, Lee Braxton. The elderly man had accomplished only an elementary education but through entrepreneurial intuition, he made a fortune during the Depression, later supporting several charitable and educational organizations. Mr. Braxton inspired Stovall with confidence and courage. One of his favorite passages from the Bible left an imprint in Stovall's mind: "God hath not given us the spirit of fear; but of power and of love and of a sound mind" (2 Timothy 1:7).

"How can I ever thank you?" Stovall asked Braxton one day.

"Some day God will give you the opportunity to encourage other people—and you'll pay me back by doing just that," he replied.

"Whatever your situation in life, you too, can step out of that safe room and proceed with faith minute by minute, hand over hand, not worrying about what lies ahead or what might happen, but trusting that God will supply you the energy and courage to cope with each experience as it arises.

But by the age of twenty-nine, Stovall had lost all his vision. Though he had set up an investment brokerage in his home and it was fairly successful, Stovall fell deeper into depression, a black mire that he could not escape. "My business was successful, and it was my intention to operate out of this room, where events would be predictable and under my control, more or less forever. I wouldn't fear being awkward or embarrassed or hurt by unknown or unfamiliar situations. I believed that I could spend my entire life here—and for a while I did."

One day while listening to a Humphrey Bogart movie and attempting to follow the scenes by listening to the dialogue, the screech of brakes and screaming resounded from the television. Stovall's frustration grew—what was happening? Why had she screamed? Then an idea came to him. *If the voice of a narrator could be added to describe what was going on, the millions of blind and visually impaired people in the United States could enjoy the movie, too.* It was time for Jim Stovall to emerge from his room of darkness and despair. It was time to pay back Mr. Braxton.

Unfortunately, the dream of a television narrative seemed to come crashing down upon Stovall as soon as it had begun. "Forget it," a professional sound technician told him. "What you're trying to do is impossible." But Stovall was determined and through the help of a teenager and an editing room, it worked. Movies with narrated dialogue were about to hit the market.

In 1988, the Narrative Television Network was officially launched. Cable networks picked it up, more movies were made available with narration, and the letters began pouring in. "For the twenty hours a week that your shows are on," one lady wrote in, "you make me forget that I'm blind."

In October 1990, Jim Stovall traveled to New York to receive an Emmy award from the National Academy of Television Arts and Sciences for his outstanding contributions to the television industry. From there, other awards followed as well as speaking engagement requests. "That meant really coming out of my safe room, navigating airports and crowded rooms, and coping with unfamiliar surroundings," he said.

Today when Mr. Stovall speaks, he reminds the audience of this. "Whatever your situation in life, you too, can step out of that safe room and proceed with faith minute by minute, hand over hand, not worrying about what lies ahead or what might happen, but trusting that God will supply you the energy and courage to cope with each experience as it arises.

"Yes, there'll be times you will fall. . . . And you'll feel like shouting, 'No, I can't.' But I've got news for you: Yes, you can!"

CONDOLEEZZA RICE: FROM SMALL-TOWN ALABAMA TO THE WHITE HOUSE

She has been called "the most powerful woman in the world." As an international studies scholar and later provost at Stanford University throughout the '80s and '90s, and now as President Bush's national security adviser, Condoleezza Rice understands walking in the faith of Jesus Christ.

As a preacher's kid and daughter of a theologian, "Condi" Rice spent many Sundays in segregated black Birmingham pews. "The church was the center of our lives [but it] was not just a place of worship. It was the place where families gathered; it was the social center of the community, too," she recently explained to a Sunday school class in Washington D.C.

But Rice did not always accept the teachings of the church or believe that God was working in her life. As a young girl who trained to be a concert pianist and a competitive ice skater and as an adult who traveled extensively throughout the world as a political specialist, Condi Rice lost the sense of her faith and the understanding that God's ways were higher than her ways. In fact, she admits that with all of her traveling, she was "always in another time zone."

Then one Sunday while she was in the Lucky's Supermarket not far from home, in the aisle of spices to be exact, her life and world as she knew it completely changed. A black man spotted her, informed her he was buying some things for his church picnic and was just wondering, did she play the piano by any chance?

She agreed to play for the little African-American Baptist church in the center of Palo Alto, California. The faith of her childhood, the memories of her father assuring her that it was okay to question Christ as the doubting disciple Thomas did, and the realization that God had such "a long reach," (from Birmingham to Palo Alto, from childhood to adulthood), drew her once again to the unchanging faithfulness of Jesus Christ.

Six months later, she was again challenged to turn to God, the god who had never left her. Sitting in a church service, she heard the pastor speak of the prodigal son, from the point of view of the elder son. The elder son had been a good son, a young man who had done all the "right" things but he had become so self-satisfied and complacent about himself and his faith. Somehow that son had seen no need to become "born again," though he had never really doubted the existence of God.

It was then that Condoleezza Rice saw herself. She, too, had become complacent, had done all the right things, had made something of herself, but she had forgotten her Creator. His hand had been on her all along; she just hadn't recognized it.

"I think people who believe in a creator can never take themselves too seriously," she says. "I feel that faith allows me to have a kind of optimism about the future. You look around you and you see an awful lot of pain and suffering and things that are going wrong. It could be oppressive. But when I look at my own story or many others that I have seen, I think, *How could it possibly be that it has turned out this way? . . .* My only answer is, it's God's plan. . . . God will never let you fall too far."

> I feel that faith allows me to have a kind of optimism about the future.

Even in her childhood where black children learned to read the COLORED ONLY signs on the Alabama restroom doors and water fountains, even when her eleven-year-old friend was killed in the 1963 dynamite blast of her black church, even when her mother died of breast cancer, and even when two towers in New York City exploded at the hands of terrorists, Condoleezza Rice knows the peace of God.

When she needs guidance, she turns to Romans 5: "hope is never disappointed, because of faith in the glory of God. When I'm concerned about something, I figure out a plan of action, and then I give it to God. I just ask to be carried through it. God's never failed me yet."

ROSA PARKS:
A QUIET WOMAN OF STRENGTH AND COURAGE

She was simply tired after a long day's work as a seamstress in Montgomery, Alabama. So when she boarded a city bus with the usual signs of "whites only" and "colored" and a white man was left standing, she refused to give up her seat for him in the "colored" section. "Our mistreatment was just not right, and I was tired of it," writes Parks in her book *Quiet Strength.* "I kept thinking about my mother and my grandparents, and how strong they were. I knew there was a possibility of being mistreated, but an opportunity was being given to me to do what I had asked of others."

The quiet strength and determination of one black woman on December 1, 1955, would redirect the course of history. After her arrest, a trial, and a 381-day Montgomery bus boycott, the Supreme Court ruled in November 1956 that segregated public transportation was unconstitutional.

. . . an opportunity was being given to me to do what I had asked of others.

Born in Tuskegee, Alabama, young Rosa Parks attended a small rural school in which one teacher taught fifty to sixty students from first to sixth grade. The children only attended school five months out of the year; the other months were spent working on the family farms. But Rosa Parks' mother was a schoolteacher and taught Rosa to read as a very young child. "The parents had to buy whatever the student used [in school]," she remembers. "Often, if your family couldn't afford it, you had no access to books, pencils, whatever. However, often the children would share. I liked to read all sorts of stories, like fairy tales—Little Red Riding Hood, Mother Goose. I read very often."

After going to a private school later in Montgomery and paying for tuition by cleaning classrooms, Rosa attended Alabama State Teachers' College for Negroes in tenth and eleventh grade. However, she failed to graduate from high school at that time because of the illness and death of her grandmother. As she prepared to return to school later, her mother became ill. It wasn't until 1934, at the age of twenty-one, that Rosa Parks received her high school diploma.

Following high school and prior to the bus incident, Rosa Parks worked quietly in a Montgomery department store performing her seamstress tasks, married Raymond Parks, served as secretary of the NAACP and later Adviser to the NAACP Youth Council. Parks also tried to register to vote on different occasions and experienced several confrontations and evictions with bus drivers. Parks recalls the humiliation of those days: "I didn't want to pay my fare and then go around the back door, because many times, even if you did that, you might not get on the bus at all."

After the December 1st ordeal, the difficulties had only begun. Rosa Parks lost her job as a seamstress, was unable to find other work, and was harassed and threatened. One year after the Supreme Court made its ruling, Rosa along with her mother and husband moved to Detroit where her younger brother Sylvester lived. But Mrs. Parks was far from giving up or losing courage. In 1965, she joined the staff of United States Representative John Conyers of Michigan, working there for twenty-three years until her retirement.

She spends much of her time today reading mail from students, politicians, and just regular people and enjoys preparing meals for others, going to church, and visiting people in hospitals. The "mother of the modern day civil rights movement," as she has been called, continues to educate people of all ages and races throughout the nation through the Rosa and Raymond Parks Institute for Self-Development, through The Rosa L. Parks Learning Center, a seniors community in Michigan that educates senior citizens on the use of computers of which Mrs. Parks was a member of the first graduating class in 1998, and through a museum and library in her honor at Troy State University in Montgomery, Alabama—the building itself located on the spot where she was arrested almost 50 years ago .

I did not feel that giving up would be a way to become a free person.

Rosa Parks has written four books, was voted by *Time* magazine as one of the one hundred most influential people of the twentieth century, and has received honorary degrees from ten colleges and universities as well as countless honors and awards. Mrs. Parks' belief in God is one message she hopes to impart to her readers and listeners. "I'd like for [readers] to know that I had a very spiritual background and that I believe in church and my faith, and that has helped to give me the strength and courage to live as I did."

When asked if she ever faced something she thought she couldn't handle, Mrs. Parks remarks, "I can't think of anything. Usually, if I have to face something, I do so no matter what the consequences might be. I never had any desire to give up. I did not feel that giving up would be a way to become a free person. That's the way I still feel."

J.C. WATTS: A SPIRIT WITHOUT FEAR

As a boy growing up in the small town of Eufala, Oklahoma, J.C. Watts failed to know the meaning of a weekly allowance. His father didn't believe in such a thing. If J.C. wanted to earn some money, he knew he had to be out mowing lawns, picking up pop bottles, hauling hay, or "whatever else that was moral, legal, and ethical to make spending money," says former United States Representative J.C. Watts, Jr.

Watts' father, nicknamed Buddy, was given the initials "J.C." when he was born in 1923. The letters did not actually stand for anything but when Buddy was in third grade, his teacher questioned him on the meaning behind the initials. "It doesn't stand for anything," he told her. "But it has to stand for *something*," the teacher insisted. Buddy quickly remembered that his sister had been studying the Roman Empire in school. Without hesitation, in a moment that would determine J.C. Watts, Jr.'s name and his son's name, J.C. Watts III, he responded, "Julius Caesar!"

"Buddy" Watts, a Baptist minister, policeman, and part-time farmer, would continue to affect his son's childhood, youth, and adulthood. When his father as a young man chose to travel across Oklahoma to be by his sister's bedside in a hospital, sleeping under bridges and waiting for visiting hours, Representative Watts learned the importance of love and family. "No matter how much we change or how far from home we find ourselves, the family is the rock on which we build our lives. . . . I know exactly where I come from. Where I come from, I was taught that I didn't spend out more money than I took in. I was taught that education was important. . . . I was taught that doing the right thing matters a lot."

Watts' parents did whatever it took to see their children receive a good education. When an elementary school near their home opened its doors to integration, Watts was one of the first two African-American children to be enrolled. At age fourteen, Watt's athletic ability was discovered. But when he once again became one of the "firsts" to join the high school football team, several white players quit the team.

"There's no one in Congress who's been called 'nigger' more times than J.C. Watts," he says today. Undaunted by discrimination, Watts received a football scholarship from the University of Oklahoma, leading the Sooners to two consecutive Big Eight championships and Orange Bowl victories. After graduating in 1981 with a journalism degree, rather than accepting a draft choice to play running back for the New York Jets, Watts opted to play as a quarterback for the Canadian Football League.

As someone who had grown up as a "geographic Democrat," Watts began to feel the pull of politics on him. He discovered that he agreed more with the Republican stance than the Democratic platform after covering a debate between a young Republican businessman (now U.S. Senator Don Nickles) and the Democratic mayor of Oklahoma City. "The Republican candidate made sense. His words resonated with the values on which I had been raised, echoing all the things my dad had taught me: work hard, play fair, be responsible, pay your own way." In 1989, Watts officially changed political parties and became the first African-American in Oklahoma to be elected to a statewide office. Nine years later, he was elected as Republican Conference Chairman, the first black Republican to be elected to a party leadership position.

After eight years of serving the Fourth District of Oklahoma, J.C. Watts, Jr. called one of the more significant press conferences in his life. He would be stepping down from his post. Conversations with President Bush, Vice President Cheney, his constituents, his staff, his wife, Frankie, and many others helped him to decide that his duties as a father of five children had to come first. His decision was made more difficult after receiving a letter from Rosa Parks who encouraged Watts to stay in office, to "remain as a pioneer on the Republican side until others come to assist you. . . . I would also like you to keep your seat," she wrote, "and not think of your mantle as heavy, but think that you are chosen to prepare the way."

But Watts had made his decision. "I've never needed anything other than the title of 'Dad' in front of my name to tell me who I am and what I should stand for," he says. Watts is also committed to his Christian faith. "I don't apologize for my personal relationship with Jesus Christ. You don't put on your faith 'suit,' then take it off when you walk in to vote on the House floor. Your carry your faith with you everywhere you go."

As also a former youth minister and ordained Southern Baptist minister, Watts encourages others to live for Christ. He reminds Christians that just as he had to remember the rules when he ran the wishbone offense for the University of Oklahoma, so too they must remember that "our Rulebook is the Bible, and Scripture says that 'God has not given us a spirit of fear.'"

Watts' has not lived in a spirit of fear against his challenges. As he admitted in his 1996 Republican National Convention speech, "In my wildest imagination, I never thought the fifth of six children born to Helen and Buddy Watts—in a poor black neighborhood, in the poor rural community of Eufaula, Oklahoma—would someday be called congressman."

It is his faith in God that brought J.C. Watts where he is today and that will continue to see him through. "My faith encourages me to believe and to trust that God is still in control," he says. " . . . In difficult times my prayers have often been, 'Dear God, I can't see Your hand in this, but I trust Your heart. I trust that You're fully in control. I trust that You are going to navigate us through this.' And in forty-three years of living, I have never been disappointed in God."

FANNY CROSBY: A FORETASTE OF GLORY DIVINE

What seemed to have been a tragic accident for a family and their six-week-old daughter in 1820 chartered a new course in American history, literature, and music. Through the blindness of a small child named Frances "Fanny" Jane Crosby would come a rare enlightenment and poetic brilliance.

Though Fanny's infant blindness was accidental, caused by a man posing as a doctor who gave her the wrong treatment, Fanny was never bitter about the stranger's error. "I have not for a moment in more than eighty-five years," she said, "felt a spark of resentment against him, because I have always believed . . . that the good Lord . . . by this means consecrated me to the work that I am still permitted to do."

Neither would she accept pity or resentment towards her handicap. A minister once remarked to her, "I think it is a great pity that the Master did not give you sight when He showered so many other gifts upon you." She immediately responded, "Do you know that if at birth I had been able to make one petition, it would have been that I should be born blind?" "Why?" he asked. "Because when I get to heaven, the first face that shall ever gladden my sight will be that of my Savior!"

> *". . . the first face that shall ever gladden my sight will be that of my Savior."*

Born into a family of sturdy New England stock whose great-grandfather had fought in the Revolution and whose distant relative had helped found Harvard College, Fanny never recognized the faces of her two sisters and one brother or her father who died when she was only one year old. But many family members surrounded Fanny, including her mother and grandmother whose love for nature, poetry, and Scripture were shared with Fanny. A pretty child with high energy and a carefree spirit, Fanny soon began to show an uncanny ability to memorize all that was told to her. At age eight, she wrote her first lines: "Oh what a happy soul am I, although I cannot see, I am resolved that in this world, contented I will be." It is said that at age ten, she could recite the first four books of both Testaments while at the same time she found time to romp outdoors with her friends, climbing fences and trees, riding horses, and listening to her grandmother's descriptions of every bud and leaf in meticulous detail.

It seemed that nothing could stifle or discourage Fanny Crosby. "My ambition," she writes in her autobiography, "was boundless, and my desires were intent to live for some great purpose in the world and to make for myself a name that should endure." But Fanny knew she could not attend school like her friends and siblings for there were neither schools nor Braille system for the blind. She became confused as to God's direction and use of her life and said later about this difficult time, "The great world that could see was rushing by me day by day and sweeping on toward the goal of its necessities and desires; while I was left stranded by the wayside." Fanny knelt with her grandmother beside her rocking chair one day and prayed, "Dear Lord, please show me how I can learn like other children." Within a year, not only had she been accepted into the New York Institute for the Blind, she also became the school's best student and later stayed on as a teacher for more thirty years.

Poetry became Fanny's passion and by the time she was twenty-four, her first book of poems *The Blind Girl and Other Poems* had been published. The name Fanny Crosby became known throughout the streets of New York as a sought-after speaker and popular poetess. But Miss Crosby felt that something was missing from her life and only through a cholera epidemic in 1849 did Crosby discover what it was. More than half of the Institute students died, and Fanny later recalled the terrible memories of small coffins lining the school's hallways. After barely escaping the illness itself, Fanny realized she was not ready to die. On November 20, 1850, she knelt at the altar at a local revival and surrendered to Jesus Christ. "For the first time I realized that I had been trying to hold the world in one hand and the Lord in the other," she said.

"For the first time I realized that I had been trying to hold the world in one hand and the Lord in the other," she said.

With a new interest in the spiritual realm, Fanny began writing hundreds of hymns and gospel songs as well as her poetry. Additional speaking invitations and developing friendships continued with such political leaders as President Van Buren, President Polk, and Grover Cleveland. But in 1858, a special man came into her life, the blind musician Alexander Van Alstyne. Soon they were married and were able to enjoy forty-four years together. Their only child died soon after birth.

Crosby, regarding the writing of her inspirational hymns, recounts many amazing stories. One day in 1868, Crosby heard a hurried knock at her door. It was a musician friend who said he had only forty minutes before the train left but he wanted her to hear a new melody that was going through his head. "What does it say, Fanny?" he asked. After a brief hesitation, she began to sing:

> *Safe in the arms of Jesus,*
> *Safe in his gentle breast,*
> *There by his love o'er-shadowed,*
> *Sweetly my soul shall rest . . .*

Twenty minutes later, the friend hurried to his train with the penciled verses of the finished hymn "Safe in the Arms of Jesus" written down. Often writing as many as six hymns a day, Crosby wrote such hymns as "Blessed Assurance," "Saved By Grace," and "Jesus My All." Fanny Crosby's faith bore fruit, producing more than eight thousand hymns and gospel songs. In her most prolific years, in fact, it was necessary for her to use close to one hundred various pseudonyms so as to avoid the numerous "Crosby" editions.

With her faith came generosity as Crosby worked with the poor and volunteered much of her time to local ministries even in her later years. As Fanny Crosby had reminded those around her, "I seem to have been led little by little, toward my work," she said, "and I believe that the same fact will appear in the life of anyone who will cultivate such powers as God has given him, and then go on, bravely, quietly, but persistently, doing such work as comes to his hands."

Fanny died peacefully in her home in Bridgeport, Connecticut, on February 12, 1915; she was ninety-five years old. Never before had people witnessed such crowds at a funeral, a testimony to the widespread influence she had had upon so many. A simple headstone marks her grave today with the name "Aunt Fanny" on it and these words: "Blessed assurance, Jesus is mine. Oh, what a foretaste of glory divine."

BILL BRIGHT:
CARRYING THE TORCH FOR CHRIST

Some said he resembled Clark Gable with his slicked-back dark hair and mustache, and trim physique, but in spite of his good looks and successful gourmet foods business, he felt something was missing from his life. In 1945, the young Bill Bright felt an urge to stop by the First Presbyterian Church in Hollywood, California. "It was almost as though an invisible hand reached out and pulled me into the church," he recalls. "It was the strangest thing, even as I think about it now."

As he silently slid into the back row of the church and listened to the sermon, the "happy pagan," as he referred to himself later, began to hear what he had never heard before. In a few months, the former agnostic, the man who was "happy in [his] ignorance" became a changed man.

A native Oklahoman, Bright was born on his family's ranch in 1921 outside the small town of Coweta. He was one of seven children and remembers his mother as "very religious" and his father as "a materialist and a humanist." Though Bill never believed in the existence of God during his childhood and teenage years, he recalls that he was "fun-loving. I enjoyed life," he says. During World War II, Bright left a job in a shipyard to start his own business. He had created clever marketing and packaging for a specialty and gourmet foods business; with his idea and a little money in hand, he moved to Los Angeles to begin Bright's Brandied Foods and Bright's California Confections, promoting the products throughout the country.

Life was hectic but fun for him during those days. Bright would put in eighteen-hour days with his business and then find time to act in amateur radio shows, ride horses, and take dates to nightspots like the Coconut Grove. But after his newly discovered Sunday morning visits to church, Bright decided to devote his life to something else, something more fulfilling, something eternal.

"I was a spiritual illiterate, so I went to seminary for five years to learn everything I could about the Bible, and Christ and religion, and in the process, God led me to put aside everything I'd worked [for] day and night to build something better."

Soon he had struck up a romantic interest in a lovely woman by the name of Vonette Zachary, a childhood friend from Coweta; and in 1948 they were married. Only three years after they had wed, Bright and Vonette drew up a contract with Jesus, vowing to give up their worldly pursuits, become Christ's slaves, and spread the Gospel of Jesus Christ through small groups on college campuses. They would call it Campus Crusade for Christ.

The Brights sold their food business and later their Oklahoma oil drilling company, investing the money into their new campus ministry. Today the organization has an annual budget of $450 million, a full-time staff of more than 26,000, and more than 225,000 trained volunteers. The investment in God's kingdom had paid off.

Throughout the years, Bright designed leadership training classes, created the religious tract "The Four Spiritual Laws," and the *JESUS* film, a feature-length documentary on the life of Christ which has been viewed by more than 5.1 billion people in 234 countries and translated into 786 languages. Campus Crusade spread from college to college, country to country, and moved beyond campuses to prisons, the military, families, and the inner city.

In 1996, Bright was presented with the prestigious Templeton Prize for Progress in Religion, worth more than one million dollars. Bright donated all of the money to causes promoting the spiritual benefits of fasting and prayer and to his organization.

["Bill Bright] has carried a burden on his heart as few men that I've ever known. A burden for the evangelization of the world," says Billy Graham, a long-time friend of the Brights. "He is a man whose sincerity and integrity and devotion to our Lord have been an inspiration and a blessing to me ever since the early days of my ministry."

In early October, 2000, Bill Bright informed his staff that he had been diagnosed with pulmonary fibrosis, an incurable disease of the lungs. The doctors had informed Bright that he might have three to five years. But the news failed to slow him down. "I'm here to do what God still has for me to do on this earth, and whenever that is finished, I am ready to be with him in heaven," Bright told his staff. "There is still so much work to be done."

Charles Colson met with his friend Bill Bright soon after he was diagnosed with the fatal disease. "It was uncanny—indeed supernatural—that Bill maintained his buoyant spirit with every breath, labored though it was, for the last two and a half years as he battled the disease," Colson says.

"'Why would God allow someone who had given over fifty years of his life to faithful ministry to die such a painful death?'" one might ask,' Colson says. 'One answer is in something that radio preacher Steve Brown once said: God allows Christians and [non-Christians] to get cancer so that the world will see a difference in how Christians deal with it."

Attached to an oxygen tank and mostly confined to his downtown Orlando condominium, Bright expressed his views on dying: "I view this as truly one of the great experiences of my life. Adversity is not something to be feared; it's something to be embraced. I've had the most incredible life. I have been married to the most wonderful woman for fifty-two years. We've seen God do miracles upon miracles, and it's just been a wonderful adventure."

On July 19, 2003, William R. Bright, age 81, joined his Savior for eternity. More than three thousand mourners gathered a few weeks later for a memorial service to recall Bill Bright as teacher, friend, and evangelist who helped change thousands of lives.

FRANKLIN GRAHAM: SON OF A PREACHER MAN, "REBEL WITH A CAUSE"

Blessed are you, O Lord, our God. Yours, O God, is the greatness and the power and the glory and the majesty and the splendor; for everything in heaven and earth is yours."

Not exactly the words one expects to hear from a rebellious son—the "rebel with a cause," the "prodigal son," the "son of a preacher man" as he has been called. But William Franklin Graham III bowed his head before millions of viewers as he prayed for President-elect George W. Bush on January 20, 2001, during the presidential inauguration.

"Yours, O Lord is the kingdom; you are exalted as head over all. Wealth and honor come from you; you are the ruler of all things. In your hands are strength and power to exalt and to give strength to all."

Though the forty-eight-year-old prodigal son stepped in for his father, Billy Graham, that cold rainy day in January, he was not always so willing to follow in his father's footsteps. Growing up in a log cabin in the Appalachian Mountains with four siblings and, most often, one parent, his mother, Ruth Bell Graham, Franklin became a mischievous boy and a rebellious teen. His sister, Anne Graham Lotz remembers the "single parent" home well: "Being raised by a single parent and giving your father up when he spends more time with a secretary or a news reporter than he does with me—that hurts. . . . We knew he preached and he went and served Jesus, so I was glad to let him go because of that."

> ". . . you are going to have to make a choice."

Without his father around much, Franklin enjoyed spending his time hunting and fishing. But later in his teen years, the outdoor hobbies became wild times of "drinking the beer, and going out to the parties, and running around with different girlfriends." His family sent him off to Stony Brook, a Christian boarding school on Long Island, New York, but he dropped out and was later expelled from another school, LeTourneau College in Longview, Texas. Then in 1974 during a trip to Switzerland, Billy Graham got serious with his twenty-two-year-old son.

Franklin recalls his father staring him straight in the eye and saying, "I want you to know that your mother and I sense there is a struggle for the soul of your life, and you're going to have to make a choice." The young Graham continued on his motorcycle tour of Europe, a bottle of scotch in his hand, but tormented in his mind by his father's conversation. The epiphany occurred one night in a hotel room in Jerusalem.

"That night instead of going to the bar for a couple of beers, I found myself alone in my room reading through the gospel of John. When I came to the third chapter, I read not just that Jesus told Nicodemus he had to be born again, but I also grasped that Franklin Graham had to be born again as well."

It was the day of his marriage to Jane Austin Cunningham on his parents' front lawn that he told all in attendance of his life-changing experience. He was now committed to God, but the last career he wanted was to become an evangelist. "I just felt that if I put myself into the pulpit, that it would be like a lightning rod for all these comparisons," he said. Graham continued his college education, graduating in 1974 from Montreat College with an Associate Degree and later in 1978 from Appalachian State University with a Bachelor of Arts Degree. But when a family friend, Bob Pierce, founder of the Christian relief organization Samaritan's Purse and World Vision, invited Graham to accompany him on a mission trip to Asia, Graham said yes.

Traveling throughout some of the most poverty-stricken and Christian-persecuted countries of the world, Franklin knew where his place needed to be. After his friend Pierce died of leukemia in 1978, Graham became president and chairman of Samaritan's Purse which today has an annual budget of $204 million with offices in Canada, Australia, the United Kingdom, the Netherlands, and Kenya and provides relief and assistance in more than a hundred countries.

> ". . . My father can go to the big stadiums, but I'll just go to the highways and the byways."

Though Franklin Graham was often encouraged to step into the pulpit or preach at his father's crusades, he continued to resist. "I'm going to travel the gutters and the ditches of the world," he said, "and I'm going to help people in the name of the Lord Jesus Christ. My father can go to the big stadiums, but I'll just go to the highways and the byways."

Then the opportunity came one November night in 1983 during a Billy Graham Crusade. Would he please join his father in the preaching of the gospel, his friend and evangelist John Wesley White, asked him? Franklin consented and preached to a crowd of more than one thousand people. And the result was phenomenal, quite phenomenal considering his father was Billy Graham. Not one person came forward to receive Christ. No one. The rebel son vowed never again to step foot in a crusade stadium or a pulpit again.

But his friend John White was convinced of the power of God, not the man himself. Later in 1989, he encouraged Franklin to once again preach—this time before thousands in Juneau, Alaska. And this time it was God's perfect timing. "They packed the place, drunks and prostitutes," said White. "He gave the invitation, and they poured down. It was a miracle, and he knew it."

Since then, Graham has committed ten percent of his time to preaching and leads as many as ten evangelistic Festivals each year for the Billy Graham Evangelistic Association. From Sydney, Australia, to Wichita, Kansas, to Nicaragua where he spoke to a crowd of 198,300, Franklin has led more than eighty-three Festivals and has spoken to more than two million people. Graham is committed to visiting many smaller areas where his father's crusades are not usually held.

Franklin has written several books including *The Name* and his autobiography *Rebel With A Cause: Finally Comfortable Being Graham*. Devoting as much time as he can with his wife in the mountains of North Carolina, and with his four children and two grandchildren, Graham gives the remainder of his time to Samaritan's Purse and his father's organization. Once the rebel without a cause, Franklin Graham now understands his calling. "I just want to be faithful to the same message that [my father's] been faithful to," he says, "and that's the preaching of the gospel."

YOU'VE READ ABOUT OTHERS
ACHIEVING THEIR DREAMS. . . .

NOW GO FIND YOURS!

INDEX

Additional copies of this book
and other titles by Honor Books
are available from your local bookstore.

If you have enjoyed this book,
or if it has impacted your life,
we would like to hear from you.
Please contact us at:

HONOR BOOKS
An Imprint of Cook Communications Ministries
4050 Lee Vance View
Colorado Springs, CO 80918

www.cookministries.com